Francisco Bruquetas & Michelle de la Calle

SPANISH FOR CALIFORNIANS

USING ENGLISH TO LEARN SPANISH

THIRD EDITION

SPANISH FOR CALIFORNIANS: USING ENGLISH TO LEARN SPANISH
THIRD EDITION
© 2008, 2010, 2012 Francisco and Michelle de la Calle

ISBN   978-0-578-10502-4

R141121

Editorial Assistants:
Meg Genoar, Tierney Genoar, Jane Lueder

Cover Art: Francisco de la Calle

Bruquetas Publishing
88 S. Third St. #162, San José, California 95112, USA
www.BruquetasPublishing.com

All rights reserved

No part of this book may be reproduced in any
manner without permission in writing from
Bruquetas Publishing.

Library of Congress Registration Number:
Txu 1-616-290

For Julián and Benjamín

Foreword

Spanish for Californians is intended for self-educated students with no previous knowledge of the language.

Its methodology takes advantage of the similarities between Spanish and English. Students will find motivation by realizing they are progressing, and they can speed up their learning by studying at their own pace, creating their own vocabulary, and observing sentences in clear examples.

As a child growing up in Spain, I still remember struggling in school to memorize random English words such as "chick pea." There was also an overwhelming task to find coherence in all the rules with that imposed vocabulary. When I moved to California, I realized two facts about learning a second language. First, sharing the class with 30 other students didn't help. Second, memorizing "chick pea" was a waste of time! The word "garbanzo," especially when you already know the word "garbanzo" in Spanish, is a piece of cake!

A significant percentage of English words have a Latin root, as do many structures. Spanish is derived from the Latin Language. This commonality is utilized extensively in this book to teach the Spanish language, its grammatical rules, and its coherence and consistency. For this reason, most of the Spanish words that the reader will find in this book are similar in English and, consequently, self-explanatory (computador, elefante, garbanzo, etc.).

The second goal of this book is to serve as a reference book, once the reader is no longer learning, and needs a book for consultation. As a reference book, *Spanish for Californians* is organized the same way the language is: first the sounds, then the words, then the sentences, then each section is categorized in coherent types of words. At the end, the reader will find a set of appendices with reference tables, special topics and vocabulary.

This book sticks to what constitutes standard Spanish. Spanish is a very unified language. The rules of spelling and grammar are the same in all of the Spanish speaking countries, and twenty two National Academies, including those of the United States, Puerto Rico and the Philippines, work to maintain this unity.

The third edition further clarifies the use of pronouns and the plural "you" (*ustedes* in Latin America, *vosotros* in Spain). Various comments and corrections have been incorporated. Special thanks go to John Trifari and Barrie Fairley for their additional support and commentary in this process.

The Book at a Glance

INTRODUCTION 18

SECTION I   SOUNDS
1. THE ALPHABET 22
2. THE VOWELS 26
3. THE CONSONANTS 30
4. SYLLABLE AND STRESS 42

SECTION II   VOCABULARY
5. SINGULAR / PLURAL 54
6. MASCULINE / FEMININE 62
7. CONJUGATION 68
8. HOW TO LEARN WORDS EFFICIENTLY 80

SECTION III   GRAMMAR
9. TYPES OF WORDS 88
10. INTERJECTIONS 92
11. DETERMINERS 98
12. ADJECTIVES 106
13. NOUNS 120
14. PRONOUNS 126
15. ADVERBS 142
16. PREPOSITIONS 152
17. CONJUNCTIONS 160
18. VERBS 166

SECTION IV   VERB TENSES

19. INFINITIVE "TO SING" 180
20. GERUND "SINGING" 186
21. PAST PARTICIPLE "SUNG" 192
22. PRESENT "I SING" 196
23. PRETERITE "I SANG" 206
24. IMPERFECT PAST "I SANG" (I USED TO SING) 214
25. FUTURE "I WILL SING" 218
26. CONDITIONAL "I WOULD SING" 224
27. IMPERATIVE "SING!" 232
28. PRESENT SUBJUNCTIVE "...THAT I SING" 238
29. PAST SUBJUNCTIVE "...THAT I SANG" 254
30. TENSES WITH TO HAVE "I HAVE SUNG" 262
31. TENSES WITH TO BE "I AM SINGING" 268
32. PERIPHRASES "I AM GOING TO SING" 272
33. REFLEXIVE VERBS 278
34. VERBS LIKE "GUSTAR" 286
35. THE PASSIVE VOICE "THE SONG IS SUNG" 292

APPENDICES

APPENDIX A: NOTES ABOUT DIALECTS 298
APPENDIX B: LOCAL WORDS OF CALIFORNIA 306
APPENDIX C: REGULAR VERBS 312
APPENDIX D: AUXILARY VERBS: HABER, ESTAR, SER, IR 316
APPENDIX E: A LIST OF REGULAR VERBS 320
APPENDIX F: A LIST OF IRREGULAR VERBS 330

GLOSSARY 342

Table of Contents

INTRODUCTION 18

SECTION I SOUNDS

1. THE ALPHABET 22
   - COROLLARY: OTHER SYMBOLS 23
   - FREQUENTLY ASKED QUESTIONS 23
     - *FAQ: Why in my dictionary are "ch" and "ll" considered single letters?* 23
   - EXERCISES 24
   - VOCABULARY 24

2. THE VOWELS 26
   - FREQUENTLY ASKED QUESTIONS 27
     - *FAQ: Is the letter "y" a vowel?* 27
   - EXERCISES 28
   - VOCABULARY 28

3. THE CONSONANTS 30
   - COROLLARY: RULES OF THUMB ON SPELLING 34
   - FREQUENTLY ASKED QUESTIONS 35
     - *FAQ 1: What are the two dots on the "u" in "lingüista?"* 35
     - *FAQ 2: I've seen both "México" and "Méjico." What's the right spelling?* .. 36
     - *FAQ 3: Why have I never heard the English "th" sound in Spanish?* 36
     - *FAQ 4: Should "y" and "ll" sound the same?* 36
   - EXERCISES 36
   - VOCABULARY 39

4. SYLLABLE AND STRESS 42
   - BREAKDOWN OF WORDS INTO SYLLABLES 43
   - RULES OF ACCENTS 45
     - *General Rules* 45
     - *Additional Rules:* 46
   - FREQUENTLY ASKED QUESTIONS 48
     - *FAQ 1: Video or Vídeo?* 48
     - *FAQ 2: Do I really need to learn how to break the words into syllables?* ... 48
     - *FAQ 3: What is the difference between accent mark and stress?* 49
     - *FAQ 4: How do I know where the stress is in words like "construimos," which has two vowels together in the stressed syllable?* 49
   - EXERCISES 49
   - VOCABULARY 50

SECTION II   VOCABULARY

5. **SINGULAR / PLURAL** 54
   - COROLLARY 1: NUMBERS 56
   - COROLLARY 2: TELLING THE TIME 59
   - COROLLARY 3 : TELLING THE DATE 60
   - FREQUENTLY ASKED QUESTIONS 60
     - *FAQ 1: What's the plural of words like "cactus?"* 60
     - *FAQ 2: Can I express years in hundreds?* 60
   - EXERCISES 61
   - VOCABULARY 61

6. **MASCULINE / FEMININE** 62
   - FREQUENTLY ASKED QUESTIONS 65
     - *FAQ 1: I've seen "el arpa" (= the harp), but my Spanish dictionary says that it is feminine. Shouldn't it be "la arpa?"* 65
     - *FAQ 2: El radio or la radio?* 65
   - EXERCISES 65
   - VOCABULARY 66

7. **CONJUGATION** 68
   - COROLLARY 1: THE PERSONAL PRONOUNS 71
   - COROLLARY 2: THE THREE SIMPLEST VERB STRUCTURES: "I AM SINGING, I AM GOING TO SING, I HAVE SUNG" 71
   - COROLLARY 3: NEGATIVE SENTENCES 75
   - COROLLARY 4: INTERROGATIVE SENTENCES 75
   - COROLLARY 5: INTERROGATIVE-NEGATIVE SENTENCES 76
   - FREQUENTLY ASKED QUESTIONS 76
     - *FAQ: "Vosotros" or "ustedes" (= you plural)?* 76
   - EXERCISES 77
   - VOCABULARY 77

8. **HOW TO LEARN WORDS EFFICIENTLY** 80
   - COROLLARY 1: PREFIXES AND SUFFIXES 83
   - COROLLARY 2: SPANGLISH 83
   - FREQUENTLY ASKED QUESTIONS 85
     - *FAQ: Where do I find the "grammatical words" I have to learn every day?* 85
   - EXERCISES 85
   - VOCABULARY 86

SECTION III   GRAMMAR

9. TYPES OF WORDS ... 88
- **FREQUENTLY ASKED QUESTIONS** ... 90
  - *FAQ: Why is this classification of words important?* ... 90
- **EXERCISES** ... 90
- **VOCABULARY** ... 91

10. INTERJECTIONS ... 92
- **COROLLARY 1: SENTENCES OF EXCLAMATION** ... 94
- **COROLLARY 2: "SO DO I," "NEITHER DO I"** ... 95
- **FREQUENTLY ASKED QUESTIONS** ... 95
  - *FAQ: What are the "Question Tags?"* ... 95
- **EXERCISES** ... 96
- **VOCABULARY** ... 96

11. DETERMINERS ... 98
- **COROLLARY 1: CONTRACTIONS** ... 100
- **COROLLARY 2: FREQUENCY OF USE OF SPANISH "EL/LA" IN COMPARISON TO THE ENGLISH "THE"** ... 101
- **COROLLARY 3: ABOUT ACCENTS MARKS** ... 102
- **COROLLARY 4: FEMININE WORDS WITH "EL:" EL AGUA** ... 102
- **FREQUENTLY ASKED QUESTIONS** ... 102
  - *FAQ: Are "possessives" a type of determiners, adjectives or pronouns?* ... 102
- **EXERCISES** ... 103
- **VOCABULARY** ... 103

12. ADJECTIVES ... 106
- **COROLLARY 1: THE VERB "TO BE"** ... 110
- **COROLLARY 2: THE VERB "TO HAVE"** ... 112
- **COROLLARY 3: COMPARATIVES** ... 112
- **COROLLARY 4: QUANTITIES** ... 114
- **COROLLARY 5: "THERE IS," "THERE'S LEFT"** ... 115
- **COROLLARY 6: ANOTHER, OTHER, OTHERS** ... 116
- **FREQUENTLY ASKED QUESTIONS** ... 117
  - *FAQ: I've seen the word "good" translated by both "bueno" and "buen;" how come?* ... 117
- **EXERCISES** ... 117
- **VOCABULARY** ... 118

13. NOUNS ... 120
- **COROLLARY 1: PREFIXES AND SUFFIXES** ... 121
- **COROLLARY 2: "BABE, BABY; JOHN, JOHNNY"** ... 122
- **FREQUENTLY ASKED QUESTIONS** ... 122
  - *FAQ 1: Are the rules to pass from masculine to feminine and from singular to plural applicable for determiners, adjectives and nouns?* ... 122
  - *FAQ 2: I've seen "United States" abbreviated as EE.UU., how come?* ... 123
- **EXERCISES** ... 123
- **VOCABULARY** ... 124

14. PRONOUNS ... 126
PERSONAL PRONOUNS: ... 127
POSSESSIVE PRONOUNS. ... 129
OBJECT PRONOUNS ... 130
Type 1. Object Pronouns with Prepositions ... 131
Type 2. Object pronouns with the preposition "con" (= with) ... 132
Type 3. Object pronouns with the preposition "entre" (= between) ... 132
Type 4. Direct Object (D.O.) pronouns ... 133
Type 5. Indirect Object (I.O.) Pronouns ... 135
REFLEXIVE PRONOUNS: ... 136
FREQUENTLY ASKED QUESTIONS ... 138
FAQ1: Again, what's the direct object? ... 138
FAQ 2: I've heard that even native speakers confuse the words: "la, le, lo." Is there a rule of thumb? ... 138
FAQ 3: I've heard that in some cases, it is accepted to use "le" as a direct object pronoun too. How come? ... 138
EXERCISES ... 140

15. ADVERBS ... 142
COROLLARY 1: THE INTERROGATIVE ADVERBS: WHAT, WHERE, WHEN, HOW, ETC. ... 145
COROLLARY 2: THE RELATIVE ADVERBS ... 146
COROLLARY 3: ADVERBS / ADVERBIAL EXPRESSIONS ... 147
FREQUENTLY ASKED QUESTIONS ... 147
FAQ 1: What does "lo que" mean? ... 147
FAQ 2: My dictionary says: "qué" means "what," and "cuál" means "which;" however, I have seen those words translated the other way round. How come? ... 147
EXERCISES ... 148
VOCABULARY ... 149

16. PREPOSITIONS ... 152
COROLLARY 1: PREPOSITIONS / PREPOSITIONAL EXPRESSIONS ... 155
COROLLARY 2: "PARA" VERSUS "POR" (= FOR) ... 155
COROLLARY 3: THE EXTENSIVE USE OF "EN" (= IN) ... 156
COROLLARY 4: THE EXTENSIVE USE OF "DE" (= OF) ... 156
COROLLARY 5: THE PERSONAL "A" (= TO) ... 156
EXERCISES ... 157
VOCABULARY ... 157

17. CONJUNCTIONS ... 160
COROLLARY: CONJUNTIONS / CONJUCTIVE EXPRESSIONS ... 163
EXERCISES ... 164
VOCABULARY ... 164

18. VERBS ... 166
ABOUT VERBS IN ANY LANGUAGE ... 166
ABOUT VERBS IN SPANISH ... 167
COROLLARY 1: ABOUT "HABER" AND "TENER" (= TO HAVE) ... 168
COROLLARY 2: ABOUT "SER" AND "ESTAR" (= TO BE) ... 169
COROLLARY 3: "HAY / QUEDA" (= THERE IS / THERE IS LEFT) ... 169
COROLLARY 4: IRREGULAR VERBS ... 170
EXERCISES ... 171
VOCABULARY ... 172

REFERENCE TABLES 174
   REGULAR VERBS *174*
   THE AUXILIARY VERBS HABER, ESTAR, SER, IR *176*

SECTION IV   VERB TENSES

19.   INFINITIVE "TO SING" 180
   COROLLARY 1: NOUNS DERIVED FROM VERBS 182
   COROLLARY 2: VERB PERIPHRASES: TWO VERBS IN TANDEM 182
   COROLLARY 3: I AM GOING TO + INFINITIVE = VOY A + INFINITIVE 183
   COROLLARY 4: IRREGULAR VERBS IN THE INFINITIVE 184
   EXERCISES 184
   VOCABULARY 185

20.   GERUND "SINGING" 186
   COROLLARY 1: ADVERBS DERIVED FROM VERBS 187
   COROLLARY 2: "I AM SINGING = "ESTOY CANTANDO" 187
   COROLLARY 3: IRREGULAR VERBS IN THE GERUND 188
      Type 1. Affects all verbs ending with -aer, -eer, -oer, -oír, -uir. e.g. atribuir *188*
      Type 2. Affects two verbs. Those IR verbs whose infinitive have an –o- in the second to last syllable. *188*
      Type 3. Affects all verbs of the third conjugation (IR verbs) whose infinitive have an -e- in the second to last syllable. *189*
      Type 4. Others *190*
   EXERCISES 191
   VOCABULARY 191

21.   PAST PARTICIPLE "SUNG" 192
   COROLLARY 1: ADJECTIVES DERIVED FROM VERBS 193
   COROLLARY 2: "I HAVE SUNG = HE CANTADO;" "I HAD SUNG" ="HABÍA CANTADO" 193
   COROLLARY 3: IRREGULAR VERBS IN THE PAST PARTICIPLE 194
   EXERCISES 195
   VOCABULARY 195

22.   PRESENT "I SING" 196
   COROLLARY 1: SPELLING-CHANGING OR FALSE-IRREGULAR VERBS 197
   COROLLARY 2: THE IRREGULAR VERBS IN THE PRESENT TENSE 199
      Type 1 Affects all verbs ending in –uir. *199*
      Type 2. Affects most verbs with an -o- in the second to last syllable. *200*
      Type 3. Affects most verbs with an –e- in the second to last syllable. *200*
      Type 4. Affects most verbs with an –e- in the second to last syllable. *201*
      Type 5. Affects all verbs ending with –cer or –cir , except "decir." *201*
      Type 6. Others. *202*
   EXERCISES 205
   VOCABULARY 205

23. PRETERITE "I SANG"... 206
   COROLLARY 1: DIFFERENCE BETWEEN THE PRETERITE AND THE IMPERFECT PAST .. 207
   COROLLARY 2: SPELLING-CHANGING OR FALSE-IREGULAR VERBS 207
   COROLLARY 3: IRREGULAR VERBS IN THE PRETERITE... 208
      Type 1 Affects all verbs ending in –aer, –eer, –oer, –oir, -uir............................. 209
      Type 3. Affects all IR-verbs with an –e- in the second to last syllable..................... 210
      Type 4. Affects all verbs ending in -cir, except "decir" and "bendecir". 210
      Type 5 Others.. 211
   EXERCISES 213
   VOCABULARY 213

24. IMPERFECT PAST "I SANG" (I USED TO SING)... 214
   COROLLARY 1: IRREGULAR VERBS IN THE IMPERFECT PAST TENSE 215
   EXERCISES 216
   VOCABULARY 216

25. FUTURE "I WILL SING"... 218
   COROLLARY 1: IRREGULAR VERBS IN THE FUTURE TENSE 219
   EXERCISES 222
   VOCABULARY 222

26. CONDITIONAL "I WOULD SING"... 224
   COROLLARY 1: IRREGULAR VERBS IN THE CONDITIONAL TENSE............................ 226
   EXERCISES 229
   VOCABULARY 229

27. IMPERATIVE "SING!" 232
   COROLLARY 1: USE OF "POR FAVOR" (= PLEASE).. 234
   COROLLARY 2: IRREGULAR VERBS IN THE IMPERATIVE 234
      Type 1. Those verbs that can form the imperative from their form in the present tense,
      i.e. acertar (= to hit with a projectile or an answer)... 234
      Type 2. Others... 235
   EXERCISES 235
   VOCABULARY 236

28. PRESENT SUBJUNCTIVE "...THAT I SING"... 238
   USE OF THE PRESENT OF SUBJUNCTIVE FOR COMMANDS 239
   INTRODUCTION TO THE SUBJUNCTIVE MOOD. 240
   COROLLARY 1: SPELLING-CHANGING OR FALSE-IRREGULAR VERBS 244
   COROLLARY 2: IRREGULAR VERBS IN THE PRESENT SUBJUNCTIVE......................... 246
      Type 1 Affects all verbs ending in –uir... 246
      Type 2. Affects most -verbs with an –o- in the second to last syllable. (verbs with –o-
      can be regular, like "co-mer")... 247
      Type 3. Affects most verbs with an –e- in the second to last syllable. (verbs with –e- can
      be regular, like "pe-sar," = to weigh).. 247
      Type 4. Affects most verbs with an –e- in the second to last syllable. 248
      Type 5. Affects all verbs ending in –cer, or –cir, except decir.............................. 249
      Type 6. Others... 249
   EXERCISES 251
   VOCABULARY 252

29. PAST SUBJUNCTIVE "...THAT I SANG" 254
   COROLLARY 1: THE CONDITIONAL SENTENCES 257
   COROLLARY 2: IRREGULAR VERBS IN THE PAST SUBJUNCTIVE 258
   EXERCISES 259
   VOCABULARY 260

30. TENSES WITH TO HAVE "I HAVE SUNG" 262
   COROLLARY 1: IRREGULARITIES IN THE COMPOUND TENSES 265
   EXERCISES 266
   VOCABULARY 266

31. TENSES WITH TO BE "I AM SINGING" 268
   EXERCISES 270
   VOCABULARY 270

32. PERIPHRASES "I AM GOING TO SING" 272
   COROLLARY: TRANSLATION OF THE ENGLISH DEFECTIVE VERBS 273
   EXERCISES 275
   VOCABULARY 276

33. REFLEXIVE VERBS 278
   Type One. Verbs that function as either reflexive or not depending on the direct object being oneself or something else. 280
   Type Two. Verbs that function as either reflexive or non-reflexive optionally, depending on the speaker's style. 280
   Type Three. Verbs that can function as either reflexive or not depending on the meaning, e.g. ir (= to go). 280
   Type Four. Verbs that can only function as reflexive, e.g. quejar (= to complain). 281
   COROLLARY 1: THE STRUCTURE "TO HAVE SOMETHING DONE" 281
   COROLLARY 2: TO GET/ TO BECOME+ ADJECTIVE/ PAST PARTICIPLE 281
   COROLLARY 3: THE ETHIC DATIVE 282
   EXERCISES 282
   VOCABULARY 283

34. VERBS LIKE "GUSTAR" 286
   COROLLARY: THE OPTIONAL EMPHASIS IN THE PERSON 289
   EXERCISES 289
   VOCABULARY 290

35. THE PASSIVE VOICE "THE SONG IS SUNG" 292
   COROLLARY: THE IMPERSONAL "SE" 293
   EXERCISES 294
   VOCABULARY 294

APPENDICES

APPENDIX A: NOTES ABOUT DIALECTS 298

APPENDIX B: LOCAL WORDS OF CALIFORNIA 306

APPENDIX C: REGULAR VERBS 312

APPENDIX D: AUXILARY VERBS: HABER, ESTAR, SER, IR 316

APPENDIX E: A LIST OF REGULAR VERBS 320

APPENDIX F: A LIST OF IRREGULAR VERBS... 330

GLOSSARY 344

INTRODUCTION
INTRODUCCIÓN

Any speaker can learn any language. No language has a specific sound or a structure that a baby cannot learn. We humans all have the same speech organs and brains. All languages have the same three components: a set of individual sounds, or **letters**, which are grouped to form **words**, which, in turn, are grouped to form **sentences**.

SOUNDS:	letters
VOCABULARY:	words
GRAMMAR:	sentences

Accordingly this book is divided into **sections**, with the following goals:

> **Section I, SOUNDS**, introduces and explains the elemental sounds. Spanish is very simple in terms of pronunciation and spelling. So simple that, at the end of Section I, you will be able to read in Spanish (though you won't know what you are saying).
>
> **Section II, VOCABULARY**, explains the rules that you need in order to learn words efficiently and advance in your personal dictionary. English and Spanish have many words in common. This section introduces the terms "number," "gender," and "conjugation" in order to recognize "word patterns." These chapters show how words change their form (e.g. lion, lioness, lions, lionesses). At the end of this section you will be able to

look up any word in the dictionary and start your own vocabulary list without mistakes.

Section III, GRAMMAR, will give you the norms that you need in order to create and understand sentences. Spanish and English have many similarities in grammar. This section devotes one chapter to each of the nine types of words (determiners, nouns, adjectives, etc.) and the structures to which they give rise. At the end of this section, you will know how to create any sentence (using only three basic verb structures).

Section IV, VERB TENSES, is devoted to the last type of words. Spanish is very intense in verbs (similar number of verbs as English, but more variable). However, verbs follow very consistent rules.

At the end of this book, you should be able to write, read, understand and speak; you will be able to communicate any thoughts you have. From that point on, to become more eloquent in Spanish, it will be only a matter of increasing your vocabulary, and confort level in speaking.

Every chapter will display:

- The core of the lesson, with: language patterns, examples, golden rules , warnings and reminders .

- **Corollaries**

- **Frequently Asked Questions**

- **Exercises**

- **Vocabulary**

Regarding which vocabulary to learn, we encourage you to **learn a consistent set of words per day** (say, ten). Some words are imposed by the language, like in English "a," "the," "to," "but," etc. (yes, the boring ones). Throughout the text we will call them *grammatical words*. These are the words that you will find in the Vocabulary at the end of each chapter.

Other words should come from your area of interest; those are the words that should make your learning process fun. However, on those days that you don't feel inspired to find your own words, you may opt to adopt words from the examples of this book. A tip to memorize is to learn in sets: words that are related, like colors, animals, cooking ingredients, sports, etc.

We discourage you to learn vocabulary systematically until completing **Chapter 8 How to Learn Words Efficiently**. Remember: "Keep it simple; when it isn't simple it doesn't work."

This book follows an academic order of chapters. This organization will help you know where you are when learning as well as look up topics when reviewing. If you find a chapter with extensive vocabulary or that is too detailed, you may go ahead and move on as long as what you leave behind is just that: memorization. However, completing chapters will give you the extra reward of confidence.

We have identified **five elements that are not found in English**, and can be obstacles in learning. With time, these five items will become easier to understand. You will find a **warning** as these are introduced in the text.

- Objects have gender (*Chapter 6*).

- The words "*le, la, lo*" are not easily translated as "him, her" (*Chapter 13*).

- There are two verbs for "to be;" "*ser*" and "*estar*" (*Chapter 11*).

- There are two types of past tense: the preterite and the imperfect past (*Chapters 22 and 23*).

- There are two extra tenses; they are called the present subjunctive and the past subjunctive (*Chapters 27 and 28*).

Without further ado, here is the Spanish Language.

SECTION I

SOUNDS
SONIDOS

In this section, you'll learn how to pronounce all of the letters in the Spanish alphabet. First, you will learn the sounds of the vowels a, e, i, o, u and then the rest (the consonants). You will then learn the basic rules of spelling.

Later we'll introduce "the word stress," the part of the word where the emphasis falls (e.g. the "a" in a̱ctress), and its representation, the accent mark. By knowing the basic rules on the accents, you will be able to pronounce the words correctly.

Goal: By the end of this section, you will be able to read any text properly.

1. THE ALPHABET
EL ALFABETO

Spanish has the same alphabet as English, which means that they use the same symbols (letters), and that they are sorted in the same order:

a b c d e f g h i j k l m n ñ o p q r s t u v w x y z

Spanish has only one extra letter: letter "ñ." This is placed after the letter "n." This is the letter of words like "jalapeño" or "piñata." It sounds like the French "gn"(e.g. co**gn**ac, filet mi**gn**on). It sounds similar to the "n" in "o**n**ion", "bu**n**ion," or "mi**n**ion; and also close to the English "nj" in i**nj**ection).

Golden Rule

> In Spanish, each letter or pair of letters (like "ch" or "qu") corresponds to one sound.

For example, in Spanish, letter "a" always sounds the same (like the "a" in father); in English, letter "a" sounds differently in "father," "cable" or "salt."

Thus, pronouncing a word in Spanish is as simple as pronouncing its letters one by one. For example, in Spanish, "cable" (= cable) sounds as c + a + b + l + e (/kábleh/).

This makes Spanish one of the simplest languages in the world, and convenient particularly for self-learners.

1. THE ALPHABET

Sounds (or "letters," to simplify) are classified mainly by **vowels**, represented by the letters: a, e, i, o, u; and **consonants**, the rest: b, c, d, f, g, etc. (Vowels are articulated solely by varying the openness of your mouth. The consonants require other organs: lips, teeth, tongue, palate, larynx etc.).

Corollary: Other Symbols

Different symbols that you will see are: the beginning of exclamations (¡) and the beginning of questions (¿):

    Hi!   Are you Pedro?
    ¡Hola! ¿Eres Pedro?

Spanish has also a symbol to mark where the stress of the word is. In English this symbol only appears in foreign-origin words, e.g. "résumé." We'll talk about this in *Chapter 4 Syllable and Stress*. For now you only need to know that all Spanish words have one, and only one, point of stress or emphasis, but this stress is not always indicated with an accent mark. This is why this book will use the underscore to indicate where the stress is (e.g. ¡H_o_la! ¿_E_res P_e_dro?).

Frequently Asked Questions

FAQ: Why in my dictionary are "ch" and "ll" considered single letters?

Considering "ch" and "ll" as single letters is an **old** rule not in use any more.

In old dictionaries letter "ch" is placed after letter "c," and "ll" is placed after letter "l."

Exercises

Knowing that the letters of the following Spanish words sound the same in English, work to pronounce them.

> bola, planta, coma, radio, elefante, kilo, sal
> (= ball, plant, comma, radio, elephant, kilo, salt)

Answers

b + o̲ + l + a
p + l + a̲ + n + t + a
c + o̲ + m + a
r + a̲ + d + i + o
e + l + e + f + a̲ + n + t + e
k + i̲ + l + o
s + a + l

(underscore indicates the stress)

Vocabulary

Since you have not learned how to pronounce the Spanish letters yet, we'll start the vocabulary section of this book with those English-origin words that have become part of Spanish and that are **written and pronounced as in English**:

OK	campus	piercing
software	camping	hobby
best seller	picnic	kleenex
email	sandwich	ipod
whisky	pizza	broker

2. THE VOWELS
LAS VOCALES

The vowel sounds in Spanish are represented by the letters a, e, i, o, u.

Letter	Sound
a	like the "a" of father
e	like the "e" of bed
i	like the "ea" of meat
o	like the "o" of open
u	like the "oo" of boot

Use this rule of thumb to memorize the sounds: they sound in English like: ah, eh, ih, oh, uh.

Warning

> Be aware that some letters, including the vowels, **don't sound identical** in both languages, but they are **close enough**. (English has a much wider range of sounds than Spanish, which gives English speakers an advantage as learners). With practice you will perfect your pronunciation.

For example, the English "oo" of "good" is slightly longer than the Spanish "u." Differences like this make the learner have an accent in Spanish. But those adjustments to the new language occur fast (and for the most part unconsciously) when trying to imitate the native speakers.

2. THE VOWELS

For now what is important is that you remember that the Spanish a, e, i, o, u always sound the same. On the contrary, in English, "a," for instance, sounds differently in "apple" and "ape."

Remember that every letter sounds independently. Thus, the combination of them must be pronounced accordingly. Examples:

>león = l +e + o +n (= lion)
>día = d + i +a (= day)

The letter "u" is silent when preceded by "q," or when preceded by "g." Examples:

>Quito   = k + i + t + o (= Quito)
>guitarra = g + i + t + a + r r + a ("g" like in "guitar")

Following this idea, if you have two vowels together, you must pronounce both. So, in Spanish, the name "Aaron" must sound as: a+a+r+o+n.

Frequently Asked Questions

FAQ: Is the letter "y" a vowel?

Vowel is defined as a type of letter or as a type of sound. The letters a, e, i, o and u always have vowel sounds. The letter "y" may sound as a vowel in certain cases.

In Spanish, the letter "y" sounds the same as the Spanish letter "i" when it means "and" (Fernando y Carlos = Fernando and Carlos); or when at the end of the word, e.g. hay (= there is), ley (= law), voy (= I go).

In those cases, letter "y" is considered as a vowel. Otherwise "y" is a consonant similar to the "j" in "major."

Exercises

a) Pronounce the words of the table of below. The table displays words of all the possible couples of vocalic sounds.

	a	e	i	o	u
a	Aarón	aéroplano	baipás	cacao	audio
e	real	proveer	freír	león	Europa
i	familia	siete	chiita	violeta	ciudad
o	boa	bohemio	coincidencia	zoo	Ourense
u	cuatro	nueve	ruina	monstruo	duunviro

In English:

	a	e	i	o	u
a	Aaron	airplane	bypass	cocoa	audio
e	real	to provide	to fry	lion	Europe
i	family	seven	Shia Muslim	violet	city
o	boa	bohemian	coincidence	zoo	Orense
u	four	nine	ruin	monster	duumviri

b) Pronounce the Spanish words: Asia, China, euro and pus (They have the same meaning in English).

When you pronounce them, if they sound like they do in English, then you did something wrong… They should sound:

$\underline{a}$ + s + i + a;
ch + $\underline{i}$ + n + a;
$\underline{e}$ + u + r o;
p + u + s

Vocabulary

Memorize the word "murciélago (= "bat," the animal). This is the only Spanish word containing all the vowels: a, e, i, o, u.

2. THE VOWELS

3. THE CONSONANTS
LAS CONSONANTES

The consonants are those letters (sounds) that are not vowels. They are:

Letter	Sound	Examples in Spanish
b	As in English.	Bolivia
c	**Two possible sounds:** When followed by *a, o, u* (ca, co, cu) or by a consonant (cr, cl) it sound as the hard "c" in English. Otherwise, it sounds like the the "c" in "cement." Only in Spain, it sounds like the "th" in "thing,"	→ capital, coma, curioso, crema, clase (= capital, comma, curious, cream, class) → cemento, cine (= cement, cinema)
d	Weaker than in English.	Diamante (= diamond)
f	As in English.	Filipinas (= Philippines)
g	**Two possible sounds:** When followed by *a, o, u* (ga, go, gu, gue, gui) or a consonant (gl, gr) as the hard "g" in English. Otherwise (ge ,gi) it sounds like the "h" in "Helen, hippo."	→ gato, golf, gurú, **gu**errilla, **gu**itarra, globo, gris (= cat, golf, guru, guerilla, guitar, balloon, gray) → general, gigante (= general, giant)

3. THE CONSONANTS

Letter	Sound	Examples in Spanish
h	Silent unless combined in "ch."	hora (= hour)
j	As the English "h" in "ham, Helen, hipo or home."	San José
k	As in English.	kilogramo (= kilogram)
l	As in English.	lámpara (= lamp)
m	As in English.	médico (= doctor)
n	As in English.	Nicaragua
ñ	Like the "gn" of "cognac."	coñac (= cognac)
p	As in English.	Perú
q	As is English (In Spanish, q is always followed by u).	Quito
r	**Two possible sounds:** Like the English "r," if not at the beginning of the word. Otherwise, at the beginning of a word, or paired, it sounds stronger.	→ hora (= hour) → rápido, carro (= rapid, car)
s	As in English.	sonido (= sound)
t	As in English.	Tijuana
v	As the English "b."	Venezuela
w	As in English.	waterpolo (= waterpolo)
x	As in English.	examen (= exam)
y	**Two possible sounds.** When either at the end of words or isolated (meaning "and") sounds like "ea" of "meal." **Otherwise**, it sounds as the English "j" in "major."	→ y (= and), Uruguay → mayor (= major)
z	Like the "c" in "cement," and only in Spain like the English "th."	zoo (= zoo)

Remember:

Letters **b** and **v** both sound like English "b."

Letter **c** has two sounds. In "**ce**," "**ci**," letter c sounds like in English. Only in Spain, it sounds as the th of **th**under. Otherwise, in "**ca, co, cu, cr, cl,**" it sounds like in English (like a "k").

Letter **d** is weaker than that of English. In Spanish "d" sounds especially weak when it's placed between vowels. Thus the words "cansado" (= tired) is pronounced "cansao" by some speakers.

Letter **g** has two sounds (as it does in English). In **ga, go, gu** sounds like the g in the English **ga**rage, **go**vernment, **gu**ru. Also like English, the combination **gue, gui** will sound: guerilla and guitar. This very sound is the one for the combinations gl, gr, like in gland, grand. However ge, gi sound like the Spanish "j" of "San José," which is a stronger than the English "h" of "ham."

Letter **h** is silent. However ch is pronounced like English of "China."

Letter **ñ** doesn't exist in English as a letter. However the sound is in popular words like "piñata," "jalapeño or "el niño" (the atmospheric phenomenon). It sounds like the gn in cog**n**ac or filet mig**n**on (close to the "nj" in i**nj**ection).

Letter **q** can only be found in the combination with "u" to form: que, qui. sounding as "k." Thus, the two spellings kilo and quilo result in the same pronunciation.

Letter **r** has two pronunciations: weak and strong r (simple and multiple vibrating r). The weak sound corresponds to that of the English "r." The strong r is represented either by the single letter r when in the beginning of the word or by "rr." English doesn't have this sound. The strong r sound has the same articulation as the weak r but the tongue vibrates (close to the onomatopoeia "brrr" or "grrr").

Letter **y** has two sounds. One as the Spanish vowel "i," (the English "ea" of meal") when meaning "and," or when at the end of a word, like "Paraguay." Otherwise it sounds as the English "j" in "major"

Letter **z** sounds as the "c" of "ceremony". Only in Spain, it sounds as the "th" of **th**under.

3. THE CONSONANTS

In addition, "**ch, ll, rr**" have one single sound each:

Pair	Sound	Examples in Spanish
ch	As in English.	Chile
ll	As the English "j" in joke.	llama (= flame)
rr	As the English "r," but it vibrates multiple times.	carro (= car)

Notice that only the **sounds** of the Spanish "ñ," "j," and the strong "r" are foreign in English. Try to pronounce the model words: co**gn**ac, San José, and "**brrr**!" Especially "**rr**" is a challenge for foreigner. Take time to learn to pronounce it.

Also notice that some letters have the same sound in Spanish. These are the pairs: b/v, ll/y, and j/g (ge, gi). Thus, these together with the silent letter "h" always become a problem of **spelling**. Examples:

gobernar (not ~~governar~~), general (not ~~jeneral~~), fallar (not ~~fayar~~), humano (not ~~umano~~)
(= to govern, general, to fail, human)

Regarding the pairs of consonants in the same syllable. Spanish only admits:

bl	cl	---	fl	gl	pl	tl *
br	cr	dr	fr	gr	pr	tr

(*) Very rarely found

Notice that all of them have either "l" or "r" as the second letter of the pair.

Examples:

blusa	clon	---	Florida	glaciar	planta	nauatl
brillo	acre	dragón	Francia	gran	primer	trío

Which mean:

blouse	clone	---	Florida	glacier	plant	nauatl
brightness	acre	dragon	France	great	first	trio

Spanish doesn't have **the sounds** for the English "sh" and "sr" (sheet, Sri Lanka).

Spanish doesn't have the pairs of **letters** "ck," and "ph." For those **sounds**, Spanish uses: "c," "qu" or "k," and "f;" for example:

>rock, check, elephant
>roca, cheque, elefante

Likewise, Spanish does not have the English pairs of **letters** bb, dd, ff, mm, pp, ss, tt or zz. For those **sounds**, Spanish uses a single letter. Examples:

>robbery, additional, difference, mommy, application, class, lottery, puzzle

>robo, adicional, diferencia, mamá, aplicación, clase, lotería, puzle.

Warning.

> In Spanish you may find cc, mb, mp, etc., but each letter of the pair belongs to different syllable. E.g.
> ac-tor, ac-ción, a-dic-to, e-le-fan-te
> (= actor, action, addict, elephant)

Now, with the rules explained, you can read any word and write (maybe misspelling) any word. The only thing left to be able to read is to learn where the stress is placed on each word, which constitutes the next chapter: *Chapter 4 Syllable and Stress.*

<u>Corollary</u>: Rules of Thumb on Spelling

Some basic rules can help you guess the right spelling in many cases (remember that there's no set of rules that covers all cases for the indistinguishable pairs v/b, g/j, ll/y, and the h).

>1) Pairs like "bb, dd, ff, pp, ss, tt, zz, sh, sr, ph" don't exist.
>E.g. abreviación, not ~~abbreviación~~; efecto, not ~~effecto~~; adicción*, not ~~addicción~~. (= effect; abbreviation, addiction)

>(*) Notice that the cc is, in reality, c-c, e.g. a-dic-ción

3. THE CONSONANTS

2) Words can't start with letter "s" followed by a consonant.
E.g. **es**pecial (= special), not ~~special~~ .

3) K and W are very rarely used (karate, kimono, okey –OK-, waterpolo, Washington and a few more). Use c or q for the k sound; and use: "gua, güe, güi, guo, gu" for the w-sound.

4) Use "ce," "ci"(sound: /theh/, /theeh/; not ~~ze, zi.~~)
E.g. **c**ero, not ~~zero~~ (as in English).

5) The plural of words ending in -z, is -ces, not –zes.
E.g. cruz → cru**ces**, not ~~cruzes~~ (= cross)

6) M (not n) goes before b or p.
E.g. bo**m**ba (= bomb or pump), not ~~bomva~~.

7) Words of the same family have similar spelling.
E.g. **h**ombre, **h**umano, **h**umanizar, **h**umanidades
(= man, human, humanize, humanities)

8) Words **ending** with "i" vowel sound in Spanish are spelled: ay, ey, oy, uy (not ai, ei, oi, ui), as long as the stress is not in the last vowel.
E.g. Paragu**ay**, ah**í**, r**ey**, re**í**, l**ey**, le**í**, h**oy**, o**í**, h**uy**, hu**í**
(=Paraguay, there, king, I laughed, , law, I read (past), today, I heard, ouch!, I fled).

9) Words starting with vowel sounds "ua," "ue," "ui," "ia," and "ie" are spelled with "h:" hua, hue, hui, hia, hie.
E.g. Huáscar, huevo, huir, hiato, hielo
(= Huascar, egg, to flee, hiatus, ice).

Frequently Asked Questions

FAQ 1: What are the two dots on the "u" in "lingüista?"

Words like lingüista or pingüino (= linguist, penguin) have this symbol called dieresis (diéresis, in Spanish). We saw that in the combination "gue" "gui" the "u" is silent. To spell a word where the "u" needs to sound, you need dieresis. It is also used in English by some newspapers to mark that a certain letter must be pronounced, like "coöperation" (the "oo" would sound like in boot, otherwise). Spanish uses this symbol with the same intent: to mark that the "u" must be pronounced.

FAQ 2: I've seen both "México" and "Méjico." What's the right spelling?

Both. The Spanish words México, Nuevo México, Texas and Oaxaca can be spelled with "x" or with "j." The **Mexican** Academy of Spanish Language decided to spell it with "x" for historical reasons, although, in any case, it is pronounced with a Spanish "j" sound. In the rest of the Spanish speaking countries, these words are spelled with "j" (Méjico, Nuevo Méjico, Tejas, Oajaca and a few others).

FAQ 3: Why have I never heard the English "th" sound in Spanish?

Using the "s" sound instead of "th" sound is also accepted. This use is found in Latin America, including Mexico and the US (See Appendix A: Notes About Dialects).

FAQ 4: Should "y" and "ll" sound the same?

Originally "ll" sounded as the English "ll" in "million" (It still sounds this way in some places of Spain and Bolivia). With time, "ll" acquired the sound of the "y." **Nowadays** both "y" and "ll" sound the same. On the other hand, there are variations in the way Spanish speakers pronounce y. In Argentina, it sounds especially strong (See Appendix A: Notes About Dialects).

Exercises

a) Taking advantage that some names of places are the same or very similar in Spanish and English, pronounce:

        Uruguay
        Paraguay
        Chile (remember, Ch is one single sound)
        Argentina (remember, here g sounds like a strong English "h")
        Ecuador
        Bolivia (remember, v and b sound identical)
        Venezuela
        Colombia
        Perú (remember, the accent gives you the stressed vowel)
        Panamá
        República Dominicana (remember, strong "r")

3. THE CONSONANTS   37

       Costa Rica
       Guatemala
       Honduras (remember, h is silent)
       El Salvador
       Nicaragua
       Méjico, México (remember, both have the same pronunciation)
       Cuba
       España (remember, the sound of ñ like in El Niño)

(The above list is that of the countries that have Spanish as their first language.)

b) Pronounce the Spanish words:

       Puerto Rico
       Estados Unidos (= United States)
       California
       Nuevo Méjico, Nuevo Méjico (same pronunciation)
       Tejas, Texas (same pronunciation)
       Colorado
       Arizona
       Nevada
       Florida (not Florida)
       Norteamérica (= North America)
       Suramérica (= South America)
       Centroamérica (= Central America)

c) Pronounce the Spanish words:

       general (same meanings as in English the opposite of "specific"
            and the military rank)
       hotel (same meaning as in English)
       zoo (same meaning as in English)

Answers

       When you pronounce them, if they sound like they do in English, then you are doing something wrong. They should sound:

       g + e+ n + e + r + a + l ("g" sounds like the "J" in "San José")
       o + t + e + l ("h" is silent)
       z + o + o ("z" sounds like th; "o" sounds twice)

d) Some English words have the same sound in Spanish, but their spelling is different. Pronounce each of the following English words, and then write them down in Spanish:

> taboo
> scanner
> O.K.
> whisky
> bypass
> snob
> standard
> stress
> sweater
> baseball

Hint. Apply the rule of thumb of the corollary of this chapter "Rules of Thumb on Spelling" to find out the right spelling.

Answers

English	Spanish
taboo	tabú
scanner	escáner
O.K.	okey
whisky	güisqui *
bypass	baipás
snob	esnob
standard	estándar
stress	estrés
sweater	suéter
baseball	béisbol

(*) whisky is also accepted by the RAE (Real Academia Española).

e) Correct the spelling of the misspelled Spanish words: addicto, ueso, rraro, invitarr, Paraguai, zírculo, zelebrar, vozes.

> adicto, hueso, raro, invitar, Paraguay, círculo, celebrar, voces
>
> (= addict, bone, rare, to invite, Paraguay, circle, to celebrate, voices)

3. THE CONSONANTS

Vocabulary

In *Chapter 8 How to Learn Words Efficiently*, you'll have the tools to start developing your own vocabulary.

Until then, you can start with:

la pal<u>a</u>bra	=	the word
la l<u>e</u>tra	=	the letter (of the alphabet)
el alfab<u>e</u>to	=	the alphabet
el son<u>i</u>do	=	the sound

Notes: Both the letters underlined here are to help you learn the right pronunciation.

"The" is sometimes translated by "**el**," and other times by "**la**" as in the table above. We will see that difference ahead in *Chapter 6 Masculine/Feminine*. By now, just notice that most words with "**el**" end with "o" (like el sonido), and most with "**la**" end with "a"(like la palabra).

You can learn **the names of the letters** of the alphabet. Note: the letter that each of them represents is here in bold.

a	jota	<u>e</u>rre
be	ka	<u>e</u>se
ce	<u>e</u>le	te
de	<u>e</u>me	u
e	<u>e</u>ne	<u>u</u>ve (also ve c<u>o</u>rta)
<u>e</u>fe	<u>e</u>ñe	<u>u</u>ve d<u>o</u>ble (also d<u>o</u>ble ve, d<u>o</u>ble u) (**w**)
ge	o	<u>e</u>kis (**x**)
h<u>a</u>che	pe	ye (also i gri<u>e</u>ga)
i	ku (**q**)	z<u>e</u>ta

You should also learn the names of some places and peoples:

Méjico, México (same pronunciation)

Pu<u>e</u>rto R<u>i</u>co

Est<u>a</u>dos Un<u>i</u>dos (= United States)

Calif<u>o</u>rnia

Nu<u>e</u>vo Méjico, Nuevo México (same pronunciation) (= New Mexico)

Tejas, Texas (same pronunciation)

Colorado

Arizona

Nevada

Florida (not Florida)

América

Norteamérica (= North America)

Suramérica (= Central America)

Centroamérica (= Central America)

mejicano, mexicano (= Mexican)

tejano, texano (= Texan)

puertoriqueño (= Puerto Rican)

americano, norteamericano, estadounidense (= American, from North America, from the US)

centroamericano (= Central American)

suramericano (= South American)

californiano (= Californian)

español (= Spanish language, Spaniard, Spanish – adjective-)

Note: Unlike English, the name of peoples are written in lower case (e.g. **m**exicano = **M**exican)

4. SYLLABLE AND STRESS
SÍLABA Y ACENTO

So far, you know how to pronounce the sound of a word but not the right intonation of it. It's not the same to say "dess<u>e</u>rt" and "d<u>e</u>sert," or <u>i</u>mport and imp<u>o</u>rt. Every word has a point of emphasis or stress.

The rules of the **accent marks** are especially useful for foreigners. With them you will be able to read any word on your own, without having listened to it before. In turn, you will be able to learn your own words from the dictionary without help.

Golden Rule

> All words, with no exception, have one, and only one, point of **stress**, and this always falls on a vowel (never on a consonant). The **accent marks** (á, é, í, ó, ú) indicate where the stressed vowel is. However, the majority of words don't require an **accent mark**.

This book uses the underline to indicate where the stress of a word is when the accent mark is not used.

The rules of the accents marks are in this chapter. They are simple to learn once you know how to break down a word into syllables.

4. SYLLABLE AND STRESS

Breakdown of Words into Syllables

Unlike English, in Spanih the breakdown of words into syllables is very intuitive.

> ca-rro, ga-to, cla-se, ac-tor, a-pén-di-ce
> (= car, cat, class, actor, appendix)

What will need some explanation are the words with syllables that have two or more vowels. For instance, you need to know why "Dios" (= God) has one syllable and "león" (= lion) has two (le-ón).

There are four elemental rules for syllabication:

One. Every syllable has **at least** one vowel: a, e, i, o, u.

Two. Only the following pair of consonants can be together in the same syllable:

bl	cl	---	fl	gl	pl	tl
br	cr	dr	fr	gr	pr	tr

And, of course, the single-sound pairs: **ch, ll, rr**.

> E.g. **"blanco"** (= white) can only be split into blan-co, since "bl" cannot be separate ("bl" is one of the pairs of the above), and since "nc" cannot be together (it is not a pair of the above.)

Three. Two vowels will stay in the same syllable if at least one of them is a weak vowel. Classification of vowels:

> a, e, o: strong vowels
> i, u: weak vowels (the "sticky ones")

Weak vowels create diphthongs (two vowels in the same syllable)

Rule of thumb: weak vowels tend to be "sticky" and glue the vowels next to them in the same syllable.

Bellow, you will see this in all possible combination of vowels:

	a	e	i/ -y	o	u
a	A-a-rón	ca-er	hay	va-ho	áu-re-o
e	re-al	le-er	ley	le-ón	Eu-ro-pa
i/ -y	re-cio	sie-te	chi-i-ta	mer-cu-rio	ciu-dad
o	ca-no-a	ro-er	hoy	di-cién-do-os	Ou-ren-se
u	cua-tro	nue-ve	rui-na	an-ti-guo	du-un-vi-ro

The rule of thumb above is also applicable to those few words that have three vowels in a row. e.g. U-ru-guay.

The translation of those words (if you are curious) is below:

	a	e	i/ -y	o	u
a	Aaron	to fall	there is	steam	golden
e	real	to read	law	lion	Europe
i/ -y	strong	seven	Shia Muslim	mercury	city
o	canoe	to gnaw	today	telling you guys (Spain)	Orense
u	four	nine	ruin	old	duunviri

Four. However, if the pair has a weak and a strong vowel (or strong and weak) and the word has the stress on the weak one, then the pair gets separated into two syllables. E.g. día → dí-a; (= day)

4. SYLLABLE AND STRESS

Rules of Accents

Remember: all words in Spanish have one, and only one, point of stress, and this always falls on a vowel. The accent mark is a mark of the stress.

The syllable that carries the stressed vowel is called the stressed syllable.

The first three rules that follow are called General Rules. These rules should be learned first; the others are their amendments.

General Rules

One. If the stress is on the **last syllable**, and the word ends with VOWEL, N or S; then the word will have an accent mark.

> autobús, Ceilán, Perú, adiós, televisión
> (= bus, Ceilan, Peru, bye, television)
>
> Examples of words with **no** accent mark: actor, actriz, cancelar, reloj (= actor, actress, to cancel, clock)

Two. If the stress is on the **second to last** and the word does **not** end with a VOWEL, N, or S, then it will have an accent mark.

> álbum, suéter, móvil, mármol, Pérez.
> (= album, sweater, mobile, marble, Perez).
>
> Examples of words with **no** accent mark: carro, torre, perfecto
> (= car, tower, perfect).

Three. If the stress is on the **third to last syllable or earlier**, it will have an accent mark, regardless of other considerations.

> apéndice, lógico, rígido, lámpara, búlgaro, teléfono, electrónico.
> (= appendix, logical, rigid, lamp, Bulgarian, telephone, electronic)
>
> **Notice** that the counting of syllables starts from the last: last, second to last, third to last (not first, second, third).

Additional Rules:

Four. When the two conditions below exist, it will have an accent mark.
- the stress is on a syllable with a strong vowel followed by a weak vowel (ai, ei, oi, au, eu, ou), or vice versa (ia, ie, io, ua, ue, uo, iu, ui), **and**
- the vowel with the stress is a weak vowel

Examples:

día, caído, búho, río, ríe, día, baúl, Seúl, biografía, García, oído.

(= day, fallen, owl, I laugh, he laughs, day, trunk, Seoul, biography, Garcia, hear)

This rule supercedes the previous ones.

Five. Single-syllable words will **not** have an accent mark.

E.g. voz, mar, sol, y, o, buey (= voice, ocean, sun, and, or, ox)

The exception of this rule are showed next.

Six. There is a list of words that have accents in order to distinguish two meanings. For example: "sí" (= yes) and "si" (= if) sound identical. The accent mark is used to leave clear which is which.

This rule supersedes the previous ones.

These words are:

Spanish	English
el / él	the / he
tu / tú	your / you
mi / mí	my / me (as in "for me")
que / qué	"what" in sentences that are not questions or exclamations, as in "This is what I want."/ "what" in sentences that are questions or exclamations, as in "What is that?"

4. SYLLABLE AND STRESS 47

Spanish	English
cual / cuál	which / which (same differentiation as with "what")
quien / quién	which / which (same differentiation as with "what")
donde / dónde	where / where (same differentiation as with "what")
cuando / cuándo	when / when (same differentiation as with "what")
como / cómo	as / how
si / sí	if / yes
aun / aún	even / still
mas / más	but / more
de / dé	of / "I give" (subjunctive)
se / sé	himself, herself, themselves / I know
te / té	your / tea

This table is updated following the *Real Academia's* recommendations on spelling of 2010. Before, for example, words as "este", would require accent mark when being a pronoun.

Seven. Other considerations. In words ending in "mente" (suffix –ly) you have to remove the suffix in order to apply the rules above. E.g. fácilmente, calmadamente. (= easily, calmly)

The Rules of Accents were created with the goal of having the lowest number of words requiring accent marks. For example, one-syllable words don't have an accent mark (rule 4).

Either explicitly or implicitly, the rules of accents tell you where the stress is.

For example, "transporte" (= transportation)

"Transporte" could be:
| tr**a**nsporte
| transp**o**rte
| transport**e**

- If it was tr**a**nsporte, it would have an accent mark (rule 3)
- If it was transport**e**, it would have an accent mark (rule 1)

Consequently, since "transporte" does not have an accent mark, the pronunciation will be: transp**o**rte.

Another example: "experimentar" (= to experience)

"Experimentar" could be:
| **e**xperimentar
| exp**e**rimentar
| expe**r**imentar
| experim**e**ntar
| experiment**a**r

- If it was **e**xperimentar, exp**e**rimentar or expe**r**imentar, it would have an accent mark (rule 3)
- If it was experim**e**ntar, it would have an accent mark (rule 2)

Consequently, since it does not have an accent mark, it will be experiment**a**r.

Frequently Asked Questions

FAQ 1: Vídeo or Video?

Just a few words can be pronounced with different stress. This is the case of vídeo/ vid**e**o (= video, video tape, DVR), and período/peri**o**do (=period). You choose.

FAQ 2: Do I really need to learn how to break the words into syllables?

Yes, if you want to learn the rules of accents you must learn to break words into syllables.

4. SYLLABLE AND STRESS

FAQ 3: What is the difference between accent mark and stress?

Stress is the elevation of intonation of a vowel in the word. An accent mark is the mark that indicates that stress. In Spanish, every word has one (and only one) stressed vowel; however, most of the words don't have an accent mark. The term "accent" is confusing since it may mean either "stress" or "accent mark." Normally "accent" refers to "accent mark."

This book uses the underline to mark the stress in those words that have no accent mark.

FAQ 4: How do I know where the stress is in words like "construimos," which has two vowels together in the stressed syllable?

In Spanish, when two weak vowels (i and u) are found together in the stressed syllable, the stress is always on the second vowel: cons-tru<u>i</u>-mos (= we build). Another example: h<u>ui</u>r (= to flee).

Exercises

Divide the following words into syllables:

	a	e	i	o	u
a	Aarón	aéreo	ahí	ahora	aún
e	marea	creer	rey	neón	eureka
i	diario	viejo	chiita	violeta	viuda
o	boa	roedor	soy	zoo	Ourense
u	cuadro	hueso	huir	búho	duunviro

The translation (if you are curious about their meaning)

	a	e	i	o	u
a	Aaron	airborne	there	now	still
e	tide	to believe	king	neon	Eureka
i	daily	old	Shia Muslim	violet	widow
o	boa	rodent	I am	zoo	Orense
u	painting	bone	to flee	awl	duumvir

Answers

	a	e	i	o	u
a	A-a-rón	a-é-re-o	a-hí*	a-ho-ra	a-ún*
e	ma-re-a	cre-er	rey	ne-ón	eu-re-ka
i	dia-rio	vie-jo	chi-i-ta	vio-le-ta	viu-da
o	bo-a	ro-e-dor	soy	zo-o	Ou-ren-se
u	cua-dro	hue-so	huir	bú-ho*	du-un-vi-ro

(*) The stress is on the weak vowel of the pair, that is why the syllable split (fourth Rule of Accents).

Notice that you can test yourself on accent marks by looking at the words of the vocabulary at the end of each chapter. All those words have the stressed vowel underlined.

Vocabulary

el ac<u>e</u>nto	=	the accent mark (also accent as in Irish accent)
la sílaba	=	the syllable
la sem<u>a</u>na	=	the week
el día *	=	the day
qué	=	what
es	=	is
hoy	=	today
¿Qué día es hoy?	=	What day is it today?
Hoy es Martes.	=	Today is Tuesday

4. SYLLABLE AND STRESS

The days of the week:

l<u>u</u>nes *	=	Monday
m<u>a</u>rtes	=	Tuesday
miércoles	=	Wednesday
ju<u>e</u>ves	=	Thursday
vi<u>e</u>rnes	=	Friday
sábado	=	Saturday
dom<u>i</u>ngo	=	Sunday

(*) In Spanish, weeks start on Monday, not Sunday.

The translation of the "on" of "**on** Monday, on Tuesday" is "**el** Lunes, **el** Martes…"

SECTION II

VOCABULARY
VOCABULARIO

Congratulations! Now you can read and write words in Spanish.

This section will teach you how to learn the meaning of those words by looking in the dictionary. Obvious? Not really. Imagine that you want to know the meaning of the English word "appendices" (not appendix). If the dictionary doesn't include the plural of words, you'd get frustrated by finding "appendix," but not appendices.

Another example would be if you wanted to look up the English word "studied" (not: study).

This short Section II will give you a guide by discussing three topics:

    Singular/plural , also called number

    Masculine/feminine, also called gender

    Person and tense, also called conjugation

In the end of this section, you will be able to find any word in the dictionary to create your own dictionary with your own vocabulary.

5. SINGULAR / PLURAL
SINGULAR / PLURAL

Like English, Spanish has "singular/plural" (identifiers for one/more than one), and both languages use the same way to identify "more than one:" they add the letter "**s**."

Like in English if the noun is plural, then the word that precedes it (determiner) is also plural. The words "a," "this," "that" and "the" are called determiners.

        <u>a</u>   <u>hotel</u>,   <u>some</u> <u>hotels</u>
        DET. NOUN   DET. NOUN

        <u>un</u> <u>hotel</u>,   <u>unos</u> <u>hoteles</u>
        DET. NOUN   DET. NOUN

    this cat, these cats
    este gato, estos gatos

    that elephant, those elephants
    ese elefante, esos elefantes

Unlike English, the determiner "the" also changes.

    the planet, the planets
    el planeta, los planetas

5. SINGULAR / PLURAL

Unlike English, in Spanish if the noun is plural, the adjective (like elegant, black or enormous) is also plural.

<u>an</u> <u>elegant</u> <u>hotel,</u>   <u>some</u> <u>elegant</u> <u>hotels,</u>
DET. ADJ. NOUN   DET. ADJ.   NOUN

<u>un</u> <u>hotel</u> <u>elegante,</u>   <u>unos</u> <u>hoteles</u> <u>elegantes</u>
DET. NOUN ADJ.   DET. NOUN   ADJ.

this black cat, these black cats (where the word black does not change).
este gato negro, estos gatos negros

that enormous elephant, those enormous elephants (where the word enormous does not change)
ese elefante enorme, esos elefantes enormes

Golden Rule

> Like English, Spanish creates the plural by adding:
> -"**s**," if the word ends in a vowel
> -"**es**," if the word ends in a consonant

Examples

One hour, two hour**s**, three hour**s**
Una hora, dos hora**s**, tres hora**s**

One album, two albums, three albums
un álbum, dos álbum**es**, tres álbum**es**

If the word ends in letter "z," then you change "z" to a "c" and add "es."

One cross, two cross**es**, three cross**es**
Una cruz, dos cru**ces**, tres cru**ces**

Only some determiners add "**os**" to create the plural. These are:

un / unos (a/some)
el / los (the/the -plural)
este / estos (this/these)
ese / esos (that/those)
aquel / aquellos (that/those*)
algún / algunos (any/some*)

(*) The translation of these words requires further explanation. This is given in *Chapter 11 Determiners.*

Corollary 1: Numbers

By paying attention to the series of numbers, you can easily deduce how to form any figure:

1	2	3	4	5	6	7	8	9	10
uno	dos	tres	cuatro	cinco	seis	siete	ocho	nueve	diez

underscore indicates stressed vowel.

10, 11, 12…19	20, 21, 22…29	30, 31, 32…39
diez	veinte	treinta
once	veintiuno	treinta y uno
doce	veintidós	treinta y dos
trece	veintitrés	treinta y tres
catorce	veinticuatro	treinta y cuatro
quince	veinticinco	treinta y cinco
dieciséis	veintiséis	treinta y seis
diecisiete	veintisiete	treinta y siete
dieciocho	veintiocho	treinta y ocho
diecinueve	veintinueve	treinta y nueve

40, 41, 42…49	50, 51, 52…59	60, 61, 62…69
cuarenta	cincuenta	sesenta
cuarenta y uno	cincuenta y uno	sesenta y uno
cuarenta y dos	cincuenta y dos	sesenta y dos
cuarenta y tres	cincuenta y tres	sesenta y tres
cuarenta y cuatro	cincuenta y cuatro	sesenta y cuatro
cuarenta y cinco	cincuenta y cinco	sesenta y cinco
cuarenta y seis	cincuenta y seis	sesenta y seis
cuarenta y siete	cincuenta y siete	sesenta y siete
cuarenta y ocho	cincuenta y ocho	sesenta y ocho
cuarenta y nueve	cincuenta y nueve	sesenta y nueve

5. SINGULAR / PLURAL

70, 71, 72…79	80, 81, 82…89	90, 91, 92…99
setenta	ochenta	noventa
setenta y uno	ochenta y uno	noventa y uno
setenta y dos	ochenta y dos	noventa y dos
setenta y tres	ochenta y tres	noventa y tres
setenta y cuatro	ochenta y cuatro	noventa y cuatro
setenta y cinco	ochenta y cinco	noventa y cinco
setenta y seis	ochenta y seis	noventa y seis
setenta y siete	ochenta y siete	noventa y siete
setenta y ocho	ochenta y ocho	noventa y ocho
setenta y nueve	ochenta y nueve	noventa y nueve

100	cien, ciento
200	doscientos/as
300	trescientos/as
400	cuatrocientos/as
500	quinientos/as
600	seiscientos/as
700	setecientos/as
800	ochocientos/as
900	novecientos/as
1000	mil
10,000	diez mil
100,000	cien mil
1,000,000	un millón
1,000,000,000	mil millones
100,000,000,000	cien mil millones
1,000,000,000,000	un billón

Notes

There is a distinction between "uno" and "un/una" (see next *Chapter 6 Masculine/Feminine*). "Uno" can only be used when it refers to a number, not a quantity of something.

       twenty one; twenty one albums, twenty one hours
       veintiuno; ventinún álbumes; ventinuna horas

The word "cien" changes to "ciento" when it is not one hundred even.

       100 albums;   101 albums;   190 albums
       cien álbumes; ciento un álbumes; ciento noventa álbumes

       100,000 albums;   1,100 albums
       cien mil álbumes; mil cien álbumes

The words doscientos (200), trescientos (300),... novecientos (900) change to doscientas, trescientas, ...novecientas if the word that follows is feminine (*Chapter 6 Masculine/Feminine*).

       Five hundred people
       Quinient**as** person**as**

The word "millón" in Spanish needs the word "de" (= of), unlike English.

       100 hours; 1,000 hours; 1,000,000 hours
       cien horas; mil horas;   un millón de horas

In Spanish figures are never expressed in terms of hundreds.

       2100 = two thousand one hundred or twenty one hundred
       2100 = dos mil cien (not veintiún cientos)

"Billón" in Spanish is <u>not</u> billion in English, but 1,000,000,000,000. "Mil millones" is one billion.

5. SINGULAR / PLURAL

Corollary 2: Telling the Time

To refer to a time or ask for the time:

>What's the time?
>¿Qué hora es?

>**At** what time is the concert?
>¿**A** qué hora es el concierto?

As in English there are **two forms** to tell the time:

>It's one fifteen.   = It's a quarter past one.
>Es la una y quince. = Es la una y cuarto.

One Form	The Other Form	Time
Son las doce y 45	Es la una menos cuarto.	12:45
Es la una.	Es la una en punto.	1:00
Es la una y 15.	Es la una y cuarto.	1:15
Es la una y 30.	Es la una y media.	1:30
Son las dos.	Son las dos en punto.	2:00
Son las dos y 5.		2:05
Son las dos y 10.		2:10
Son las dos y 15.	Son las dos y cuarto.	2:15
Son las dos y 20.		2:20
Son las dos y 25.		2:25
Son las dos y 30.	Son las dos y media.	2:30
Son las dos y 35.	Son las tres menos 25.	2:35
Son las dos y 40.	Son las tres menos 20.	2:40
Son las dos y 45.	Son las tres menos cuarto.	2:45
Son las dos y 50.	Son las tres menos 10.	2:50
Son las dos y 55.	Son las tres menos 5.	2:55

Corollary 3: Telling the Date

In Spanish, when telling the date, the day always precedes the month

>What day of the week is today? Today is Saturday.
>¿Qué día es hoy?　　　　　　　Hoy es Sábado.

>What date is today? Today is February 21, 2007.
>¿Qué día es hoy?　　　Hoy es 21 de Febrero de 2007.

Month	Mes	Month	Mes
January	Enero	July	Julio
February	Febrero	August	Agosto
March	Marzo	September	Septiembre
April	Abril	October	Octubre
May	Mayo	November	Noviembre
June	Junio	December	Diciembre

Frequently Asked Questions

FAQ 1: What's the plural of words like "cactus?"

Like English, Spanish has a reduced number of words that have an irregular plural, like cactus.

>un cactus, dos cactus, tres cactus
>(= a cactus, two cacti, three cacti)

In general, Spanish words ending in "–us," "–is" don't change. An exception is gris-grises (= gray).

>crisis - crisis, análisis - análisis, tesis -tesis
>(= crisis - crises, analysis - analyses, thesis - theses)

FAQ 2: Can I express years in hundreds?

No, in Spanish no quantity (not only years) is expressed in hundreds.

>In nineteen forty (1940)...
>En mil novecientos cuarenta... (not ~~En diecinueve cuarenta~~)

5. SINGULAR / PLURAL

Exercises

Spell out:

    253   153   1,101   1,929   2,128   5,100

Answers

253	doscientos cincuenta y tres
153	ciento cincuenta y tres
1,101	mil ciento uno
1,929	mil novecientos veintinueve
2,128	dos mil ciento veintiocho
5,100	cinco mil cien

Vocabulary

Learn the numbers and how to write the figures. Learn the months of the year. The translation of "in" (in January) is "en" (en Enero).

el ac<u>e</u>nto	=	the accent mark
el mes	=	the month
el <u>a</u>ño	=	the year
la f<u>e</u>cha	=	the date
de	=	of
la h<u>o</u>ra	=	the hour
y	=	and
cu<u>a</u>rto	=	quarter (1/4)
m<u>e</u>dia	=	half
son	=	they are
m<u>e</u>nos	=	minus

    (<u>Underlined</u> indicates the stress of the word).

Notice that Spanish doesn't use the ordinals (first, second, third...) for dates, as English does (e.g. first of June).

6. MASCULINE / FEMININE
MASCULINO / FEMENINO

Some nouns have gender. In both Enlgish and Spanish, there are words that reflect this.

>boy/girl,   lion/lioness,   actor/actress
>niño/niña,   león/leona,   actor/actriz

However English nouns referring to things generally don't have gender. There are exceptions (lion/lioness). Generally, English divides the world into living and non-living. Gender applies only to living things (he, she, man, woman, etc.). Spanish categorizes all entities into masculine and feminine.

English makes no additional distinction whether the word is masculine or feminine. Spanish does. In Spanish all words around a noun (i.e. determiners and adjectives) must have the same gender as the noun.

>`a` lion   / `a` lioness
>`un` león/ `una` leona

>`the` `small` boy   / `the` `small` girl
>`el` niño `pequeño` / `la` niña `pequeña`

6. MASCULINE / FEMININE

In addition, Spanish assigns a gender to **every noun**, i.e. every object, material or immaterial, can be masculine or feminine. Examples:

- Masculine: cemento, kilo, carro, sonido, yate
  (= cement, kilo, car, sound, yacht)

- Feminine: guitarra, isla, hora, avenida, luz
  (= guitar, island, hour, avenue, light)

However, the words around the noun (determiners and adjectives) don't have an **intrinsic** gender. The same word can change masculine and feminine. Example: americano (= American) is an adjective, and it can be americano (masculine) or americana (feminine).

niño americano (= American boy)
niña americana (= American girl)

Some rules were found to help students to recognize if a noun is masculine or feminine. These rules are based on the endings of words (meaningful endings of words are called "suffixes").

Golden Rule

> Words ending with an **"o" tend** to be masculine; ending with an **"a" tend** to be feminine.

For example: el cemento, la guitarra. There are exceptions, for instance: (el) mapa, (la) mano.

Other basic rules of gender are:

- Words ending in "**-ma**" tend to be masculine, e.g. el dilema (= dilemma), el problema (= problem). There are some exceptions: (la) calma (= calm).

- Words ending in "**-dad**," and "**-ción**" are feminine, e.g. la identidad, la diversidad, la realidad, la solución, la intervención, la atracción (= identity, diversity, reality, solution, intervention, attraction). Notice that "-dad" and "-ción" correspond to the English "-ty" and "-tion."

- Words ending in "**-ista**" ("-ist" in English) will be masculine or feminine depending on the person who is referred to, e.g. el artista (= artist) Pablo Picasso, la artista Frida Kahlo.

Besides, certain groups of nouns have a defined gender:

- The names of the letters are feminine, e.g: la A, la Be, la Ce, etc.

- The names of the numbers are masculine: el uno, el dos, el tres, etc. (= one, two, three, etc.)

- The names of countries tend to be masculine unless ending in "a." e.g. Brasil (masculine), España (feminine); "Brasil es lindo, España es linda" (= Brazil is beautiful, Spain is beautiful").

- Foreign words tend to be masculine, unless ending in "a." e.g. el software; la pizza

Collections are masculine: When you have a collection of names, with masculine **and** feminine elements in it, use the masculine gender.

> I have four daughters and one son: they are my children.
> Tengo cuatro hijas y un hijo: son mis hijos.
>
> My uncles and aunts live in Texas.
> Mis tíos viven en Texas.
>
> Spain and Brazil are beautiful.
> España y Brasil son lindos.

From now on, it's important that you memorize nouns with their proper gender. In Spanish dictionaries, the first information that is presented about a noun is whether it is masculine or feminine.

Warning

> Here are some basic rules that will help you. However, there are many exceptions. It is important when you learn a new word from the dictionary, you learn it with its gender (Remember: only nouns have gender).

6. MASCULINE / FEMININE

Frequently Asked Questions

FAQ 1: I've seen "el arpa" (= the harp), but my Spanish dictionary says that it is feminine. Shouldn't it be "la arpa?"

It's "el arpa," even if the word "arpa" is feminine. We change "la" to "el" to avoid a bad sound of two a's together. This rule is applicable only if the word starts with a stressed "a," like <u>a</u>rpa, <u>a</u>gua, <u>á</u>guila (eagle), <u>a</u>ncla (anchor). This is explained in *Chapter 11 Determiners*.

FAQ 2: El radio or la radio?

A few words in the Spanish language can have two genders. One example is *radio* (= radio). You can say "el radio" (masculine) or "la radio" (feminine). Both are correct.

There are other set of words (a few) that are very similar but have different gender. Examples are: "el computador" /" la computadora" (= the computer) and "el televisor"/ "la televisión" (= the TV set).

Exercises

a) Put the right article: "el" or "la."

software   pizza
hardware   piercing
email   hobby
whisky   kleenex
campus   ipod
hippy   broker
picnic   camping
sandwich   best seller

Each of the following words is an English word that Spanish has adopted as is. Thus, regardless of their spelling, they must be pronounced as English words.

Answers

el software	la pizza
el hardware	el piercing
el email	el hobby
el whisky	el kleenex
el campus	el ipod
el/la hippy	el broker
el picnic	el camping
el sandwich	el best seller

b) The following words have a gender that you can deduce out of the rules. Put the right article: el, la.

Europa, hijo, papá, nueve, hache
(= Europe, son, dad, nine, h)

Answers

(la) Europa*, el hijo, el papá, el nueve, la hache

(*) The names of countries have gender although article el/la many times is not used. "Francia es linda" (not: La Francia es lindo).

Vocabulary

If you have started your vocabulary list, make sure that you know the right gender of every word on it.

In addition, these words are suggested to be included.

el/la hijo/a	=	the son, the daughter
el/la niño/a	=	the boy, the girl
el/la hermano/a	=	the brother, the sister
el/la tío/a	=	the uncle, the aunt
el/la abuelo/a	=	the grandfather, the grandmother
el/la sobrino/a	=	the nephew, the niece
el/la nieto/a	=	the grandson, the granddaughter
los hijos	=	the children (sons and daughter)

6. MASCULINE / FEMININE

los nietos	=	the grandchildren
el hombre	=	the man
la mujer	=	the woman
el/la suegro/a	=	the father-in-law/ the mother-in-law
el/la cuñado/a	=	the brother-in-law/ the sister-in-law
el yerno	=	the son-in-law/
la nuera	=	the daughter-in-law
el papá *	=	the father
la mamá *	=	the mother

(*) In Spain, it's used "padre" and "madre" for father and mother.

7. CONJUGATION
CONJUGACIÓN

If you looked up the words "studied," "studies" or "studying" in the English dictionary you may not find them. This is because all tenses of the verb "to study" are represented only by the word "study." The form of the verb with the preposition "to" (to study) is called the infinitive.

Golden Rule.

> In Spanish, the infinitive (the proxy of the verb) **always** ends with -AR, -ER or –IR.

For example:

> estudi**ar**, correspond**er**, distribu**ir**
> (= to study, to correspond, to distribute)

Those three endings correspond to three patterns called "conjugaciones" (= conjugations). It's important that you learn these names:

- Verbs ending in -AR are called **AR-verbs,** or verbs of the **first conjugation.**

- Verbs ending in -ER are called **ER-verbs**, or verbs of the **second conjugation**.

- Verbs ending in -IR are called **IR-verbs**, or verbs of the **third conjugation.**

7. CONJUGATION

Thus although you may find the word "estudia" (= he studies), you probably won't find it in the dictionary. You must look for "estud**iar**" (= to study) which is the infinitive, the representative of its family.

The dictionary will also tell you if the verb is regular or irregular, in other words, if the verb follows the rules when it is conjugated.

English puts the information of who makes the action (I, you, he/she/it, we, you, they) before the verb (I do something). On the contrary, Spanish puts this information within the verb, at the end of the verb, as a suffix.

<u>We adore</u> theatre. <u>They paint</u> houses.
<u>Adoramos</u> el teatro. <u>Pintan</u> casas.

Golden Rule

In Spanish the subject of the sentence is always **in** the verb The translations of the English personal pronouns are suffixes: particles at the end of the verb. These are:

English	Spanish	Example
I	= VOWEL* or –y	plane**o**, so**y** (= **I** plan, **I** am)
You (singular)	= –s **	invita**s** (= **you** invite)
he/she/it	= –VOWEL*	cuent**a** (= **he/she** counts)
We	= –mos	convence**mos** (= **we** convince)
You guys (Spain)	= –is	aparecé**is** (= **you** appear)
You guys/ They***	= –n	estudia**n** (= **you/ they** study)

(*) These VOWELS can be: a, e, i, o, depending on the tense. For example: canto (= I sing), canté (= I sang)

(**) As it will be explained in the Section IV, Verbs, this form has three exceptions: the Preterite and the Imperative tenses, and the verb "ser" (= to be).

(***) In Latin America the forms of "you guys" and "they" coincide. For example, "aparece**n**" means "you guys appear" and "they appear." The words "ustedes" (= you guys) and "ellos" (= they) are used to avoid ambiguity. See Apendix A, Notes about Dialects.

Let's see examples of the presente tense of verbs of the three Spanish conjugations:

>admir**ar** (= to admire) is an **AR**-verb, also called a verb of the **first** conjugation.
>respond**er** (= to respond) is an ER-verb, also called a verb of the **second** conjugation.
>describ**ir** (= to describe) is an **IR** verb, also called a verb of the **third** conjugation.

to admire	= admirar
I admire	admir**o**
You admire	admir**as**
He/She/It admires	admir**a**
We admire	admir**amos**
You guys admire	admir**áis** (Spain)
You guys/ They admire	admir**an**

to respond	= responder
I respond	respond**o**
You respond	respond**es**
He/She/ It responds	respond**e**
We respond	respond**emos**
You guys respond	respond**éis** (Spain)
You guys/ They respond	respond**en**

to describe	= describir
I describe	describ**o**
You describe	describ**es**
He/She describes	describ**e**
We describe	describ**imos**
You guys describe	describ**ís** (Spain)
You guys / They describe	describ**en**

7. CONJUGATION

Corollary 1: The Personal Pronouns

Spanish does have personal pronouns such as: I, you, he, she, etc., but it doesn't use them much. It would be redundant because the information on who makes the action is already in the verb itself. So, we recommend not to use them unless necessary to avoid confusion.

The personal pronouns are:

I	yo
you (singular)	tú
he, she, It	él, ella, ello*
we	nosotros, nosotras
you guys (Spain)	vosotros, vosotras
you guys/ they	ustedes/ ellos, ellas

(*) "ello" (= it) is normally omitted. For example: "It describes" would be "Describe," not: ~~Ello describe~~

The pronouns are only used to either answer "who?" to emphasize, or to avoid ambiguity.

> Who responds? We respond, but she can't.
> ¿Quién responde? Nosotros respondemos, pero ella no puede.
>
> They must re-write the letter.
> Ellos deben reescribir la carta .
>
> I paid.
> Yo pagué.

Appendix A, Notes about Dialects, shows the use of the pronouns according to the three main dialects.

Corollary 2: The Three Simplest Verb Structures: "I am singing, I am going to sing, I have sung"

Let's look at three easy tenses: one for the present, one for the future, and one for the past. With these structures, you will loosen up and start creating your first sentences. They will also help you translate many examples from this book until we reach Section IV, Verbs.

These are the constructions to study:

I am going to sing [future]	"Voy a cant**ar**"
I am singing [present]	"Estoy cant**ando**"
I have sung [past]	"He cant**ado**"

In bold we have marked the endings that correspond to the verb "cantar" (and all verbs of the group of the "first conjugation"). Below, you'll see the ending for the three conjugations.

These three structures are the simplest in the sense that the number of irregular verbs in those tenses are none or very limited.

Every conjugation (AR or first, ER or second, and IR or third) has its own set of **endings**.

AR Verbs	ER Verbs	IR Verbs
-**ar** e.g cantar (= to sing)	-**er** e.g beber (= to drink)	-**ir** e.g vivir (= to live)
-**ando** e.g. cantando (= singing)	-**iendo** e.g bebiendo (= drinking)	-**iendo** e.g viviendo (= living)
-**ado** e.g. cantado (= sung)	-**ido** e.g bebido (= drunk)	-**ido** e.g vivido (= lived)

These three tenses (I'm singing, I am going to sing, and I have sung) use three auxiliary verbs, which are: to be (estar), to go (ir) and to have (haber). In order to use them appropriately you need to know the present tense of those three verbs.

Ir = to go

English	Spanish
I go	voy
you singular go	vas
he/she/it goes	va
we go	vamos
you guys go	vais (Spain)
you guys/ they go	van

7. CONJUGATION

English		Spanish	
I am going	to sing	Voy	a cantar
You are going	to sing	Vas	a cantar
He/she is going	to sing	Va	a cantar
We are going	to sing	Vamos	a cantar
You guys are going	to sing	Vais	a cantar (Sp.)
You guys/ They are going	to sing	Van	a cantar

Notice that the translation doesn't occur word for word: "*Voy a cantar*" is literally "I go to sing," but the translation is "I am going to sing."

Other examples:

> I am going to establish a record.
> Voy a establec**er** un récord.
>
> They are going to divide the property.
> Van a divid**ir** la propiedad.

Estar = to be

English	Spanish
I am	est<u>o</u>y
You singular are	estás
He/she/it is	está
We are	est<u>a</u>mos
You guys are	estáis (Spain)
You guys are/ they are	están

Thus, "I am singing, You are singing"...would be:

English		Spanish	
I am	singing	Estoy	cantando
You are	singing	Estás	cantando
He is /she is	singing	Está	cantando
We are	singing	Estamos	cantando
You guys are	singing	Estáis	cantando (Spain)
You guys/ They are	singing	Están	cantando

Unlike the structure we had before ("I am going to sing"), this is a direct translation: I am = *estoy*; singing = *cantando*. Other examples:

I am establishing a record.
Estoy estable**ciendo** un récord.

They are dividing the property.
Están divid**iendo** la propiedad.

Haber = to have (auxiliary)

English	Spanish
I have	he
You singular have	has
He/she/it has	ha
We have	hemos
You guys have	habéis (Spain)
You guys / They have	han

Thus, "I have sung, you have sung..." would be

English		Spanish	
I have	sung	He	cantado
You have	sung	Has	cantado
He/she has	sung	Ha	cantado
We have	sung	Hemos	cantado
You guys have	sung	Habéis	cantado (Spain)
You guys/ They have	sung	Han	cantado

This structure is a literal translation: I have = *he*; sung = *cantado*.

Other examples:

I have established a record.
He estable**cido** un récord.

They have divided the property.
Han divid**ido** la propiedad.

7. CONJUGATION

Corollary 3: Negative Sentences

To convert a sentence into negative you just need to add the word "no" before the verb.

>That acrobatics does <u>not appear</u> possible.
>Esa acrobacia <u>no parece</u> posible.
>
>Juan is <u>not going</u> to cancel an interview.
>Juan <u>no va</u> a cancelar una entrevista.

In Spanish, you have to use a double negative. The exception is when the negative word" nunca," "nadie" or "ninguno" (= never, nobody, none) is placed before the verb.

>Juan has **never** cancelled an interview.
>Juan **no** ha cancelado una entrevista **nunca**.[double negation]
>Juan **nunca** ha cancelado una entrevista. [single negation]
>**Nunca** Juan ha cancelado una entrevista. [single negation]
>
>Nobody administers that office.
>No administra esa oficina **nadie**.[double negation]
>**Nadie** administra esa oficina. [single negation]

Corollary 4: Interrogative Sentences

Unlike English, to convert a sentence into interrogative, in the majority of cases, requires only to put the right intonation.

If the question has a question word (like what, where, when, which etc), the subject normally goes after the verb.

>At what time is the director leaving the hospital?
>¿A qué hora está saliendo del hospital **el director**?

Otherwise (when there's no interrogative word), the location of the subject is optional

>Is Carlos going to study at the library?
>¿**Carlos** va a estudiar a la biblioteca?
>¿Va **Carlos** a estudiar a la biblioteca?
>¿Va a estudiar **Carlos** a la biblioteca?
>¿Va a estudiar a la biblioteca **Carlos**?

Corollary 5: Interrogative-Negative Sentences

When a sentence is both negative and interrogative, the rules of above overlap.

>Has Juan never canceled an interview?
>¿Juan no ha cancelado una entrevista nunca?
>¿Juan nunca ha cancelado una entrevista?
>¿Nunca Juan ha cancelado una entrevista?

Frequently Asked Questions

FAQ: "Vosotros" or "ustedes" (= you plural)?

"Vosotros" (= you guys) is only used in Spain. **It uses the form of the second person of plural,** e.g.

>vosotros cantáis (= you guys sing)

"Ustedes" means "you guys" (informal) in Latinoamerica and means "you, sirs" or "you, ma'ams" (formal) in Spain. Regardless of this, "ustedes" doesn't use the forms of the second person plural, but the forms of the third person of plural, e.g.

>ustedes cantan (= you guys sing)   not ~~ustedes cantáis~~

In the same way, "usted " means "you singular (and formal) in Latinoamerica, and means "you, sir" or "you, ma'am" (formal) in Spain. Regardless of this, "usted" doesn't use the forms of the second person of singular, but the forms of the third person of singular, e.g.

>usted canta (= you -singular- sing)   not ~~usted cantas~~.

This book teaches the complete range of verb forms: the six persons (all the verb tables of this book have six rows). The forms of "vosotros," i.e. the forms of the second person plural, are exceptionally regular.

The use of "usted" and "ustedes" is also explained in Appendix A, Notes About Dialects.

7. CONJUGATION

Exercises

a) Identify the following verbs with their conjugation. Write AR, ER, or IR accordingly.

   aceptar (= to accept), distribuir (= to distribute), estudiar (= to study), entretener (= to entertain), pintar (= to paint).

b) With the meanings given above, translate the following:

   She has accepted the position.
   We are going to distribute the property.
   We are studying Mathematics.
   You (singular) are going to entertain the public.
   They have painted a lot.

Answers

   a) AR, IR, AR, ER, AR

   b) (ella) Ha aceptado la posición.
       Vamos a distribuir la propiedad.
       Vamos a estudiar Matemáticas.
       Vas a entretener al público.
       Han pintado mucho.

Vocabulary

The verb "to be" use two verbs: *ser* and *estar* in Spanish. *Ser* is used for permanent attributes; *estar* for non-permanent attributes. Example:

   Martin **is** from the Unites States. Martin **is** in Italy now.
   Martín **es** de los Estados Unidos. Martin **está** en Italia ahora.

The following is the conjugation for the present tense of the verbs "ser" and "estar."

English	Spanish	
to be	ser	estar
I am	soy	est<u>o</u>y
You (singular) are	<u>e</u>res	estás
He/She/It is	es	está
We are	s<u>o</u>mos	est<u>a</u>mos
You guys are	s<u>o</u>is (Spain)	estáis (Spain)
You guys/ They are	son	están

Remember that the underscore mark is just a hint of this book to tell you where the stressed vowel is, and make it easy to learn the words with their correct pronunciation (you don't need that aid if you know the rules of accents already).

8. HOW TO LEARN WORDS EFFICIENTLY
CÓMO APRENDER PALABRAS EFICIENTEMENTE

As we saw in the last three chapters, when you look up a word in the dictionary, you must look for the proxy of that word.

> e.g. "carro" (singular), not "carros" (plural)
> e.g. "gato" (masculine), not "gata" (feminine)
> e.g. "estudiar" (infinitive), not "estudié" (= to study, not studied).

The proxy must be singular and masculine (if the word is a noun, determiner or adjective) and infinitive (if the word is a verb).

As for the meaning, we can classify words in two main categories:

> **Non-grammatical words** are those words with an actual meaning by itself: dog, white, walking, Peter, fast, attitude,... These are the words that you can describe when you play the party game charades.
>
> **Grammatical words** are those words that create the structure of the sentence: the, a, at, to, over, however, on, another, by...

You could only communicate very primitively without grammatical words. Grammatical words form the structure of the sentence. For example, in the sentence "Your cat is on the table," if you removed the grammatical words the result would be absurd:

> (Your) cat is (on the) table → cat is table

8. HOW TO LEARN WORDS EFFICIENTLY

Regarding the non-grammatical words: now you will have to choose which of these words you want to learn every day according to your areas of interest (cooking, business, art, cars etc). There's a reason for this: The words that you pick yourself will be the ones that you will enjoy memorizing, and the ones that you will end up utilizing. This book will give you recommendations and clues to look up non-grammatical words in the dictionary.

Regarding the grammatical words, Section III, Grammar, will go over these words extensively. Some will be explained in the body of each chapter, others will appear in the vocabulary section of each chapter.

We recommend the following method. Take it as a **golden rule**.

- **Learn a consistent number of words a day** (say ten). Flash cards are a great idea to test yourself; in turn, using a computer spreadsheet for those words is the best way to keep a record. It enables you to sort your learned words and keep them organized.

- **Pick your own words**. Select the grammatical words from this book, and the non-grammatical words from your areas of interest. Lists or families of words work better than unlinked words. For example, if you are keen on painting, learn the list of basic colors as part of your daily set of words (vs., one color and nine other words today, and another color with another nine words tomorrow).

- **Notice if the words you are picking have similarities with English in any form**. Being aware of the commonalities will help you not only memorize the word but also memorize other words of its family.

A distinction can be made regarding the similar words in both languages. On one hand, there are "**cognates**," those words from Spanish that are easy to translate and recognize, for instance teléfono/telephone or artista/artist. On the other hand, there is what we can call "indirect cognates," those words whose similarities are not evident, but are based on other words of the same family. For instance, "agua" is not a cognate of "water;" however, you can find the meaning through the cognate: aquarium/acuario.

There are hundreds of cognates, and hundreds of indirect cognates. Below you will find a list of indirect cognates:

Spanish	English	Cognate English/ Spanish
agua	water	aquarium = acuario
año	year	annual = anual
araña	spider	arachnid = arácnido
árbol	tree	arboretum = arboreto
avión	plane	aviation = aviación
bailar	to dance	ballerina = bailarina
beber	to drink	beverage = bebida
campo	field	to camp = acampar
carne	meat	carnivore = carnívoro
cerebro	brain	cerebral = cerebral
cien	hundred	cent = céntimo
cuerpo	body	corporal = corporal
diente	tooth	dentist = dentista
dormir	to sleep	dormant = durmiente
escalera	ladder	escalator = escalera mecánica
gemelo	twin	Gemini (zodiac) = géminis
grande	big	grand = gran
hombre	man	human = humano
leche	milk	lactose = lactosa
lengua	tongue	language = lenguaje
luna	moon	lunar = lunar
mano	hand	manual = manual
mar	sea	submarine = submarino
mes	month	semester = semestre
mil	thousand	mile = milla
muerto	dead	morgue = morgue
nacer	to be born	native = nativo
nave	vessel	navigate = navegar
pez	fish	Pisces (zodiac) = piscis
piel	skin	to peel = pelar
polvo	dust	to pulverize = pulverizar
pueblo	village	popular = popular

8. HOW TO LEARN WORDS EFFICIENTLY

Spanish	English	Cognate English/ Spanish
refugio	shelter	to refuge = refugiar
sentir	to feel	sentiment = sentimiento
sol	sun	solar = solar
toro	bull	Taurus (zodiac) = tauro
uno	one	unit = unidad
vender	to sell	vendor = vendedor
ver	to see	visible = visible
vivir	to live	to survive = sobrevivir

Corollary 1: Prefixes and Suffixes

A prefix is an initial particle of a word with meaning. It is called suffix if it goes at the end of the word. For example the prefix "un" means "opposite." Thus, for example: "unnecessary" means "not necessary."

The vast majority of prefixes and suffixes are the same or very similar in both Spanish and English. Below, you will find just a sample:

Spanish		English	
in-	e.g. innecesario	un-	e.g. unnecessary
pre-	e.g. prenatal	pre-	e.g. prenatal
post-	e.g. post operación	post-	e.g. post operation
ex-	e.g. exconvicto	ex-	e.g. exconvict
anti-	e.g. antidroga	anti-	e.g. antidrugs
-dad	e.g. integridad	-ty	e.g. integrity
-ción	e.g. preparación	-tion	e.g. preparation
-ismo	e.g. comunismo	-ism	e.g. comunism

Corollary 2: Spanglish

Spanglish is what results when you insert an English word (genuine or altered) in a Spanish speech.

Si tomo la **freeway**, llego allí antes.

This means: "If I take the freeway, I get there sooner;" where "freeway" is not a Spanish word.

In some cases the word has been taken from English as is (in spelling and pronunciation):

>(la) freeway, (el) bypass,(el) SUV, (el) bill, (los) taxes,
>(el) VCR, (el) U-turn, (el) e-mail, (el) zip code

Other times, the words have suffered some adaptation to the Spanish pronunciation:

>la troca (= truck), la marketa (= market), la carpeta (= carpet), la yarda (= yard), las utilidades (= utilities), las partes (= auto-parts), lonchear (= to have lunch), parkear (= to park), likear (= to leak)

Occasionally, the newborn word can conflict with another word existing in the Spanish standard:

Non-standard Spanish	Standard Spanish
carpeta (= carpet)	carpeta (= folder)
remover (= to remove)	remover (= to stir)
ordenar (= to order food)	ordenar (= to command)

Those words that sound similar in both languages but have different meanings are called false cognates or "false friends." You can't trust them: their meaning is different to that what you would expect.

In Spanish	sounds like...	but it means...
embarazada	embarrassing	pregnant
recuerdo	record	a memory
consistente	consistent	firm, fix

This corollary is just to warn you that those words exist and that they are part of the California speech. Appendix B, Local Words of California, shows a list of some of the most popular terms.

8. HOW TO LEARN WORDS EFFICIENTLY

Frequently Asked Questions

FAQ: Where do I find the "grammatical words" I have to learn every day?

In the vocabulary at the end of each chapter, you will find a summary of the grammatical words related with the topic of the chapter in question. Occasionally, the vocabulary includes other words, non-grammatical words, which are important. The chapters of the last section, Section IV, Verb Tenses, show verbs that are of very common use.

Which non-grammatical words to learn is a personal choice. For example, one can enjoy learning words related with cars, cooking, business, etc.

Conversely, the grammatical words are not really a choice: you need to memorize them all in order to construct sentences.

Exercises

Write a sample of what will be your daily vocabulary list.

 Sample of a 15-word daily list

 (Grammatical words)

 un/una/unos/unas = a, some
 el/la/los/las = the

 (Non-grammatical words)

 el carro * = car
 la compañía = company
 resistente = resistant
 estudiar (regular verb **) = to study
 querer (irregular verb **) = to want
 amarillo/a = yellow
 rojo/a = red
 azul (masc. & fem.) = blue
 verde (masc. & fem.) = green
 blanco/a = white
 negro/a = black
 gris (masc. & fem.) = gray
 naranja = orange (color), la naranja = orange (fruit)

(*) If you have not learned the rules of accents, use a sign (like the underscore in this book) to mark where the stress of each word is.

(**) If the word is a verb, it is convenient to mark whether it is regular or irregular. Use appendices E, "A list of Regular Verbs" and F, "A List of Irregular Verbs."

Vocabulary

Some Spanish words are **only** found in the US. They are adaptations of Latin root words in the English language. They do not belong to the standard Spanish. However, they are very common in the Spanish of the US.

Some of the most popular ones are:

aplic_a_r	=	to apply (for a job)
la aplicación	=	the application
la f_o_rma	=	the form
la carp_e_ta	=	the carpet
la tr_o_ca	=	the truck
la elegibilid_a_d	=	the eligibility
la r_e_nta	=	the rent
la y_a_rda	=	the backyard
las utilid_a_des	=	the utilities
las p_a_rtes	=	the auto-parts

You can find an extensive list in Appendix B: Local Words of California.

SECTION III

GRAMMAR
GRAMÁTICA

Remember, from today on, it is recommended that you learn a number of words a day. Your daily set of words should be divided into two categories. One category is the grammatical words. You will find them at the end of every chapter. The other category, the non-grammatical words, you can pick on your own (carro, Argentina, melón, lámpara, hora etc), depending on your areas of interest. Learn these words in groups (sports, colors, tools, etc.).

When you finish Section III, you will know all the grammatical words, with the exception of the auxiliary verbs.

The first chapter of this section gives a classification of words in eight types.

Every chapter describes one type and the variations within that type. For example, within the adjective (e.g. tall), you'll study the comparative structures (as tall as…, taller than…, the tallest…).

Verbs have been saved for last, as they require several chapters. Nevertheless, by now you know three verb tenses (the equivalent of "I am doing…" "I am going to do…" and "I have done…"). With those, you can build sentences in the present, future, and past.

9. TYPES OF WORDS
TIPOS DE PALABRAS

According to their functions in the sentence, words can be:

- **Interjections** (interjecciones): Hello!
- **Determiners** (determinantes): the, a, an, five, these...
- **Adjectives** (adjetivos): green, large, true, productive...
- **Nouns** (nombres): Peter, house, truth, productivity...
- **Pronouns** (pronombres): we, us, ours, ourselves, me...
- **Adverbs** (adverbios) rapidly, quietly, strongly...
- **Prepositions** (preposiciones): of, for, at, on, in, under...
- **Conjunctions** (conjunciones): and, or, yet, but, what, if...
- **Verbs** (verbos): am, have, goes, worked, forgotten...

Let's see one example in one sentence:

<u>Wow!</u> <u>that</u> <u>gray</u> <u>dog</u> <u>that</u> <u>she</u> <u>bought</u> <u>in</u> <u>Germany</u> <u>runs</u> <u>fast!</u>
INTERJ. DET. ADJ. NOUN CONJ PRON. VERB   PREP. NOUN   VERB ADVERB

For now, you just need to know that each type of word identifies a function, and that a word can have different roles in different sentences. In the following example, the word "milk" has different uses (i.e. it functions as different types)

Noun:	**Milk** is the product from cows.
Adjective	**Milk** products sell well.
Verb:	The farmers **milk** the cows everyday.

9. TYPES OF WORDS

In this book, some relevant words that accept different functions can be covered in more than one chapter or only in the chapter of the type that fits more commonly.

The above classification of words overlaps that of grammatical words and non-grammatical words. **Grammatical words** are: determiners, pronouns, prepositions, conjunctions, a few adverbs, and the auxiliary verbs (to have, to be and to go). **Non-grammatical words** are: interjections, nouns, adjectives, most adverbs and verbs.

Some books on English grammar consider **determiners** as a type of **adjective** based on their similarities. However, when learning Spanish, distinguishing the difference is important. In Spanish, the determiner goes before the noun, and the adjective after the noun. (In English, both the determiner and adjective go before the noun).

<u>Many</u> <u>violet</u> flowers
DET.   ADJ.

<u>Muchas</u> flores <u>violetas</u>
DET.   ADJ.

You may be familiar with the term "article" as a type of word. Articles are the words "the," a," "an," and they are a type of what we call "determiners."

You may also be familiar with the term "possessive." This is a subtype of words as well. This label is ambiguous since there are: possessive determiners (like "my"), possessive pronouns (like "mine"), etc.

The following table displays the most important features of each type of words. You will learn them in detail in next chapters.

Type	Gramm. Words?	Masc./ fem.	Singu./ plural	Person & tense
Interjections	no	no	no	no
Determiners	yes	yes	yes	no
Adjectives	no	yes	yes	no
Nouns	no	yes (**)	yes	no
Pronouns	yes	yes	yes	no
Adverbs	a few (*)	no	no	no
Prepositions	yes	no	no	no
Conjunctions	yes	no	no	no
Verbs	a few (*)	no	no	yes

(*) Because of their grammatical value we can consider grammatical words adverbs like "muy" (= very), "aquí" (= here), and the four auxiliary verbs: "ser," "estar" (both meaning "to be"), haber (= to have) and "ir" (= to go).

(**) Nouns have an intrinsic gender. They have a fixed gender: either masculine or feminine. Other types, like determiners they have both.

Frequently Asked Questions

FAQ: Why is this classification of words important?

Every type of word represents one function in the sentence, and has different properties. For example, thanks to that categorization, we can make statements like:

- All interjections are sentences by themselves.
- All nouns have an intrinsic gender.
- All determiners precede the nouns; adjectives go after them.
- All determiners and adjectives correspond to the noun in number (singular, plural) and gender (masculine, feminine).

Exercises

a) Categorize the following words into the categories to which they normally belong:

    elefante (= elephant), garbanzo (= garbanzo bean), nosotros (= we), Pedro (= Peter), computador (= computer), hola (= hi), el (= the– masculine), la (the– feminine), ser (= to be), resistente (resistant), rápidamente (= rapidly), y (= and), de (= of), en (= in), Argentina (=Argentina), estudiar (= to study).

Answers

    Interjections: hola
    Determiners: el, la
    Adjectives: resistente

9. TYPES OF WORDS

>Nouns: elefante, garbanzo, Pedro, computador, Argentina
>Pronouns: nosotros
>Adverbs: rápidamente
>Prepositions: de, en
>Conjuctions: y
>Verbs: ser, estudiar

b) Categorize the same set of words into grammatical or non-grammatical words.

Answers

>non-grammatical words: elefante, garbanzo, Peter, computador, resistente, rápidamente, Argentina, estudiar
>grammatical words: nosotros, hola, el, la, ser, y, de, en

Vocabulary

We recommend that you learn some useful sentences. The following are expressions that can't be translated literally. Learn each structure as is.

>What's your name? My name is Antonio Smith.
>¿Cómo te llamas? Me llamo Antonio Smith.
>
>How old are you? I'm 40 years old.
>¿Cuántos años tienes? Tengo 40 (cuarenta) años.
>
>Where are you from? I'm from San Jose, California.
>¿De dónde eres? Soy de San José, California.
>
>How long have you been here? I've been here for 3 years / I've been here since 2005.
>¿Cuánto tiempo llevas aquí? Llevo aquí tres años. / Llevo aquí desde el 2005.

10. INTERJECTIONS
INTERJECCIONES

Interjeccions are those expressive words that constitute a sentence by themselves: Wow, Ah, Ouch, OK, Bye, etc. and are invariable. The main reason why we treat them first in this book is because they are not related to any other type of words.

Golden Rule

> Interjections make up sentences by themselves, and they are invariable. They don't change regardless of occuring in the past, present or future, or for having one subject or another. As a consequence, each interjection is to be learned as is, with no further analysis.

For example, the English expression "Wow!" means "I am surprised by that," regarless of the context being in the present, past or future; regardless of who speaks (one or more people, masculine or feminine). Conversely, the equivalent sentence "I am surprised by that" is formed by pieces (each word) that are subject to grammar rules to be combined and have different meanings: "I was surprised by that," "He is surprised by that..."

Not all words that make sentences by themselves are interjections. For example, the word "run" can form a sentence by itself as a command "Run!;" however, it is not a interjection because it can vary. "Run" can become part of a sentence with a different meaning: "They **run** everyday."

10. INTERJECTIONS

For simplicity, we can include in this category, every **invariable** expression that makes up **a sentence by itself**, for example:

H<u>o</u>la	=	Hello
<u>O</u>key	=	Okay
Adiós	=	Goodbye
Ojalá	=	I wish!

Notice that "Adios" is a single word in Spanish, but "good bye" is not a single word in English.

Also for simplicity, we can take as interjections the following words, even though they can have other functions.

¡Ay<u>u</u>da!	=	Help me!
¡Soc<u>o</u>rro!	=	Help me!
Perdón	=	I'm sorry
Gr<u>a</u>cias	=	Thank you

(In Spanish they can also work as nouns: ayuda = aid, socorro = aid, perdón = forgiveness, gracias = grace).

The following are multiple-word expressions that function as interjections since they make up an invariable sentence.

M<u>u</u>chas Gr<u>a</u>cias	=	Thank you very much
De n<u>a</u>da	=	You're welcome
Por fav<u>o</u>r	=	Please
Con perm<u>i</u>so	=	Excuse me
Lo si<u>e</u>nto	=	I'm sorry
¿De verd<u>a</u>d?	=	Really?
Bu<u>e</u>nos días	=	Good morning (until lunch time)
Bu<u>e</u>nas t<u>a</u>rdes	=	Good afternoon (until dusk)
Bu<u>e</u>nas n<u>o</u>ches	=	Good evening, or Good night
H<u>a</u>sta la v<u>i</u>sta	=	See you later
H<u>a</u>sta lu<u>e</u>go	=	See you later
H<u>a</u>sta pr<u>o</u>nto	=	See you soon

The following expressions are also worth while learning now in order to have some all-occasion vocabulary.

Sí	= Yes
No	= No
Tal vez	= Maybe
Quizás (or quizá)	= Maybe
Yo también	= Me too
Yo tampoco	= Me neither
No lo sé (or No sé)	= I don't know

Remember that, in Spanish, every time you use either exclamation or question marks, you need to put the mark in the beginning too, e.g. ¡Hola! ¿De verdad?

Corollary 1: Sentences of Exclamation

Like in English, in Spanish you can convert a sentence into an exclamation sentence by raising the tone.

> It's 7:00 already. → It's 7:00 already!
> Son las 7:00 ya. → ¡Son las 7 ya!

Remember. Spanish uses a ¡ symbol to mark the beginning of the exclamation.

When the you want to make an exclamation emphasizing an adjective, a noun, or an adverb, you need to use "qué." This is equivalent to "what/how" in English.

How big!	¡Qué grande!
What a house!	¡Qué casa!
What a big house!	¡Qué casa tan grande! Or: ¡Qué casa más grande!
How fast!	¡Qué rápido!
How fast you run!	¡Qué rápido corres!

10. INTERJECTIONS   95

Corollary 2: "So do I," "Neither do I"

Spanish is simpler than English when expressing agreement and disagreement. In Spanish these type of responses are fixed.

> So do I. So will I. So would I. So am I.
> Yo también. Yo también. Yo también. Yo también.
>
> Neither do I. Neither will I. Neither would I. Neither am I.
> Yo tampoco. Yo tampoco. Yo tampoco. Yo tampoco.

In these constructions, the use of the pronoun, like "yo" (= I) is mandatory.

Other examples:

> So does he. So did you. So will they. So would she.
> Él también. Tú también. Ellos también. Ella también.
>
> Neither do we. Nether did you guys. Neither will she.
> Nosotros tampoco. Ustedes tampoco. Ella tampoco.

On other occasions, the pronoun is mine, yours… which, in Spanish, is translated by el mío / la mía / los míos / las mías…

> — My son is going to come. — So is mine.
> — Mi hijo va a venir. — El mío también.
>
> — My daughters have come. — So have mine.
> — Mis hijas han venido. — Las mías también.
>
> — Our parents are not working. — Neither are Maria's.
> — Nuestros papás no estan trabajando. — Los de María tampoco.

Frequently Asked Questions

FAQ: What are the "Question Tags?"

Question tags are those mini sentences that you add in order to give some reinforcement, like: "isn't it?" "are you?" "shouldn't she?"

Spanish lacks these question tags. However, it has "¿verdad?" which is equivalent to "right?" and can be used in place of the English tags.

>You're kidding, right?
>Estás bromeando, ¿verdad?

Notice that the translation of question tags is a fixed expression, "¿verdad?" So are the expressions "Yo también" and "Yo tampoco."

Exercises

Translate:

>You're kidding me, aren't you?
>She is not working tomorrow, is she?
>The test is going to start at 3:00, isn't it?

Answers
>(tú) Estás bromeando, ¿verdad?
>(ella) No está trabajando mañana ¿ verdad?
>El test va a comenzar a las tres ¿verdad?

Vocabulary

Hola	=	Hello
Okey	=	Okay
Adiós	=	Goodbye
Ojalá	=	I wish!
¡Ayuda!	=	Help me!
¡Socorro!	=	Help me!
Perdón	=	I'm sorry
Gracias	=	Thank you
Muchas Gracias	=	Thank you very much
De nada	=	You're welcome
Por favor	=	Please
Con permiso	=	Excuse me

10. INTERJECTIONS

Lo siento	=	I'm very sorry
¿De verdad?	=	Really?
Buenos días	=	Good morning (until lunch time)
Buenas tardes	=	Good afternoon (until dusk)
Buenas noches	=	Good evening, or Good night
Hasta la vista	=	See you later
Hasta luego	=	See you later
Hasta pronto	=	See you soon
Sí	=	Yes
No	=	No
Tal vez	=	Maybe
Quizás (or quizá)	=	Maybe
Yo también	=	Me too
Yo tampoco	=	Me neither
No lo sé (, No sé)	=	I don't know
¿Verdad?	=	…, right?
qué	=	What (What a..!)
tan	=	so (in exclamations)
más	=	so (in exclamations), more

11. DETERMINERS
DETERMINANTES

The determiners are those words that complement the noun, like: the, a, some, this, our... In Spanish, unlike the adjectives (whose also qualify the noun), determiners go before the noun.

> **The** difficult lesson
> DET.   ADJ.   NOUN

> **La** lección difícil
> DET. ADJ.   NOUN

Golden Rule

> All determiners go before the noun, and they correspond to the noun in number (singular/plural) and in gender (masculine/feminine).

The translations of the English A (AN) and SOME are the following:

> a boy/ a girl / some boys /some girls
> **un** niño /**una** niña/ **unos** niños / **unas** niñas

UNO in Spanish only means "one" as a number.
> How many? One.
> ¿Cuántos? Uno.–not *Un-*

11. DETERMINERS

The translation of the English THE is the following

    The boy/ The girl / The boys /The girls
    El niño/ **la** niña/ **los** niños / **las** niñas

The translations of the English THIS and THESE are:

    This boy/ This girl / These boys /These girls
    Este niño/ **esta** niña/ **estos** niños / **estas** niñas

The translations of the English THAT and THOSE are:

    That boy/ That girl / Those boys /Those girls
    Ese niño/ **esa** niña/ **esos** niños / **esas** niñas

Less often, you would use another version of THAT/THOSE (ese / esa / esos / esas). They are: aquel/ aquella / aquellos / aquellas. They are used for persons and things that are placed farther away.

    that boy/ that girl / those boys /those girls
    aquel niño/ **aquella** niña/ **aquellos** niños / **aquellas** niñas

Other determiners are those that denote possession, the possessives:

English	Spanish
my	mi / mis
your	tu / tus
his, her, its	su / sus
our	nuestro / nuestra / nuestros/ nuestras
your (Spain)	vuestro / vuestra / vuestros/ vuestras
your, their	su / sus

Examples of possessives are:

    My cat is black, my turtle is yellow, my dogs are white, my salamanders are red
    Mi gato es negro, **mi** tortuga es amarilla, **mis** perros son blancos, **mis** salamandras son rojas

Spanish uses the articles "el, la, los, las" instead of the possessives when there is no ambiguity on who is the owner or when the subject of the sentence is also the owner of the object possessed.

    I have repaired **my** car.
    He reparado **el** carro (instead of "**mi**").

Fernando is preparing **his** taxes.
Fernando está preparando **los** impuestos (instead of "**sus**").

This is not applicable when the object possessed is a person, e.g.

Finally I have contacted **my** son.
Finalmente he contactado con **mi** hijo.

Here it is pertinent to introduce another set of words related to possessive determiners:

English	Spanish
mine	mío / mía / míos /mías
yours	tuyo / tuya / tuyos /tuyas
his, hers, its	suyo / suya / suyos / suyas
ours	nuestro/ nuestra / nuestros / nuestras
yours (Spain)	vuestro/ vuestra / vuestros / vuestras
yours/ theirs	suyo / suya / suyos / suyas

Examples are:

This cat is mine, that turtle is mine, those dogs are mine, those salamanders are mine.
Este gato es **mío**, esa tortuga es **mía**, esos perros son **míos**, esas salamandras son **mías**.

Remember that the pronoun refers to what is possessed not to the person who posseses it.

This house is his.
Esta casa es suya (not suyo).

These cars are theirs (of Mary and Helen).
Estos carros son suyos (not suyas).

Corollary 1: Contractions

Contractions are the fusion of two words in one: aren't, don't, doesn't, they're...

11. DETERMINERS

Golden Rule

> Spanish only admits two contractions:
> a el → **al** (= to the)
> de el → **del** (= of the)
> They are mandatory. You can't choose not to contract (with one exception –see below).

Examples:

> Director's documentation goes to the hospital.
> La documentación **del** director va **al** hospital.
>
> I have received this letter from the patient's father.
> He recibido esta carta **del** padre **del** paciente.
>
> At the end of the month, I am going to the lab.
> **Al** final del mes, voy **al** laboratorio.

Exception: Only if "el" doesn't equal "the", you don't contract:

> Fernando is from El Salvador.
> Fernando es de El Salvador.
>
> This depends on him.
> Esto depende de él.
>
> I have responded with that letter to him.
> He respondido con esa carta a él.

Corollary 2: Frequency of Use of Spanish "el/la" in Comparison to the English "the"

In English, there are many instances where "the" is omitted e.g. " ~~the~~ Patience is a virtue;" however, Spanish uses el/la as long as it is not the name of a person or the name of a place.

> Patience is a virtue. Peter is at school.
> **La** paciencia es una virtud. Peter está en **el** colegio.

Other examples:

> Dogs bark; This is Marta's house.
> **Los** perros ladran. Esta es **la** casa de Marta.

The name of a person or the name of a place will have "the" only if you are emphasizing that particular one among others with the same name:

> This is neither the Marta nor the Peru that I knew.
> Esta no es ni **la** Marta ni **el** Perú que yo conocía.

Corollary 3: About Accents Marks

If you went over the Rules of Accents (*Chapter 4 Syllable and Stress*), you'll remember that the words "este, esta, estos, estas, esa, esos, esas, aquel, aquella, aquellos, aquellas" will have accent only if they function as nouns.

> **This** is the agent that has cooperated. **This** agent is Peter.
> **Éste** es el agente que ha cooperado. **Este** agente es Peter.

Corollary 4: Feminine Words with "el:" el agua

If you see a word that is feminine with the article EL (masculine), instead of "la," it's because the word after starts with another stressed "a," and this "a-a" sounds bad in Spanish.

> ~~la agua~~ → el agua (= water)
> ~~la águila~~ → el águila (= eagle)
> ~~la arpa~~ → el arpa (= harp)

Notice that, in all cases, the word after has the stress (with accent or not) in the "a." Otherwise this is not applicable: la abeja (the bee).

Frequently Asked Questions

FAQ: Are "possessives" a type of determiners, adjectives or pronouns?

All of the above. Possessive is an attribute that indicates ownership or relation. It is an ambiguous term since it is used for different subtypes of words.

11. DETERMINERS

Possessives can be:

- a type of determiner, like "my" in "**My** house is this."
- a type of adjective, like "mine" in "The house is **mine**."
- a type of pronoun, like "mine" in "**Mine** is this."

In this book, for simplicity, they all are grouped as determiners.

Exercises

Translate:

>The cats are hers.
>The lamp is his.
>This documentary on the tiger is going to explore its habits.
>Pablo has painted his sister's friend.
>In California, the voters of the south are a majority.

Answers

>Los gatos son suyos.
>La lámpara es suya.
>Este documental del tigre va a explorar sus hábitos.
>Pablo ha pintado al amigo de su hermana.
>En California, los votantes del sur son una mayoría.

Vocabulary

el, la, los, las	= the
un , una	= a
unos, unas	= some
este, esta	= this
estos, estas	= these
ese, esa	= that
esos, esas	= those
aquel, aquella, aquellos, aquellas	= that = those (farther)
del	= of the

al	=	to the, at the
mi / mis	=	my
mío / mía /míos /mías	=	mine
tu / tus	=	your (singular)
tuyo / tuya /tuyos /tuyas	=	yours (of you, singular)
nuestro/ a / os/ as	=	our, ours
vuestro/ a / os/ as (Sp.)	=	of you guys, your (you guys),
su / sus	=	his (as in "his house"), her, its, their, of you guys, your (you guys)
suyo / a / os /as	=	his (as in "This is his"), hers, its, theirs

11. DETERMINERS

12. ADJECTIVES
ADJETIVOS

The adjectives are the words that inform us about qualities of the noun e.g. blue, large, expensive, happy, etc.

As a rule of thumb: adjectives are the words that can go after the verb "to be," e.g. "His house will be blue." "It was large." "That is expensive." " I am happy." Words like "tired" function as adjectives, although derived from verbs ("to tire"). For more detail see *Chapter 21 Past Participle*, Corollary 1, "Adjectives Derived from Verbs."

Unlike English, in Spanish the adjectives are placed after the noun.

> an <u>automatic</u> <u>transmission</u>
>   ADJ.   NOUN

> una <u>transmisión</u> <u>automática</u>
>   NOUN   ADJ.

Notice a main difference between determiners and adjectives. Determiners always go before the noun.

Golden Rule

> Adjectives correspond with the noun in number (singular/plural) and in gender (masculine/feminine). They go after the noun, with the exception of five words.

12. ADJECTIVES

The exceptions are: "buen" (= good) "mal"(= bad), "primer" (= first), "tercer" (= third), and "gran" (= great). See the Frequently Asked Questions of this chapter.

Unlike English, Spanish adjectives must correspond with their noun in number and gender. Example, "automático:"

>an automatic watch; some automatic watches
>un reloj automático, unos relojes automático**s**

>an automatic machine; some automatic machines
>una máquina automática, unas máquinas automática**s**

	SINGULAR	PLURAL
MASCULINE	automático	automáticos
FEMININE	automática	automáticas

In the two examples of above "automático" needs to add an "s" when it is plural.

>the fantastic man; the fantastic woman; the fantastic men; the fantastic women

>el hombre fantástico; la mujer fantástic**a,** los hombres fantástico**s**; las mujeres fantástica**s**

Another example:

>the white satellite, the white satellites; the white jungle; the white jungles

>el satélite blanco, los satélites blanco**s**; la jungla blanca, las junglas blanca**s**

The adjectives that end in "-o" (in the masculine-singular) form the feminine by switching the "-o" to an "-a."

	SINGULAR	PLURAL
MASCULINE	-o	-os
FEMININE	-a	-as

Notice that this is also applicable to possessivess that function as adjectives (Possessives can function as determiners, adjectives or pronouns).

My car is white. The car is mine. Mine is white.
DET.   ADJ.   PRON.

El carro es blanco. El carro es mío. El mío es blanco.

	SINGULAR	PLURAL
MASCULINE	**mío**	míos
FEMININE	mía	mías

	SINGULAR	PLURAL
MASCULINE	**nuestro**	nuestros
FEMININE	nuestra	nuestras

The adjectives that don't end with "-o" (in the masculine-singular) will have the same form for the feminine. For example "verde" (= green)

	SINGULAR	PLURAL
MASCULINE	**verde**	verdes
FEMININE	verde	verdes

the green car, the green cars; the green jungle; the green jungles

el carro verde, los carros verdes; la jungla verde, las junglas verdes

Other examples:

	SINGULAR	PLURAL
MASCULINE	**violeta**	violetas
FEMININE	violeta	violetas

	SINGULAR	PLURAL
MASCULINE	**importante**	importantes
FEMININE	importante	importantes

The main exception to this rule are the adjectives related to nationalities.

	SINGULAR	PLURAL
MASCULINE	**inglés**	ingleses
FEMININE	inglesa	inglesas

12. ADJECTIVES

Notice that, in Spanish, the adjectives of countries are not capitalized.

Also notice if the adjective doesn't end with "o" you will still add an "a" to make the feminine.

inglés inglesa	ingleses inglesas	= English
japonés japonesa	japoneses japonesas	= Japanese
alemán alemana	alemanes alemanas	= German
español española	españoles españolas	= Spanish
portugués portuguesa	portugueses portuguesas	= Portuguese
danés danesa	daneses danesas	= Danish
francés francesa	franceses francesas	= French
irlandés irlandesa	irlandeses irlandesas	= Irish
ceilanés ceilanesa	ceilaneses ceilanesas	= Sri Lankan
neocelandés neocelandesa	neocelandeses neocelandesas	= New Zealander
finlandés finlandesa	finlandeses finlandesas	= Finish

The above explains how the adjective changes to feminine in order to match the gender of the noun it follows (casa blanca).

The adjective will also change to plural in order to match the number of the noun it follows (casas blancas). (See *Chapter 5 Singular/Plural*). Thus, if the adjective ends with a vowel (a, e, i, o, u) you will add s, otherwise you will add es. If the adjective ends with z, you will change to –ces.

Example: audaz (= audacious)

	SINGULAR	PLURAL
MASCULINE	audaz	audaces
FEMININE	audaz	audaces

Notice that "audaz" doesn't change in the feminine. It doesn't end with "o."

As we mentioned, one word may have more than one function. This also happens in English.

>This motor functions <u>slow</u> ("slowly" better). This motor is <u>slow</u>.
><u>   ADVERB   ADJECTIVE</u>

       Este motor funciona <u>lento</u>. Este motor es <u>lento</u>.
                                ADVERB   ADJECTIVE

However, in Spanish this is far less common.

       Whisky is a valuable <u>export</u>. We <u>export</u> it.
                                 NOUN   VERB

       El whysky es un <u>producto de exportación</u> valioso. Lo
              <u>exportamos</u> (where both are different words).

       You have <u>language</u> skills and the Spanish <u>language</u> is easy.
                  ADJECTIVE   NOUN

       Tú tienes habilidad para los <u>idiomas</u>. El <u>idioma</u> español es fácil (where idioma works as a noun in both cases).

The equivalent of the English word **very** is "**muy**." "Muy" is not an adjective and it doesn't change number (singular/plural) or gender (masculine/feminine) of the adjective it correspond to.

       This chapter is **very** long. These chapters are **very** long.
       Este capítulo es **muy** largo. Estos capítulos son **muy** largos.

<u>Corollary 1</u>: The verb "to be"

There is a strong relationship between the verb "to be" and the adjectives, We will start to explain the verb here. Spanish has two verbs for "to be:" "*ser*" and "*estar.*"

The basic rule to distinguish them is that "ser" is used for permanent adjectives; and "estar" is used for temporary adjectives.

12. ADJECTIVES

ser (= to be -permanent)	estar (= to be -temporary)
Es de Perú. (He is from Peru).	Está en Perú. (He is in Peru).
Es aburrido. (He is boring).	Está aburrido. (He is bored).
Es callado. (He is a quiet person).	Está callado. (He is being quiet).
Es feliz. (He is a happy person).	Está feliz. (He feels happy).

Unfortunately, the general rule of "ser" vs "estar" has exceptions. So, don't get surprised if you read or hear something diferent, for example:

>He's crazy. (as a permanent illness).
>Está loco.

As we saw in the vocabulary of *Chapter 7 Conjugation*, the present tense for "ser" and "estar" are:

	ser
I	soy
you singular	eres
he/she/it	es
we	somos
you guys (Spain)	sois
you guys/ they	son

	estar
I	estoy
you singular	estás
he/she/it	está
we	estamos
you guys (Spain)	estáis
you guys/ they	están

Remember, there are words for I, you, he, she...them, but you don't need them. The ending of the verb is giving you that information already.

Warning

> "*Ser*" and "*estar*" are especially challenging to learn. Take time to learn the basic rule provided above, and learn more as your Spanish develops.

Corollary 2: The verb "to have"

Another verb that is very useful is **to have**: "tener". English has the same verb with two meanings. One means "to posses" or "to be related to;" the other is the auxiliary verb (in expressions like "I have sung").

In Spanish these two meanings are indicated separately by **tener** (for possession) and **haber** (auxiliary). Haber was introduced in *Chapter 7 Conjugation*. Let's introduce the verb tener.

Tener represents just possession, "to have."

>I **have** a car. I **have** visited my mother today.
>Tengo un carro. He visitado a mi madre hoy.

The table for the present tense of "tener" is:

	TENER
I	tengo
you singular	tienes
he/she/it	tiene
we	tenemos
you guys (Spain)	tenéis
you guys/ they	tienen

Example:

>We have many cars, but they have more.
>Nosotros tenemos muchos carros pero ellos tienen más.

Other than possesion, "tener" is also used in the following expressions:

>I am hungry/ thirsty/ cold/ hot/ sleepy/scared/40 years old/ in a hurry/ right/ careful
>Tengo hambre/ sed/ frío/ calor/ sueño/miedo/ 40(cuarenta) años, prisa/ razón/ cuidado.

Corollary 3: Comparatives

In these structures, you compare one noun to another with respect to a certain quality (the adjective). There are three types: "as..., as...", "more.. than..." ", the most..." Comparatives are adverbs; however they have a strong relation with adjectives.

12. ADJECTIVES

> Madrid is **as** important **as** Barcelona.
> Madrid is **tan** importante **como** Barcelona.
>
> This video is **more** relevant **than** that photo.
> Este video es **más** relevante **que** esa foto.
>
> This city is **the most** beautiful (**of** the region).
> Esta ciudad es **la más** bonita (**de** la región).

You can also use negative comparison, such as:

> This photo is **less** relevant **than** that video.
> Esta foto es **menos** relevante **que** ese video.
>
> This city is the least beautiful (**of** the region).
> Esta ciudad es **la menos** bonita (**de** la región).

Also as in English, some Spanish comparatives use one single word to express "more + Adjective…" and "most + Adjective…"

> Peter is ~~more good~~ than him. → Peter is **better** than he is..
> Pedro es más bueno que él. → Pedro es mejor que él.

The entire list is below:

~~more good~~	→ better	~~more bad~~	→ worse
más bueno	→ mejor	más malo	→ peor
~~the most good~~	→ the best	~~the most bad~~	→ the worst
el más bueno	→ el mejor	el más malo	→ el peor
~~more big~~	→ bigger	~~more small~~	→ smaller
más grande	→ mayor	más pequeño	→ menor
~~the most big~~	→ the biggest	~~the most small~~	→ the smallest
el más grande	→ el mayor	el más pequeño	→ el menor
~~more old~~	→ older	~~more yourg~~	→ younger
más viejo	→ mayor	más pequeño	→ menor
~~the most old~~	→ the oldest	~~the most young~~	→ the youngest
el más viejo	→ el mayor	el más joven	→ el menor

Corollary 4: Quantities

As in English, Spanish distinguishes between quantities of the countable (like cars), and the uncountable, like sugar.

For the countable, the expressions are:

>How many guests are there?
>¿Cuántos invitados hay?
>
>How many stamps do you have?
>¿Cuántas estampillas tienes?
>
>I have all the stamps (of the collection).
>Tengo **todas** las estampillas (de la colección).
>
>I have most (= the majority) of the stamps in my collection.
>Tengo **la mayoría** de las estampillas de mi colección.
>
>I have no stamps.
>No tengo **ninguna** estampilla.
>
>I have some stamps.
>Tengo **algunas** estampillas. = Tengo **unas** estampillas.
>
>I have many stamps.
>Tengo **muchas** estampillas.
>
>I have few stamps.
>Tengo **pocas** estampillas.
>
>I have a few stamps.
>Tengo **unas pocas** estampillas.

For the uncountable, the expressions are:

>I have all the lemonade (that I ordered).
>Tengo **toda** la limonada (que ordené).
>
>I have most of the lemonade.
>Tengo **la mayoría** de la limonada.
>
>I have no lemonade.
>No tengo **nada** de limonada.

12. ADJECTIVES

> I have some lemonade.
> Tengo **algo** de limonada.
>
> I have a lot of lemonade.
> Tengo **mucha** limonada.
>
> I have little lemonade.
> Tengo **poca** limonada.
>
> I have a little lemonade.
> Tengo **un poco de** limonada.
>
> I have a little bit of lemonade.
> Tengo **un poquito** de limonada.

Unlike English, the Spanish negative sentences with quantities have double nagation:

> I have no stamps.
> **No** tengo **ninguna** estampilla.
>
> I have nothing.
> **No** tengo **nada.**

Corollary 5: "There is," "there's left"

This is the appropriate moment to learn three words useful with the sentences that describe quantities. These are: hay, queda / quedan

there is	hay
there are	hay
there is…left	queda
there are…left	quedan

Examples:

> There is one potato in the bag.
> **Hay** una patata en la bolsa.
>
> There are three people in the line.
> **Hay** tres personas en la fila.

Aren't there any bottles left?
¿No **queda** ninguna botella?

There are three tomatoes left in the bag.
Quedan tres tomates en la bolsa.

They are the simple verbs since they are impersonal (as in English).

Corollary 6: Another, other, others

English	Spanish
another, other, others	otro, otra, otros, otras
the other, the others	el otro, la otra, los otros, las otras

Like in English, the word "otro" precedes the noun.

I am considering another option.
Estoy considerando **otra** opción.

Remember that Spanish adjectives change if they are singular or plural.

The giraffes are tall.
Las girafas son alt**as** (not "alta").

Have this in mind when you use "otro" and its forms:

I am investigating other clues now.
(yo) Estoy investigando otr**as** pistas ahora (not "otra").

To learn how to use this, simply make coordination between the gender and the number. In the above example "noticias" is feminine and plural, so should be otr**as.**

(Notice that "others" and "the others" are never adjectives but nouns. However, they are studied in this chapter to increase understanding).

12. ADJECTIVES

Frequently Asked Questions

FAQ: I've seen the word "good" translated by both "bueno" and "buen;" how come?

There are five words that lose their last letters when they have a noun following them (This is called "*apócope*").

>That is the third floor.
>Ese es el piso **tercero.** or Ese es el **tercer** piso.

Notice that when you do this transformation the adjective has to precede the noun!

>**Third** floor
>Piso **tercero**
>**Tercer** piso

The list of adjectives that can be shortened are:

>bueno   buen   (= good)
>malo   mal   (= bad)
>primero primer (= first)
>tercero   tercer (= third)
>grande   gran   (= big / great *)

>(*) grande = big; gran = great. E.g. "Esa es una casa grande." "Pedro es un gran amigo."

They are only shortened in the masculine-singular form (so, words as buena, buenos, buenas, are never shortened to "buen").

Exercises

Translate:

>Somebody else is in charge of the department.
>I am not the first athlete on the team.
>These directors are very intelligent but they are disorganized.
>The Eiffel tower is higher than the Leaning Tower of Pisa.
>Isn't there any beer left in the box?

Answers

Otra persona está a cargo del departamento.
Yo no soy el primer atleta del equipo.
Estos directores son muy inteligentes pero están desorganizados.
La torre Eiffel es más alta que la de Pisa.
¿No queda ninguna cerveza en la caja?

Vocabulary

tan… como	=	as…as
más..que	=	more…than
menos…que	=	less… than
malo	=	bad
pequeño	=	small
mayor	=	bigger, biggest, older, oldest
menor	=	smaller, smallest, younger, youngest
cuántos	=	how many
la mayoría	=	the majority
todo	=	everthing
todos los / todas las	=	all
nada	=	nothing
ninguno / ninguna	=	none
ningún /ninguna	=	no…
ninguno/a de	=	none of
algo	=	something
alguno /a/os/as de	=	some
algún /a /os/ as	=	some…
algúno/a/os/as de	=	some of …
mucho	=	a lot
mucho / mucha	=	much
muchos / muchas	=	many
poco	=	little (amount)
poco / poca	=	little (amount)…
un poco de	=	a little of…
un poquito de	=	a little bit of
los dos	=	both
cualquier	=	any…, whichever

12. ADJECTIVES

cualqui<u>e</u>ra	=	any, whichever
hay	=	there is/ there are
qued<u>a</u>r	=	to be left
<u>o</u>tro/ <u>o</u>tra/ <u>o</u>tros /<u>o</u>tras	=	another, other, others
bu<u>e</u>no	=	good
bu<u>e</u>n	=	good…
s<u>a</u>nto	=	saint
san	=	saint…
prim<u>e</u>ro / prim<u>e</u>ra	=	first
prim<u>e</u>r	=	first…
terc<u>e</u>ro / terc<u>e</u>ra	=	third
terc<u>e</u>r	=	third…
gr<u>a</u>nde	=	big
gran	=	big…

The ellipsis mark after the translation indicates that the word is followed by a noun, e.g.

> I am eating something. I am eating some pears.
> Estoy comiendo algo. Estoy comiendo algunas peras.

13. NOUNS
NOMBRES

Nouns are all words that represent entities, such as persons, animals, plants, objects, places or ideas. For example:

>Jose, woman, zebra, pear, California, milk, love, velocity

Remember that those words can occasionally have other functions.

>I like <u>milk</u> and <u>milk</u> cake. The farmers <u>milk</u> their cows.
>   NOUN   ADJECT.   VERB

Golden Rule

> All nouns in Spanish have an intrinsec gender regardless of whether or not they denote persons, animals or objects.

Example:

>José [masc.], mujer [fem.], cebra [fem.], pera [fem.], California[fem.], leche [fem.], amor [masc.], velocidad [fem.]
>
>(= Jose, woman, zebra, pear, California, milk, love, velocity)

The difficulty of a noun having gender (masculine/feminine) is that it is not seen by the noun itself. You must identify it by the determiners or adjectives that may "orbit" the noun.

13. NOUNS

José *, la mujer, la cebra, la pera, California*, la leche, el amor, la velocidad

(*) Names os people or places are not generally accompanied by the words "el/la"

Unlike nouns, determiners and adjectives accommodate themselves to the corresponding nouns.

Example: "Otras islas blancas:" (= Other white islands)

The noun **isla** (= island) is feminine. Use "blancas" plural because it refers here to more than one island.

The adjective **blanco** (= white) will adapt to the noun that follows. So it will be blanc**as** when it is with "isl**as**."

The determiner **otro** (= another) will also have to adapt to "islas" and I'll write "otr**as**."

Something more about the gender is that some names of professions use the same word for male and female.

Maria is a dentist, her spouse is a dentist too.
María es dentista, su esposo es dentista también.

In English, many meanings are formed by combining two words: Spanish prefers to add endings instead:

shoe maker, shoe shop, little shoe, big shoe
zapat**ero**, zapat**ería**, zapat**ito**, zapat**ón**

Corollary 1: Prefixes and Suffixes

English and Spanish have many prefixes and suffixes in common, as we saw in *Chapter 8 How to Learn Words Efficiently*.

Examples of prefixes:

prehistory, **post**war, **in**humane, **dis**order, **ex**-husband,...
prehistoria, **post**guerra, **in**humano, **des**orden, **ex**marido,...

Examples of suffixes:

>possibi**lity**, distrib**ution**, elemen**tal**, evid**ent**, dent**ist**, plumb**er**, initia**tive**, curi**ous**, automa**tic**...

>posibili**dad**, distribu**ción**, elemen**tal**, evid**ente**, dent**ista**, plom**ero**, inicia**tiva**, curi**oso**, automá**tico**...

Corollary 2: "babe, baby; John, Johnny

One of the most used suffixes in English is "-y." So in Spanish, the most common suffix is "–ito." "Ito" can also be translated by "little:"

>a little house, little Richard, a little baby, a little bit of
>una casita, Ricardito, un bebito, un poquito de

Don't be surprised if you hear: -ico, -in, -ino, -illo (e.g.: casica, Ricardín, bebino, poquillo). Although "-ito" is the most commonly used by far, those others are local terms in some areas of the Spanish-speaking world.

Frequently Asked Questions

FAQ 1: Are the rules to pass from masculine to feminine and from singular to plural applicable for determiners, adjectives and nouns?

Basically, yes, but nouns don't change gender. They are the pivot of the sentence. When you are going to describe "carros"(= cars), the determiners and adjectives that orbit around the noun will have to adopt the form accordingly (masculine-plural in this case).

Nouns are either masculine or feminine. They can only change their number (singular /plural). The determiners and adjectives are the ones that have masculine **and** feminine so that they match with the noun they accompany in the sentence. In the following example, you can see how the determiner "el" and the adjective "alto" accommodate with the noun chico, and then with the noun casa.

13. NOUNS

El carr**o** alto
los carr**os** altos

La cas**a** alta
Las cas**as** altas

FAQ 2: I've seen "United States" abbreviated as EE.UU., how come?

In Spanish, the entities that have more than one word are abbreviated by repeating their initials:

    Estados Unidos   EE.UU. (= USA)
    Juegos Olímpicos   JJ.OO. (= Olympic Games)

Otherwise, they are formed out of their initials or significant letters:

    Organización de Países Exportadores de Petróleo, OPEP
    (= OPEC)

    Organización de las Naciones Unidas, ONU
    (= UN)

    Real Academia Española de la Lengua, RAE
    (= Royal Academy of the Spanish Language)

Exercises

Translate:

    My children are: Maria, Marta, Fernando, and Isabel.
    Noah has included in his ark: a bull and a cow, a tomcat and a she-cat, a male deer and a female deer...
    Canada, USA and Mexico form North America.
    The Canary Islands are volcanic and are in the Atlantic Ocean.
    Liberty, equality, and fraternity are the pillars of the French Revolution.

Answers

Mis hijos son María, Marta, Fernando e Isabel.
Noé ha incluído en su arca: un toro y una vaca, un gato y una gata, un ciervo macho y un ciervo hembra...
Canadá, EE.UU. (Estados Unidos/ Los Estados Unidos) y México forman Norteamérica.
Las Islas Canarias son volcánicas y están en el océano atlántico.
La Libertad, la igualdad y la fraternidad son los pilares de la revolución francesa.

Vocabulary

Nouns are essentially non-grammatical words, so no vocabulary list is given here.

As for your personal vocabulary list, we recommend that you learn words in sets, such as:

Countries: Argentina, India...

Organs of the body: las arterias (= arteries), los pulmones (= lungs)...

Sciences: la Economía (= Economics), la Física (= Physics), la Medicina (= Medicine)...

Professions: el/la economista (= econosmist) , el/la ingeniero (= engineer)...

Arts: la arquitectura (= Architecture), la música (= Music), la literature (= Literature)...

13. NOUNS

14. PRONOUNS
PRONOMBRES

Pronouns are those words that substitute for a noun. Thanks to them, when the subject of the sentence is known, you avoid repeating the noun:

Mary said **Mary** bought **the car**, now **the car** is **Mary's**.
She said **she** bought **it**, now **it** is **hers**.

In English, they all are:

Personal pronouns	Possessive pronouns	Object pronouns	Reflexive pronouns
I	mine	me	myself
you	yours	you	yourself
he, she, it	his, hers, its	him, her, it	himself, herself, itself
we	ours	us	ourselves
you	yours	you	yourselves
they	theirs	them	themselves

⟵—————⟶ ⟵—————————⟶
Same position Spanish/English   Position can be different

We'll group the pronouns by types in four tables (each group corresponds to a column of the above table).

14. PRONOUNS

Personal Pronouns:

English	Spanish
I	yo
you	tú
he, she, it	él *, ella, ello
we	nosotros, nosotras
you guys (Spain)	vosotros, vosotras
you guys / they	ustedes/ ellos, ellas

(*) Notice that él (= he) has an accent mark. This is to distinguish it from "el" (= the).

The personal pronouns are commonly placed before the verb, as in English.

>I work very much.
>Yo trabajo mucho.

The use of these words in Spanish is very limited due to the golden rule:

Golden Rule 1

> Spanish doesn't use the **personal** pronouns (I, you, he...) in normal speech. Instead, the information of "who does" is carried by the verb in its ending. If you use them, they must go before the verb, with only two optional exceptions: the imperative mood and questions.

Example:

>I study at three o'clock → (yo) Estudio a las tres.

Notice that, in the examples of this book yo, tú, él, etc are in parenthesis, since they are commonly omitted. This is explained in *Chapter 18 Verbs*.

- Imperative mood:
    Prepare it!
    ¡Prepáralo **tú**! (more common)
    ¡**Tú**, Prepáralo! (less common)

- Questions:
    Where do you study?
    ¿Dónde estudias **tú**? (more common)
    ¿**Tú** dónde estudias? (less common)

There are two extra personal pronouns, "usted," with the same meaning of "tú" ("you" singular), and its plural: "ustedes."

Golden Rule 2

> There are two differences between **tú and usted**, as per their use:
>
> "Tú" is the common and **in**formal way of treatment.
> "Tú" is conjugated with its own verb forms (the forms of "tú" that appear in this book).
>
> "Usted is used only to address someone very formally (like a stranger on the street or an official in court)
> "Usted" **is conjugated with the verb forms of "he/she/it"**
>
> There are two differences between **vosotros and ustedes**, as per their use:
>
> "Vosotros" (used only in Spain) is the common and informal way of treatment equivalent to "you guys."
> "Vosotros" is conjugated with its own verb forms (the forms of "Vosotros" that appears in this book)
>
> "Ustedes in Spain is used only to address someone very formally (like strangers on the street or officials in court). **In Latin America**, "ustedes" doesn't make this distinction formal/informal. It simply means "you plural."
> "Ustedes" **is conjugated with the verb forms of "they."**

Appendix A: Notes about Dialects shows the use of the pronouns according to the three main dialects.

As an example, lets see again the idiomatic sentences of the vocabulary of *Chapter 9 Types of Words*.

        What's your name?
        ¿Cómo te llamas (tú)?
        ¿Cómo se llama (usted)?

14. PRONOUNS

How old are you?
¿Cuántos a̱ños ti̱enes (tú)?
¿Cuántos a̱ños ti̱ene (usted)?

Where are you from?
¿De dónde e̱res (tú)?
¿De dónde es (usted)?

How long have you been here?
¿Cuánto ti̱empo lḻevas (tú) aquí?
¿Cuánto ti̱empo lḻeva (usṯed) aquí?

Possessive Pronouns

They indicate possession (mine, yours, his, hers, ours, theirs). These were explained together with the possessive determiners in *Chapter 11 Determiners*.

English	Spanish
mine	mío, mía, míos, mías
yours	tuyo, tuya, tuyos, tuyas
his, hers, its	suyo, suya, suyos, suyas
ours	nuestro, nuestra, nuestros, nuestras
yours	vuestro, vuestra, vuestros, vuestras (Spain)
yours / theirs	suyo, suya, suyos, suyas

The possessive pronouns are placed as in English.

Examples are:

My car is gray. → Mine is gray.
Mi carro es gris. → El mío es gris. (carro is singular, masc.)

My turtles are gray. → Mine are gray.
Mis tortugas son grises. → Las mías son grises. (plural, femin.)

Object Pronouns

The **English** object pronouns are:

>   me
>   you (singular)
>   him, her, it
>   us
>   you (plural)
>   them

Unlike English, in Spanish they can be classified in turn, into:

> 1. After a preposition, e.g. "That gift is for **her**."
> 2. After the preposition "with" e.g. "He may go with **her**."
> 3. After the preposition "between" e.g. "Between **you** and **me** there are no secrets.
> 4. Direct Object (D.O), e.g. "I have written **it**".
> 5. Indirect Object (I.O.), e.g. "I have written it to **her**".

The pronouns after prepositions are placed in the sentence as in English.

> That document is for **her**.
> Ese documento es para **ella**.

The direct and indirect pronouns are <u>not</u> always placed as in English.

> I have seen **it**.
> **Lo** he visto.

Type 1: pronoun after a preposition	Type 2: pron. after the prep. "con" (= with)	Type 3: pron. after the prep. "entre" (= between)	Type 4: Direct Object pronoun	Type 5: Indirect Object pronoun
mí	conmigo *	yo	me	me
ti	contigo *	tú	te	te
él, ella, ello	con él, ella, ello	él, ella, ello	lo, la, lo/la	le
nosotros/ as	con nosotros/ as	nosotros/ as	nos	nos
vosotros/ as (Spain)	con vosotros/ as (Spain)	vosotros/ as (Spain)	os (Spain)	os (Spain)
ustedes, ellos/ ellas	con ustedes, ellos/ ellas	ustedes, ellos/ ellas	los/ las	les

14. PRONOUNS

Examples:

> That document is for **her**.
> Ese documento es para **ella**.
>
> I am going to register with **her**.
> Voy a registrarme con **ella**.
>
> Between **you** and **me** there are no secrets.
> Entre **tú** y **yo** no hay secretos.
>
> I have seen **her**.
> **La** he visto.
>
> I have told **her** that that is impossible.
> **Le** he dicho que eso es imposible.

Classification

Type 1. Pronouns with Prepositions different than "con" (= with), and "entre" (between)

> The pronouns after prepositions (for, from, etc.) are placed in the sentence as in English.
>
> Examples:
> for me, by me, to me, from me...
> para mí, por mí, a mí, de mí...
>
> The object pronouns with preposition are:

English	Spanish
me	mí
you	ti
him, her, it	él, ella, ello
us	nosotros, nosotras
you guys	vosotros, vosotras (Spain)
you guys / them	ustedes/ ellos, ellas

> Notice that "mí" (= me) has an accent mark. This is to distinguish it from "mi" (= my). Also notice that the table looks like that of the Personal Pronouns, with the exception of "mí" and "ti."

Type 2. Pronouns with the preposition "con" (= with)

When the preposition is "con" (= with), the pronouns to use are the following:

English	Spanish
with me	conmigo *
with you	contigo *
with him, her, it	con él/con ella/ con ello
with us	con nosotros/con nosotras
with you guys	con vosotros/ con vosotras (Sp.)
with you guys/ with them	con ustedes/ con ellos, ellas

Notice that "conmigo" is a single word, so is "contigo." Also notice that the table looks like that of the Personal Pronouns, with the exception of "conmigo" and "contigo."

Remember that the pronouns after prepositions are placed in the sentence as in English. Example:

Peter is going to sing with her and with you.
Peter va a cantar con ella y contigo.

Type 3. Object pronouns with the preposition "entre" (between)

When the preposition is "entre" (= between, among), the pronouns to use are the following:

Spanish

yo
tú
él/ ella/ ello
nosotros/ nosotras
vosotros/ vosotras (Spain)
ustedes/ ellos, ellas

Notice that the table looks like that of the Personal Pronouns.

Remember that the pronouns after prepositions are placed in the sentence as in English. Example:

Between you and me, that debate has no sense.
Entre tú y yo, ese debate no tiene sentido.

Type 4. Direct Object (D.O.) pronouns

The Direct Object is the part of the sentence that respond to "what." In "I sing a song," what do I sing? The D.O. is "a song."

The D.O. pronouns are:

English	Spanish
me	me
you	te
him, her, it	lo, la
us	nos
you guys (Spain)	os
you guys / them	los, las

To translate "it" into Spanish, use "lo" if masculine, and "la" if feminine.

Example:
>I have seen **it** (a book).
>**Lo** he visto (el libro).

The placement of the direct and indirect object (D.O.) pronouns are not always the same as in English. In the next subse are pleced in the sentence before or after the verb

Warning

In the following two subsections (types 1 and 2), we will discuss the difference between the direct object and the indirect object: when to use "*la*", "*lo*" or "*le*" (= him or her). This difference is confusing even for native speakers, and it is a real challenge for English speakers. If you find it too hard in the beginning, **learn the rule of thumb** that is provided in the FAQ 2 of this chapter, and take time to learn more as your Spanish develops.

The preposition "a" (= to) precedes the D.O. when the following circumstances occur simultaneously: the D.O. is a person (versus an animal or a thing),and the name is not substituted by the pronoun.

>I have seen Maria.
>He visto **a** María.

I am calling Maria now.
Estoy telefoneando a María ahora.

But you do **not** use the preposition "a" in sentences as:

I am phoning **her** now.
La estoy telefoneando ahora.

I have seen **cats** there.
He visto **gatos** allí.

In English, both the D.O. and the I.O. pronouns are always placed after the verb (e.g. I saw **them**). In Spanish, they commonly go before the verb. This makes another golden rule:

Golden Rule

> In Spanish, you can always place the D.O. the I.O. pronoun: before the verb. This rule has three exceptions: the imperative form, and, when isolated (not functioning as a verb), the infinitive and gerund.
> If the pronoun goes after the verb, it is written as part of the verb.

Example:

The doctor has told **me** that I'm not sick.
El doctor **me** ha dicho que no estoy enfermo.

These are all the possible cases:

- I saw **her** (single-verb form, not the imperative).
  La vi

- I have seen **her** (double-verb form with past part.).
  (yo) **La** he visto.

- He is going to analyze **it at the office** (double-verb structure with infinitive).
  (él) **Lo** va a analizar en la oficina. Or:
  (él) Va a analizar**lo** en la oficina.

- He is analyzing **it** at the office (double-verb structure with gerund).
  (él) **Lo** está analizando en la oficina. Or:
  (él) Está analizándo**lo** en la oficina.

14. PRONOUNS

Examples of the exceptions indicated in the rule are:

- Sing it!
  ¡Cántalo! (imperative form).

- After seeing it, I believe it (infinitive, here isolated -not fuctioning as a verb).
  Despues de verlo, lo creo.

- Repeting it, you memorize it.
  Repitiéndolo, lo memorizas (gerund, here isolated - not fuctioning as a verb).

Type 5. Indirect Object (I.O.) Pronouns

The Indirect Object (I.O.) answers "to whom?" In the sentence "I said that to Mary," "that" is the D.O. , and "Mary" is the I.O.

The I.O. pronouns are:

English	Spanish
Me	me
You	te
him, her, it	le
Us	nos
You guys (Spain)	os
You guys / Them	les

Notice that "le" and "les" are the only differences from the previous set of pronouns (the D.O. pronouns).

The placement of the I.O. follow the same golden rule of above.

The Indirect Object pronouns in Spanish can be repeated and you can have both the noun and its pronoun in the same sentence.

Le he contado el secreto a ella ["le" is required]
(Le) he contado el secreto a mi madre. ["Le" is the common]
I have told the secret to her/ to my mother.

The Direct Object pronouns can also be repeated but this is not so common:

> La vi a ella ayer. ["la" is required]
> La vi a tu madre ayer. [*]
> I saw her/ your mother.

> El periódico lo compra mi hijo todos los días
> My son buy the newspaper every day.

> (*) Very rarely found in Spain. Example: "A veces la odio a Elsa" -from Ramón J. Sender- (Sometimes I hate Elsa).

Use of D.O and I.O. combined in the same sentence

Golden Rule

> You can have two object pronouns together (e.g. "He said **it** to **us**"). In English and Spanish, the order is reversed. In Spanish, the I.O. pronoun goes first.
> In addition, you can have neither the combination "le lo," "le los" nor "le la", "le las." In these cases, you must substitute "le/les" for "**se**:" se lo, se la, se los, se las.

Example:

> He has said **it** to **us.**
> **Nos lo** ha dicho. (nos = to us, lo = it)

> I have said **it** to **him.**
> ~~Le lo~~ he dicho → **Se lo** he dicho.

Reflexive Pronouns:

The reflexive pronouns are:

English	Spanish
myself	me
yourself	te
himself, herself, itself	se /se /se
ourselves	nos
yourselves (Spain)	os
yourselves/ themselves	se

14. PRONOUNS

Example:

> Pedro have looked at **himself** in the mirror.
> Pedro **se** ha mirado en el espejo

Regarding the placement, the reflexive pronouns follow the same rule as the D.O. and I.O. pronouns, which is:

Golden Rule

> In Spanish, you can always place the D.O. and/or the I.O. pronoun: before the verb. This rule has three exceptions: the imperative form, and, when isolated (not functioning as a verb), the infinitive and gerund.
> If the pronoun goes after the verb, it is written as part of the verb.

Examples:

> He hasn't convinced **himself** of it.
> Él no **se** ha convencido de ello.

In Spanish, these pronouns are also used to express **reciprocity**: "one another" or "each other."

> Peter and José are going to attack **each other.**
> Peter y José **se** van a atacar.
>
> Lucia, Marcos and I have looked at **one another**.
> Lucía, Marcos y yo **nos** hemos mirado.

A last comment about reflexive pronouns is the translation of sentences like: "I'll have my hair cut," "I'll have my car fixed" etc… which are reflexive in Spanish, even though the subject is not actually the barber or the mechanic:

> I'm going to have my hair cut; I'm going to have my car repaired.
> **Me** voy a cortar el pelo; **Me** voy a reparar el coche.

Frequently Asked Questions

FAQ1: Again, what's the direct object?

It is the part of the sentence over which the action of the verb falls. In the sentence, **He wrote a letter to Mary yesterday**, the Direct Object would be "a letter," since this is what "he" wrote.

In general, a complete clause follows the pattern:

[Someone or something] does [Something or someone] to [Someone or something] in a place, time or manner

Someone or something	(Subject)	He
does	(Verb)	wrote
Something or someone	(Direct Object)	a letter
to someone or something	(Indirect Object)	to Mary
in a time, place or manner	(Circumstantial Object)	yesterday

FAQ 2: I've heard that even native speakers confuse the words: "la, le, lo." Is there a rule of thumb?

Many native speakers confuse *la, le* and *lo* in certain occasions.

The subconscious rule of thumb that those speakers use is:

    le or lo   for masculine
    la   for feminine

FAQ 3: I've heard that in some cases, it is accepted to use "le" as a direct object pronoun too. How come?

As said, it is accepted in Spanish, but it is recommended that you use the proper rule (*lo/la* for D.O., and *le* for I.O.).

This question requires a deeper understanding of Spanish and a long explanation.

As we saw, there are two types of object pronouns: direct and indirect object pronouns, D.O. and I.O. Roughly, direct pronouns respond to the question "what/who;" indirect pronouns respond to "to what/to whom?"

14. PRONOUNS

> I've written <u>a letter</u> to <u>the senate.</u>
>   DIRECT   INDIRECT

> **What** have you written? A letter
> **To whom** have you written? **To** the senate

Spanish distinguishes the direct object from the indirect object for the following pronouns: la le, lo, las, les, los. The others (me, te, nos) are invariable.

English	Spanish D.O	I.O.
me	me	me
you	te	te
him	lo	le
her	la	le
it	lo/la	le
us	nos	nos
you guys (Spain)	os	os
you guys/ them	**los /las**	**les**

We can write:

	D.O.	I.O.
masculine	lo	le
feminine	la	le

	D.O.	I.O.
masculine	los	les
feminine	las	les

Examples:

> Regarding the plants, that gardener has watered them.
> En cuanto a las plantas, ese jardinero **las** ha regado.

> The mailman is going to distribute them [the packets].
> El cartero **los** va a distribuir.

> The mailman is going to put labels on them [the packets].
> El cartero **les** va a poner etiquetas.

The straightforward way to know if an object is direct or indirect is to pass the sentence to passive voice. This will result in the subject of the sentence being the direct object.

The postman put **labels** on the packets.
Labels are put on the packets by the postman.

The use of "le" as a D.O. is accepted when the D.O. is a person and it is masculine.

	D.O.	I.O.
masculine	lo/le	le
feminine	la	

	D.O.	I.O.
masculine	los	les
feminine	las	

I saw him
Le vi. (accepted)
Lo vi. (as per the norm)

The tendency in many cases is to use a pattern that doesn't depend on D.O./I.O.

	D.O.	I.O.
masculine	le	
feminine	la	

	D.O.	I.O.
masculine	les	
feminine	las	

I saw it
Le vi. (popular use, although not correct)
Lo vi. (as per the norm)

Exercises

Translate:

We are preparing a surprise party for him.
We are preparing a surprise party for her.
I am going to explain it to him later.
I am going to explain it to her later.
– Who is going to go? – I am. – You too?

14. PRONOUNS

Answers

Le estamos preparando una fiesta sorpresa.*
Le estamos preparando una fiesta sorpresa.*
Se lo voy a explicar más tarde.**
Se lo voy a explicar más tarde.**
– ¿Quién va a ir?   – Yo. –¿Tú también?

(*) Notice that the first two sentences are identical in Spanish.
(**) Likewise, second and third sentences.

Vocabulary

The table below is a summary of the words dealt in this chapter.

yo	= I
tú	= you (singular)
él	= he
ella	= she
ello *	= it
nosotros	= we
vosotros (Spain)	= you guys
ustedes	= you guys
ellos	= they
me	= to me, to myself
te	= to you (singular), to yourself
le, la, lo *	= to him, to her, to it
se **	= to himself, to herself, to itself, to themselves, to you guys
nos	= to us, to ourselves
os (Spain)	= to you guys, to yourselves
les, las, los *	= to them, to you guys
mí	= (for/by/ from/of...) me
ti	= (for/by/ from/of...) you (singular)
conmigo	= with me
contigo	= with you (singular)

(*) See the use of "le, la, lo" in this chapter
(**) See the use of "se" in this chapter

15. ADVERBS
ADVERBIOS

Adverbs answer the questions: how, where and when.

> They are reducing the cost of the product **effectively**.
> Están reduciendo el coste del producto **eficazmente**.

In the above example, the adverb answers the question "how" (How are they reducing the cost of the product? Effectively).

An adverb is a word that describes a verb, an adjective or another adverb.

Examples:

> She has aborted the operation **drastically**.
> Ella ha abortado la operación **drásticamente.**
>
> That machine is **really** complex ("complex" is an adjective).
> Esa amáquina es **realmente** complicada.
>
> This new computer is going to calculate **more rapidly**.
> Esta computadora nueva va a calcular **más rápidamente.**

While adverbs explain the action of the verb, adjectives describe nouns.
Examples:

> The green house is his. (How is his house? green).
> He runs fast (How does he run? fast).

15. ADVERBS

Golden Rule

> Adverbs function in a similar way as adjectives. The main difference is that adverbs are invariable: They don't change masculine/feminine or singular/plural.

Thanks to this rule, we can apply many of the characteristics of the adjectives to the adverbs. We can apply the word "muy" (= very) and the comparatives:

> These chapters are **very** long.
> Estos capítulos son **muy** largos.
>
> Madrid is growing **as** rapidly **as** Barcelona.
> Madrid está creceindo **tan** rápidamente **como** Barcelona.
>
> This camera is going to work **more** efficiently **than** that one.
> Esta cámara va a funcionar **más** eficientemente **que** esa.
>
> This is the TV that is functioning **the best**.
> Esta es la televisión que está funcionando **mejor**.

Sometimes adverbs looks like adjectives but this should not constitute a difficulty for the student, since both have similar characteristics.

> This car is slow (slow, adjective).
> Este carro es <u>lento</u>.
>
> This car is functioning slowly (slowly, adverb).
> Este carro está funcionando <u>lentamente</u>.

In many cases, in both Spanish and English, we can use the adverb that looks like the adjective. This happens when we don't use the suffix "ly" ("mente").

> This car is functioning slow (slow, adverb).
> Este carro está funcionando <u>lento</u>.

In English, an adjective becomes an adverb when you add **<u>ly</u>**. In Spanish, you add **<u>mente</u>** to make it an adverb.

> poor → poorly;   happy → happily
> pobre → pobre**mente**;   feliz → feliz**mente**

If the adjective ends with "o" then you must change to "a."

> serious → seriously; ample → amply
> serio → seriamente; amplio → ampliamente

Most adverbs have an actual meaning (rapidly, slowly, happily…); however, there are a few that have only grammatical value. Those adverbs that are grammatical words are listed in the vocabulary of this chapter. Here are the different types:

- Place and time adverbs, like: here, there, now, yesterday etc.

- The words sí (= yes) and no (= no, not), for example:

    > Are you marking the pages of that book? Yes, I am
    > ¿Estás marcando las páginas de ese libro? Sí.
    >
    > No, I prefer not to study.
    > No, prefiero no estudiar.

- The interrogative adverbs, which are:

    > where, when, how, what, which, who
    > dónde, cuándo, cómo, qué, cuál/cuáles, quién/quiénes

    And:

    > How much/ how many
    > Cuánto/cuánta/cuántos/cuántas

- The relative adverbs are essentially identical, but they have no accent mark. They have one only when they are in questions or exclamations.

    > Where do you study? I study where I can.
    > ¿Dónde estudias? Estudio donde puedo.

- The comparatives (which are shown in Chapter 12, Corollary 3): más (= more), menos (= less), tan (= so), etc.

Corollary 1: The Interrogative Adverbs: What, Where, When, How, etc.

The words to ask for something, someone, some place, some time, etc. are also adverbs.

In *Chapter 7 Conjugation*, the Spanish interrogative sentences were explained. The order of the sentence doesn't change.

The list of adverbs are:

> What, Which, How, Where, When, Who
> Qué, Cuál, Cómo, Dónde, Cuándo, Quién ("Quiénes," if plural)

Example:

> What have you studied?
> ¿Qué has estudiado?

As in English, in Spanish you can create questions with prepositions; however, in Spanish, the preposition never goes at the end of the sentence but at the beginning.

> Where are you **from**?
> ¿**De** dónde eres?

Other interrogative expressions are:

English	Spanish
At what time...?	¿A qué hora...?
How many...?	¿Cuántos/cuántas...?
How much...?	¿Cuánto...?
(for) How long...?	¿(durante) Cuánto tiempo...?
How long ago...?	¿Cuánto tiempo hace...?
How often...?	¿Con qué frecuencia...?

Note for linguists: "Who" is used here as a pronoun, not as an adverb. However, in this book "quién," "quiénes" are grouped with the other interrogative adverbs for simplicity.

Corollary 2: The Relative Adverbs

Roughly all the adverbs of the above corollary can also function to link clauses in one sentence, as relative adverbs. The words are:

>what, which, how, where, when, who
>que, el/la cual, como, donde, cuando, quien ("quienes," if plural)
>
>"Quien" and "quienes" are commonly replaced by "el/la que" and "los/las que" respectively.

Examples

>Barcelona is the city **where** I was born.
>Barcelona es la ciudad **donde** nací.
>
>That's the person **with whom** I have had the accident.
>Esa es la persona con **quien** he tenido el accidente.
>
>He is showing me an old photo, **which** has my face.
>Me está mostrando una foto vieja; **la cual** tiene mi cara.

Notice the spelling without any accent of the relative adverbs (it's because they are not either in interrogative, or in exclamatory sentences).

When those words are at the beginning of the sentence, they have another function: they are pronouns.

>Madrid is the city **where** I have studied. **Where** have you studied?
>Madrid es la ciudad donde (yo) he estudiado. ¿Dónde has estudiado (tú)?

In Spanish you can't omit the relative adverb "that" (= "que"), as is possible in English.

>I believe (that) you are right.
>Creo **que** tienes razón.

15. ADVERBS

Corollary 3: Adverbs / Adverbial Expressions

An adverbial expression is the part of the sentence that responds to how or where or when. So it works as an adverb.

>She has governed **with respect**.
>(ella) ha gobernado **con respeto**.

Here "with respect" responds to "how," which constitutes an adverbial expression; however, "with" is a prepostion" and "respect" is a noun. Neither are adverbs. In many instances, the proper adverb can substitute the adverbial expressions.

>She has governed **respectfully**.
>(ella) ha gobernado **respetuosamente**.

Adverbs are a type of word, so, strictly speaking, we cannot call expressions such as "con respeto" (= with respect) adverbs, since they are not single words. The vocabulary below includes adverbial expressions.

>Sometimes = a veces
>Anywhere = en cualquier parte
>Once = una vez

Frequently Asked Questions

FAQ 1: What does "lo que" mean?

"Lo que" is translated by "what" in any sentence that is **not** interrogative.

>What I am asking is necessary.
>Lo que estoy pidiendo es necesario.
>
>This is what we are going to do...
>Esto es lo que vamos a hacer...

FAQ 2: My dictionary says: "qué" means "what," and "cuál" means "which;" however, I have seen those words translated the other way round. How come?

Basically, the rule to differentiate "Qué"/ "Cuál" is the same as that in English: what (qué) is used when you ask from a large selection and which (cuál) from a limited one.

> **What** color is that? (among the **limitless** number of possible colors)
> ¿**Qué** color es ese?
>
> **Which one** do you prefer (among the limited number of options)
> ¿**Cuál** prefieres?

There are two main exceptions:

1. "Cuál" can **not** be followed by a noun; so you would use "qué" instead.

   > Which <u>city</u> is your favorite: Madrid or Barcelona?
   >   NOUN
   >
   > ¿**Qué** ciudad es tu favorita: Madrid o Barcelona? (not "cuál")

2. "Qué" can **not** be followed by the verb "ser" (= to be), unless what you mean is "What's the meaning of…"

   > What <u>is</u> your telephone number?
   > ¿**Cuál** es tu teléfono? (not "qué")
   >
   > What is "metaphysics?" or What does "metaphysics" mean?
   > ¿**Qué** es la metafísica?

Exercises

Translate:

> I am sure that tomorrow, he is going to bring the other car.
> Pedro is the engineer who is in that project.
> The law is going to permit pedestrians to cross in the red, which is perilous.
> Before cooking them, I'm going to peel the potatoes.
> After cooking them, I'm going to prepare the sauce.

Answers

> Estoy seguro que mañana va a traer el otro carro.
> Pedro es el ingeniero que* está en ese proyecto
> La ley va a permitir a los peatones cruzar en rojo, lo cual es peligroso.

15. ADVERBS

Antes de cocinarlas, voy a pelar las papas.
Después de cocinarlas, voy a preparar la salsa.

(*) Notice that "que " is used instead of "quien."

Vocabulary

sí	=	yes
si	=	if
no	=	no, not
qué	=	what (in interrogative and exclamatory sentences)
que	=	what (in other cases "this is what I want")
cuál/cuáles	=	which (in interrogative and exclamatory sentences)
cual/cuales	=	whose, which (in other cases)
quién/quiénes	=	who (in interrogative and exclamatory sentences)
quien/quienes	=	who (in other cases)
dónde	=	where (in interrogative and exclamatory sentences)
donde	=	where (in other cases)
cuándo	=	when (in interrogative and exclamatory sentences)
cuando	=	when (in other cases)
cómo	=	how (in interrogative and exclamatory sentences)
como	=	as, how (in other cases)
cuánto/a	=	How much
cuántos/as		How many
mucho/a/os/as	=	many /much
aquí, acá	=	here
ahí, allí, allá	=	there
en todas partes	=	everywhere
en ninguna parte	=	nowhere

en alguna parte	=	somewhere
en cualquier parte	=	anywhere
todas las veces	=	every time
cada vez	=	each time, every time
muchas veces	=	many times
pocas veces	=	few times
a veces	=	sometimes
en cualquier momento	=	anytime
ninguna vez	=	no time
una vez al año	=	once a year
dos veces a la semana, dos veces por semana	=	twice a week
ayer	=	yesterday
hoy	=	today
mañana	=	tomorrow
anteayer, antier	=	the day before yesterday
pasado mañana	=	the day after tomorrow
la semana pasada	=	last week
la semana anterior	=	the previous week
la semana próxima	=	next week
la semana siguiente	=	the following week
suficiente	=	sufficient
bastante	=	enough
demasiado	=	too
siempre	=	always
nunca	=	never
jamás	=	never
casi	=	almost
tarde	=	late
pronto	=	early
temprano	=	early
a tiempo	=	on time
puntual	=	punctual
antes	=	before
ahora	=	now
después	=	afterwards
cuanto antes	=	as soon as possible
ya	=	already, yet
no más	=	not any more

15. ADVERBS

todavía	=	still
aún	=	still
aun	=	even
¿(durante) Cuánto tiempo...?	=	(for) How long...?
¿Cuánto tiempo hace...?	=	How long ago...?
¿Con qué frecuencia...?	=	How often...?

The following also function as adverbs:

dentro	=	inside
fuera	=	outside
alrededor	=	around
al lado	=	side by side
cerca	=	near, close to, circa, around
lejos	=	far
en medio	=	in the middle
al principio	=	at/in the beginning
al final	=	at/in the end
encima	=	on top
debajo	=	under

You will see a similar list in the next chapter. This is because those adverbial expresions also may function as prepositions.

I am in the middle. (Where are you? In the middle; adverb)
    ADVERBIAL
Estoy en medio.
    ADVERBIAL

I am in the middle of the street
    PREPOSITIONAL
Estoy en medio de la calle.
    PREPOSITIONAL

16. PREPOSITIONS
PREPOSICIONES

Together with the determiners and the conjunctions (in next chapter), prepositions are grammatical words, which means they don't have a "tangible" meaning, only a structural value in the sentence they are in.

They can be single-word prepositions: at, in, on, over, under, below, etc., or multiple-word expressions functioning as prepositions: on top of, in the middle of,...

The prepositions are:

a	(= to, at)	hacia	(= to, towards)
ante	(= before)	hasta	(= until, up to)
bajo	(= under)	para	(= for, to)
con	(= with)	por	(= for, by, to)
contra	(= against)	según	(= according to)
de	(= of, from, off)	sin	(= without)
desde	(= from)	sobre	(= on)
en	(= in, on, at)	tras	(= after)
entre	(= between, among)		

16. PREPOSITIONS

Examples:

I am going to go to class **at** 3 o'clock.
Voy a clase **a** las 3.

I have said "hi" **to** John many times, but he has never responded to me.
Le he dicho a John "hola" muchas veces, pero nunca me ha respondido.

He has spoken **before** the judge.
Ha hablado **ante** el juez.

The cat is **under** the table.
El gato está **bajo** la mesa.

The temperature is **below** zero.
La temperatura es **bajo** cero.

He's María**'s** brother (Spanish doesn't have this structure).
Es el hermano **de** María.

I have arrived here **from** Canada.
He llegado aquí **de** Canadá.

It's a Coca-Cola ad.
Es un anuncio **de** Coca Cola.

I am going to eat **in** one hour.
Voy a comer **en** una hora.

I have lived **in** Los Angeles.
He vivido **en** Los Ángeles.

Three is **between** 2 and 4.
El tres está **entre** el 2 y el 4.

Juan is **among** the crowd.
Juan está **entre** la multitud.

He is walking **to** (towards) the door.
Está caminando **hacia** la puerta.

I am going to study **until** 3 o'clock.
Voy a estudiar **hasta** las 3.

Peter has sailed **up to** Cuba.
Peter ha navegado **hasta** Cuba.

A hammer is **for** hammering.
El martillo es **para** martillear.

For here or **to** go.
Para aquí o **para** llevar.

I am going there **for** one reason: ...
Estoy yendo allí **por** una razón: ...

He has been devoured **by** a lion.
Ha sido devorado **por** un león.

He is dancing **on** the roof.
Está bailando **sobre** el tejado.

His plane is going to fly **over** the city.
Su avión va a volar **sobre** la ciudad.

He has run **after** him.
Ha corrido **tras** él.

After the incident, he has declared.
Tras el incidente, ha declarado.

The multiple-word expressions that function as prepositions are:

dentro de ...*	= inside ...
fuera de...	= outside...
alrededor de...	= around...
junto a...	= next to...
al lado de...	= side by side...
cerca de ...	= near, close to, circa, around...
lejos de ...	= far from...
en medio de...	= in the middle of...
al principio de...	= at/in the beginning of...
al final de...	= at/in the end of...
encima de...	= on top of...
debajo de...	= under...

(*) Ellipses points (...) are written to indicate that there should be some words after them. Otherwise, they would not be functioning as a preposition but an adverb. Remember: an adverb answers where, when, or how.

16. PREPOSITIONS

I'm <u>inside</u> the house.
     PREP.

Estoy <u>dentro de</u> la casa.
      PREP.

I am <u>inside</u>.
    ADV.

Estoy <u>dentro.</u>
     ADV.

Notice that if you learn the prepositional expression (like "in the middle of"), then you have learned the adverbial expression ("in the middle").

Corollary 1: Prepositions / Prepositional Expressions

As we have just seen at the asterisk on the previous page, the particle of the sentence that works as a preposition is a prepositional expression and its constituents may not be prepositions.

    I'm <u>inside </u>the house. I am <u>inside.</u>
       PREP.   ADV.

    Estoy <u>dentro de</u> la casa. Estoy <u>dentro.</u>
         PREP.   ADV.

We cannot call multiple-word expressions prepositions because, strictly speaking, prepositions are a type of single words. The vocabulary below includes prepositional expressions.

    al principio de = in the beginning of

    detrás de (algo) = behind (something)

Corollary 2: "*Para*" versus "*Por*" (= for)

The translation of "for" can be either "para" or "por." A first approach to distinguish them is the following:

    Para expresses: finality or use
    Por expresses: cause or reason

For nailing that, you are going to need a hammer.
Para clavar eso, (tú) vas a necesitar un martillo.

Thank you **for** singing (-cause, reason-).
Gracias **por** cantar.

Corollary 3: The Extensive Use of "*En*" (= in)

In many cases "en" is translated not only by "in," but also by "on," "at"

The book is on the table. She is working at the hospital.
El libro está en la mesa. Está trabajando en el hospital.

Corollary 4 : The Extensive Use of "*De*" (= of)

Unlike English, Spanish doesn't have the structure called Saxon genitive: Peter**'s** house; the cat**'s** basket.

However, Spanish uses the same alternative that English has, the preposition "of" (de).

The house **of** Peter; the basket **of** the cat
La casa **de** Pedro; la cesta **del** gato

Corollary 5: The Personal "*A*" (= to)

In Spanish, when the Direct Object is a person, then it is preceded by "a." (as explained in *Chapter 14 Pronouns*). This use is called the personal "a" (la "a" personal). Examples:

I have seen Maria at the ball.
He visto **a** María en el baile.

16. PREPOSITIONS

He has embraced my father.
Ha abrazado **a** mi padre.

I have admired Madrid and I have admired Picasso.
He admirado Madrid y he admirado **a** Picasso.

The exception of the rule is when the person is abstract, as in: "Estamos buscando el mejor candidato" (We are looking for the best candidate).

Exercises

Translate:

Peter's car is from Japan.
From here to the ocean is 20 miles.
Tom has had an accident and is in the hospital.
The ambulance is at the hospital.
The dish is on the table.

Answers

El carro de Pedro es de Japón.
Desde (= de) aquí hasta (= al) océano hay 20 millas.
Tom ha tenido un accidente y está en el hospital.
El ambulancia ya está en el hospital.
El plato está en la mesa.

Vocabulary

a	=	to, at
bajo	=	under
con	=	with
contra	=	against
de	=	of, from, off
desde	=	from
en	=	in, on, at
entre	=	between, among
hacia	=	to, towards
hasta	=	until, up to

para	=	for, to
por	=	for, by
según	=	according to
sin	=	without
sobre	=	on
tras	=	after
dentro de	=	inside
fuera de	=	outside
alrededor de	=	around
junto a	=	next to
cerca de	=	near, close to, around
lejos de	=	far from
debajo de / abajo de	=	underneath
al lado de	=	side by side
en medio de	=	in the middle of
al principio de	=	at/in the beginning of
al final de	=	at/in the end of
encima de	=	on top of

Below are some common expression of time that carry an specific preposition, both in Spanish and in English:

A las 3:00	=	**at** 3:00
el martes	=	**on** Tuesday
en octubre	=	**in** October
en 2007	=	**in** 2007
el 2 de octubre de 2007	=	**on** October 2, 2007
en el siglo XVI	=	**in** the XVI century
por la mañana	=	**in** the morning
dentro de 2 horas	=	**within** 2 hours
en 2 horas	=	**in** 2 hours
hace 2 horas	=	2 hours ago
en Navidad	=	**at** Christmas
un rato	=	**for** a while
mucho tiempo	=	**for** a long time

16. PREPOSITIONS

17. CONJUNCTIONS
CONJUNCIONES

Conjunctions are grammatical words that joins two elemental clauses to create a compound sentence:

<u>I studied enough.</u> and <u>I passed the test.</u>
    CLAUSE 1   CLAUSE 2

<u>I'll have to fix it myself</u> since <u>you don't want to help me.</u>
      CLAUSE 1   CLAUSE 2

Notice that the conjunction doesn't need to be between the two in order to join them:

Since <u>you don't want to help me</u>, <u>I'll have to fix it myself</u>.
        CLAUSE 2   CLAUSE 1

Conjunctions are: and, or, but, however, nevertheless, if... The translation English-Spanish is quite straightforward. For example, in every instance that you use "**and**," it can be translated into "**y**."

As we saw with other functions like the adverbs or prepositions, the actual conjuctions are those single words that join; however you can have multiple-word expressions that function as conjunctions.

17. CONJUNCTIONS

This table is followed by some comments.

y	and
o	or
o...o...	either...or...
ni...ni...	neither ...nor...
pero	but (*)
sino	but (*)
aunque	although
a pesar de	in spite of
sin embargo	however
no obstante	nevertheless
en otras palabras	in other words
como	as
a medida que	as
al igual que	like
a diferencia de	unlike
según	according to
porque	because
por	because of
por causa de	because of
debido a	due to
puesto que, ya que	Since
en vista de que, visto que	in view of
entonces	then
luego	then, afterwards
en el caso de que	in case of
a condición de que	under the condition that
suponiendo que	supposing that
a menos que	unless
dado que	given that
incluso	even
aun	even
en cuanto	as soon as; as per
tan pronto como	as soon as
para que	so that
si	if
mientras	while; as long as

The conjunction **y** (and) changes to **e** if the word that follows starts with an "i" (this is to avoid having two consecutive equal sounds i-i).

>Maria **and** Lucas have studied hard.
>María **y** Lucas han estudiado duro.

>María **and** Isabel have studied hard.
>María **e** Isabel han estudiado duro.

Notice that, although it looks like only one sentence, underneath, there are two clauses and one conjunction in between: Maria studies hard (1) **and** Lucas studies hard (2).

As before, the conjunction **o** (or) changes to **u** if the word that follows starts with an "o" (this is to avoid having two consecutive sounds o-o).

>You are coming with Juan or with me.
>(tú) Estás viniendo con Juan o conmigo.

>With my program of Spanish, I am going to visit Madrid or Oviedo.
>Con mi programa de español, voy a visitar Madrid u Oviedo.

The English conjunction **as** has two translations as per the context: either **como** or **a medida que**:

>**As** the baby is crying, I am going to give him the pacifier.
>**Como** el bebé está llorando, le voy a dar la chupeta.

>**As** the fire is advancing, the smoke is reaching the last floor.
>**A medida que** el fuego está avanzando, el humo está alcanzando el último piso.

Similar to "as" is "since" (ya que):

>**Since** you are not going to help me, I am going to repair it myself.
>**Ya que** no vas a ayudarme, voy a repararlo yo mismo.

The English conjunction **but** has two translations as per the context: **"pero"** if the sentence is affirmative; **"sino"** if the sentence is negative:

>The satellite is okay **but** in the wrong position.
>El satellite está okey **pero** en una mala posición.

17. CONJUNCTIONS 163

Not only have I gained the scholarship, **but** I got the position.
No sólo he ganado la beca, **sino** que he conseguido el puesto.

In Spanish, the equivalent to neither...nor...can have more than two elements:

Neither Felipe nor Adolfo have studied enough.
Ni Felipe ni Adolfo han estudiado suficiente.
Felipe y Adolfo no han estudiado suficiente.

Felipe, Adolfo and Pedro haven't studied enough.
Ni Felipe, ni Adolfo ni Pedro han estudiado suficiente.
Felipe, Adolfo y Pedro no han estudiado suficiente.

Examples of other main conjuntions are:

Although Pirro has won the battle, he has lost the war.
Aunque Pirro ha ganado la batalla, ha perdido la guerra.

Caesar has adopted Brutus; **however,** Brutus is wanting more.
César ha adoptado a Brutos; **sin embargo** Bruto está queriendo más.

This telescope is old; **nevertheless,** it has been in use for many years.
Este telescopio es viejo; no obstante, ha estado en uso muchos años.

Corollary: Conjuntions / Conjuctive Expressions

We must remember that a conjuction is a type of word; however it also defines a function within the sentence.

As we saw when dealing with adverbs (*Chapter 15* in Corollary 1) and prepositions (*Chapter 16* in Corollary 1), some multiple-word expressions can function as adverbs and prepositions respectively. Some multiple-word expressions can function as conjuctions.

In spite of his attempts, he has failed.
A pesar de sus intentos, (él) ha fallado.

Where "in," "spite" and "of" are not conjuctions, the expression itself function as a conjunction.

Exercises

Translate:

> According to the experts, we are in a recession time.
> This car has a good price, but it's not the car of my dreams.
> The failure of this business is not because of the idea but because of the situation of the market.
> As time is passing by, I am becoming more and more happy.
> As you are insisting on it so much, I am going to accompany you.

Answers

> Según los expertos, estamos en un tiempo de recesión.
> Este carro tiene un buen precio pero no es el carro de mis sueños.
> El fallo de este negocio no es por la idea sino por la situación del mercado.
> A medida que el tiempo está pasando, estoy siendo más y más feliz.
> Como estás insistiendo tanto, voy a acompañarte.

Vocabulary

y	=	and
o	=	or
o...o..	=	either...or...
ni...ni...	=	neither ...nor...
pero	=	but (*)
sino	=	but (*)
aunque	=	although
a pesar de	=	in spite of
sin embargo	=	however
no obstante	=	nevertheless
en otras palabras	=	in other words
como	=	as (*)

17. CONJUNCTIONS

a medida que	=	as (*)
al igual que	=	like
a diferencia de	=	unlike
según	=	according to
porque	=	because
por	=	because of
por causa de	=	because of
debido a	=	due to
puesto que, ya que	=	since
en vista de que, visto que	=	in view that
entonces	=	then
luego	=	then, afterwards
en el caso de que	=	in case that
a condición de que	=	under the condition that
suponiendo que	=	supposing that
a menos que	=	unless
dado que	=	given that
en cuanto	=	as soon as; as per
tan pronto como	=	as soon as
para que	=	so that
si	=	if
mientras	=	while, as long as

(*) Although they have the same translation they have different uses.

18. VERBS
VERBOS

About Verbs in any Language

Verbs are the nuclei of the sentence. A sentence can lack nearly anything but a verb. Verbs are all those words that describe what the subject (the person or thing) does. Examples of verbs:

> to repeat, to posses, to declare, to prefer, to toast
> repetir,   poseer,   declarar,   preferir,   tostar

Let's see a verb in action with other elements:

> <u>He</u>   <u>cancelled</u>   <u>his</u>   <u>ticket.</u>
> NOUN   VERB   DET.   NOUN

Every verb is, in reality, a set of words: For example, the English verb "to sing" consists of the words:

> sing, sings, sang, sung, singing

We change the form of the verb depending on who is doing the action (I sing, he sings, ...), and depending on when the action occurs (I sing, I sang, I will sing...).

18. VERBS

Conjugating a verb means to put the verb in its different forms. For example, in English, the **conjugation** of the verb "to be" in the present tense is:

> I am
> You are
> He/she/it is
> We are
> You guys are
> They are

About the Verbs in Spanish

As we saw in *Chapter 7 Conjugation*, Spanish puts the information as to who does the action (I, you, he, she, it, we and they) in the end of the verb, as a suffix.

Remember the Golden Rule:

The translation of the English personal pronouns are not words but suffixes: particles at the end of the verb. These are:

English	Spanish	Example
I	–VOWEL* or –y	plane**o**, so**y** (= **I** plan, **I** am)
you (singular)	–s **	invita**s** (= **you** invite)
he/she/it	–VOWEL*	cuent**a** (= **he/she** counts)
we	–mos	convence**mos** (= **we** convince)
you guys (Spain)	–is	aparecé**is** (= **you guys** appear)
you guys / they***	–n	estudia**n** (=**you/ they** study)

(*) These VOWELS can be: a, e, i, o, depending on the tense. For example: canto (= I sing), canté (= I sang)

(**) As it will be explained in the Section IV: Verb Tenses, this form has three exceptions: the Preterite and the Imperative tenses, and the verb "ser" (= to be)

(***) In Latin America the forms of "you guys" and "they" coincide. For example, "apare**cen**" means "you guys appear" and "they appear." The words "ustedes" (= you guys) and "ellos" (= they) are used to avoid ambiguity. See *Apendix A, Notes about Dialects*.

Examples:

We study drama. **They** paint their houses.
Estudia**mos** drama. Pinta**n** sus casas.

Besides the person, the other piece of information that also goes at the end is the tense (when the action occurs).

We **will** study drama. They paint**ed** houses.
Estudi**are**mos drama. Pint**aro**n sus casas.

As an example, to compare English and Spanish, let's see the conjugation of the verb "admirar" (= to admire) in the present tense:

	English	Spanish
I	admire	admiro
You	admire	admiras
He	admires	admira
We	admire	admiramos
You guys	admire	admiráis (Spain)
You guys / They	admire	admiran

Corollary 1: About "Haber" and "Tener" (= to have)

Spanish has two verbs for "to have:" haber and tener. Haber is only used to create the compound tenses (I **have** gone.) "Tener" means to posses (I have a computer). Other examples:

I **have** established a record before. I **have** a cat.
He [haber] establecido un récord. **Tengo** [tener] un gato.

However, the expression "I have to" in Spanish uses the verb "tener," not "haber."

I have to cancel the tickets.
Tengo que cancelar los tiquets.

Corollary 2: About "Ser" and "Estar" (= to be)

As we saw in *Chapter 12 Adjectives*, "to be" has two translations, "ser" and "estar." You will use the verb "ser" when the attribute is permanent, and "estar" when the attribute is temporary:

> **I am** from Peru.   **I am** content.
> **Soy** de Perú.   **Estoy** contento.

Warning

> Certain expressions that use "to be" in English, use another verb in Spanish: "tener."

For example:

> **I am** hungry/ thirsty/ cold/ hot/ sleepy/scared/40 years old/ in a hurry/ right/ careful
> **Tengo** hambre/ sed/ frío/ calor/ sueño/miedo/ 40(cuarenta) años/ prisa/ razón/ cuidado

Corollary 3: "Hay / Queda" (= there is / there is left)

We saw this structure in *Chapter 12 Adjectives*, when seeing constructions to express quantities.

This structure is impersonal, which means that there's no person doing the action.

> **There is** water in my car.
> **Hay** agua en mi carro.

"Hay" is an impersonal form of the verb "haber." To use other tenses like there was, and there will be, you simply have to use the pattern of the verb haber (it's conjugated completely in the Reference Table in the end of this section).

> **There was** water in my car.
> **Había** agua en mi carro.

> **There will be** a war if there's no agreement now.
> **Habrá** una guerra si no hay un acuerdo ahora.

> **There would be** an agreement if the romans wanted.

> **Habría** un acuerdo si los romanos quisiesen.

Likewise is "queda"

> **There is** water left in the bottle.
> **Queda** agua en la botella.
>
> **There are** lemons left in the basket.
> **Quedan** limones en la cesta.

Corollary 4: Irregular Verbs

A verb is irregular when it doesn't exactly follow all the endings that correspond to its conjugation. If a given verb has one single irregularity in one tense, it is enough to call it irregular.

Some verbs are very irregular, and they don't meet the patterns in multiple instances.

In the end of every chapter of this section, you will find a corollary with the verbs that are irregular in the tense described in that chapter.

Golden Rule

> If a verb is irregular, all verbs that derive from it are irregular too, and they have the same irregularities.

Let's see some examples: de**tener** (= to detain), con**tener** (= to contain), and man**tener** (= to maintain) have the same irregularities as the verb that they derive from: **tener** (= to have).

Thus:

tener	detener	contener	mantener
tengo	detengo	contengo	mantengo
tienes	detienes	contienes	mantienes
tiene	detiene	contiene	mantiene
tenemos	detenemos	contenemos	mantenemos
tenéis	detenéis	contenéis	mantenéis
tienen	detienen	contienen	mantienen

18. VERBS

A rare exception is the verb "decir" (= to say) and its derivatives, like: bendecir, predecir, contradecir.

> I will say "no."   I will predict the future.
> Diré que no.   Predeciré el futuro (not, "prediré").

Verb tenses are linked by their irregularities. These groups follow similar rules.

- Present, Present Subjunctive and Imperative
- Future and Conditional
- Preterite, Past Subjunctive and Gerund

The next chapters are devoted to verb tenses. These relationships will be explained in detailed in three golden rules.

Exercises

a) Give the type of conjugation of the following verbs. Identify if they are: AR, ER or IR verbs.

> multiplicar, verificar, comprender, prohibir, estudiar, experimentar

b) Write the stems of the verbs above.

c) According to their conjugation, add the following suffix.

> If AR verb, then add -amos
> If ER verb, then add -emos
> If IR verb, then add -imos

d) Knowing that the endings of above correspond to the present tense of the person "we," translate (guess!).

Answers

	a)	b), c)	d)
multiplicar	AR	multiplic-amos	we multiply
verificar	AR	verific-amos	we verify
comprender	ER	comprend-emos	we comprehend
prohibir	IR	prohib-imos	we prohibit
estudiar	AR	estudi-amos	we study
experimentar	AR	experiment-amos	we experiment

Vocabulary

As we established, the vocabulary part of each chapter of this book only will focus on **grammatical words**: those words that are essential to the structure of the sentence.

The only grammatical words among the verbs are the **auxiliary verbs**: to have (haber), to be (ser and estar), and to go (ir). However the knowledge of the three conjugations of the regular verbs (AR verbs, ER verbs and IR verbs) are also basic, and they have been added.

The following two Reference Tables display all the forms of the regular verbs and the complete conjugation of the auxiliary verbs (haber, ser, estar, and ir).

These tables are repeated in Appendix D, Auxiliary Verbs, for quick consultations.

You may decide to memorize the auxiliary verbs straight and then learn their details as they appear in the chapters about the tenses. On the contrary, you may prefer to learn them step by step. Whichever method you chose is good as long as you make sure that you learn each tense before entering a new chapter, and as long as you learn the regular form before learning the irregular. Also use those tables to see the similarities in Spanish verbs.

If you decide the former, and learn the table by heart before moving on, you may want to have an overview of the Reference Tables:

- The first set of tables are only endings for the regular verbs, and the second is for only the four auxiliary verbs.

- There are three "moods" called: indicative, imperative and subjunctive. In general, English lacks the subjunctive. This is explained in *Chapter 28 The Present Subjunctive*.

- There are two past tenses in the indicative mood. These are the preterite and imperfect (I sang, and I was singing / I used to sing). The details are in *Chapter 23 The Preterite*.

- The imperative tense functions only in the second person ("you"). You can't give orders to yourself.

18. VERBS

- The last two forms are for one tense: the Past Subjunctive. They have identical meaning and identical use.

- Haber is translated by "to have" as "I have sung" (not as "I have money"). It's very irregular (notice that the endings don't match with those of the Regular verbs for the most part). This is explained in *Chapter 30 The Tenses with To Have*.

- Ser and estar are translated by "to be." Ser is used to create the passive voice ("The song was sung by me" versus "I sing the song"). This is explained in *Chapter 35 The Passive Voice*. The other "to be," estar, is the auxiliary verb for the structure "I'm singing," as explained in *Chapter 31 The Tenses with To Be*.

- Ir means "to go" but works also as an auxiliary in structures like "I'm going to sing," I was going to sing." Notice that "ir" and "ser" have some forms that are identical (like it was in Latin).

REFERENCE TABLES
(also at Appendices C & D):
REGULAR VERBS
&
THE AUXILIARY VERBS HABER, ESTAR, SER, IR

REGULAR VERBS

Impersonal Forms of the Verb

Infinitive (to sing)

AR verbs	ER verbs	IR verbs
-ar	-er	-ir

Gerund (singing)

AR verbs	ER verbs	IR verbs
-ando	-iendo	-iendo

Past Participle (sung)

AR verbs	ER verbs	IR verbs
-ado	-ido	-ido

Personal Forms of the Verb: Indicative Mood

Present (I sing)

	AR verbs	ER verbs	IR verbs
(I)	-o	-o	-o
(you singular)	-as	-es	-es
(he/she/it)	-a	-e	-e
(we)	-amos	-emos	-imos
(you guys) -Spain-	-ais	-éis	-ís
(you guys/ they)	-an	-en	-en

Preterite (I sang)

	AR verbs	ER verbs	IR verbs
(I)	-é	-í	-í
(you singular)	-aste	-iste	-iste
(he/she/it)	-ó	-ió	-ió
(we)	-amos	-imos	-imos
(you guys) -Spain-	-asteis	-isteis	-isteis
(you guys/ they)	-aron	-ieron	-ieron

Imperfect Past (I sang*)

	AR verbs	ER verbs	IR verbs
(I)	-aba	-ía	-ía
(you singular)	-abas	-ías	-ías
(he/she/it)	-aba	-ía	-ía
(we)	-ábamos	-íamos	-íamos
(you guys) -Spain-	-abais	-íais	-íais
(you guys/ they)	-aban	-ían	-ían

18. VERBS

Future (I will sing)	AR verbs	ER verbs	IR verbs
(I)	-aré	-eré	-iré
(you singular)	-arás	-erás	-irás
(he/she/it)	-ará	-erá	-irá
(we)	-aremos	-eremos	-iremos
(you guys) -Spain-	-aréis	-eréis	-iréis
(you guys/ they)	-arán	-erán	-irán

Conditional (I would sing)	AR verbs	ER verbs	IR verbs
(I)	-aría	-ería	-iría
(you singular)	-arías	-erías	-irías
(he/she/it)	-aría	-ería	-iría
(we)	-aríamos	-eríamos	-iríamos
(you guys) -Spain-	-aríais	-eríais	-iríais
(you guys/ they)	-arían	-erían	-irían

Personal Forms of the Verb: Imperative Mood

Imperative (Sing!)	AR verbs	ER verbs	IR verbs
(I)			
(you singular)	-a	-e	-e
(he/she/it)			
(we)			
(you guys) -Spain-	-ad	-ed	-id
(you guys/ they)			

Personal Forms of the Verb: Subjunctive Mood

Present (...that I sing)	AR verbs	ER verbs	IR verbs
(I)	-e	-a	-a
(you singular)	-es	-as	-as
(he/she/it)	-e	-a	-a
(we)	-emos	-amos	-amos
(you guys) -Spain-	-éis	-áis	-áis
(you guys/ they)	-en	-an	-an

Past (...that I sang)	AR verbs	ER verbs	IR verbs
(I)	-ara	-iera	-iera
(you singular)	-aras	-ieras	-ieras
(he/she/it)	-ara	-iera	-iera
(we)	-áramos	-iéramos	-iéramos
(you guys) -Spain-	-arais	-ierais	-ierais
(you guys/ they)	-aran	-ieran	-ieran
-or-			
(I)	-ase	-iese	-iese
(you singular)	-ases	-ieses	-ieses
(he/she/it)	-ase	-iese	-iese
(we)	-ásemos	-iésemos	-iésemos
(you guys) -Spain-	-aseis	-ieseis	-ieseis
(you guys/ they)	-asen	-iesen	-iesen

THE AUXILIARY VERBS *HABER, ESTAR, SER, IR*

Impersonal Forms of the Verb

	HABER	ESTAR	SER	IR
Infinitive (to sing)	haber	estar	ser	ir
Gerund (singing)	habiendo	estando	siendo	yendo
Past Participle (sung)	habido	estado	sido	ido

Personal Forms of the Verb: Indicative Mood

	HABER	ESTAR	SER	IR
Present (I sing)				
(I)	he	estoy	soy	voy
(you singular)	has	estás	eres	vas
(he/she/it)	ha	está	es	va
(we)	hemos	estamos	somos	vamos
(you guys) -Spain-	habéis	estáis	sois	vais
(you guys/ they)	han	están	son	van
Preterite (I sang)				
(I)	hube	estuve	fui	fui
(you singular)	hubiste	estuviste	fuiste	fuiste
(he/she/it)	hubo	estuvo	fue	fue
(we)	hubimos	estuvimos	fuimos	fuimos
(you guys) -Spain-	hubisteis	estuvisteis	fuisteis	fuisteis
(you guys/ they)	hubieron	estuvieron	fueron	fueron
Imperfect (I sang*)				
(I)	había	estaba	era	iba
(you singular)	habías	estabas	eras	ibas
(he/she/it)	había	estaba	era	iba
(we)	habíamos	estábamos	éramos	íbamos
(you guys) -Spain-	habíais	estabais	erais	ibais
(you guys/ they)	habían	estaban	eran	iban

18. VERBS

Future (I´ll sing)	HABER	ESTAR	SER	IR
(I)	habré	estaré	seré	iré
(you singular)	habrás	estarás	serás	irás
(he/she/it)	habrás	estará	será	irá
(we)	habremos	estaremos	seremos	iremos
(you guys) -Spain-	habréis	estaréis	seréis	iréis
(you guys/ they)	habrán	estarán	serán	irán

Conditional (I´d sing)	HABER	ESTAR	SER	IR
(I)	habría	estaría	sería	iría
(you singular)	habrías	estarías	serías	irías
(he/she/it)	habría	estaría	sería	iría
(we)	habríamos	estaríamos	seríamos	iríamos
(you guys)	habríais	estaríais	seríais	iríais
(they)	habrían	estarían	serían	irían

Personal Forms of the Verb: Imperative Mood

Imperative (Sing!)	HABER	ESTAR	SER	IR
(I)				
(you singular)		estate	sé	ve
(he/she/it)				
(we)				
(you guys) -Spain-		estad, estaos	sed	id
(you guys/ they)				

Personal Forms of the Verb: Subjunctive Mood

Pres. (...that I sing)	HABER	ESTAR	SER	IR
(I)	haya	esté	sea	vaya
(you singular)	hayas	estés	seas	vayas
(he/she/it)	haya	esté	sea	vaya
(we)	hayamos	estemos	seamos	vayamos
(you guys) -Spain-	hayáis	estéis	seáis	vayáis
(you guys/ they)	hayan	estén	sean	vayan

Past (...that I sang)	HABER	ESTAR	SER	IR
(I)	hubiera	estuviera	fuera	fuera
(you singular)	hubieras	estuvieras	fueras	fueras
(he/she/it)	hubiera	estuviera	fuera	fuera
(we)	hubiéramos	estuviéramos	fuéramos	fuéramos
(you guys) -Spain-	hubierais	estuvierais	fuerais	fuerais
(you guys/ they)	hubieran	estuvieran	fueran	fueran
-or-				
(I)	hubiese	estuviese	fuese	fuese
(you singular)	hubieses	estuvieses	fueses	fueses
(he/she/it)	hubiese	estuviese	fuese	fuese
(we)	hubiésemos	estuviésemos	fuésemos	fuésemos
(you guys) -Spain-	hubieseis	estuvieseis	fueseis	fueseis
(you guys/ they)	hubiesen	estuviesen	fuesen	fuesen

SECTION IV

VERB TENSES
TIEMPOS VERBALES

So far you know three structures with verbs: I am singing, I have sung, and I am going to sing (Estoy cantando, He cantado, Voy a cantar). To state that you know a verb completely, you need to know all the persons (I, you, he, etc.) of all tenses (present, past, future, conditional, etc.).

In this section you'll learn all the forms of the verbs organized by tenses. This section starts with those tenses that are impersonal (to sing, singing and sung), and then, those that have a person (I sing, I sang, I will sing, etc). Every chapter corresponds to a tense, and shows the patterns of that tense and its rules, as well as the use of that tense and those verbs.

The types of irregularities for that given tense and some rules to help you memorize them are displayed at the end of each chapter. An additional aid is the fact that certain tenses have common irregularities (e.g. future and conditional tenses).

Verbs are non-grammatical words, as defined in this book, and have meaning (with the exception of the auxiliary verbs). However at the end of each chapter there will still be some suggested vocabulary.

Appendix E provides an extensive list of regular verbs; appendix F provides a table of irregular verbs indicating the types of irregularities that they have.

At the end of this section, you will be able to speak Spanish.

19. INFINITIVE "TO SING"
EL INFINITIVO "CANTAR"

Infinitive (to sing)	AR Verbs	ER Verbs	IR Verbs
	-ar	-er	-ir
	cantar	beber	partir
	cant**a**r	beb**e**r	part**i**r

The infinitive is the form that represents the verb. (You **don't** say "This is the verb sung, or the verb singing, but this is the verb **"to sing"**).

As it was introduced in *Chapter 7 Conjugations*, every Spanish verb fits in one of the following categories:

- **AR Verb,** or first conjugation, when its infinitive ends in AR , e.g. cant**ar** (= to sing)
- **ER Verb**, or second Conjugation, when its infinitive ends in ER, e.g. beb**er** (= to drink)
- **IR Verb,** or third conjugation, when its infinitive ends in IR , e.g. part**ir** (= to split)

Golden Rule

> **All** verbs have their infinitive ending in **AR**, **ER** or **IR**. The stem of the verb is what is left when you take out the ending AR, ER, or IR, from its infinitive.

19. INFINITIVE

For example, the stems of the verbs "cantar," "beber" and "partir" are: "cant," "beb" and "part."

No Spanish verb, not even the most irregular one, ends in anything different than AR, ER or IR. (On the contrary, English infinitives can have any endings, e.g. to study, to jump, to be). Let's see an example: the verb "de**cir**" (= to say) is very irregular, as we'll see in the next chapter; however its infinitive still ends in one of the three models, in this case IR.

Warning

> You may see the particle "**se**" at the end of the infinitives after AR, ER or IR. "Se" means "self." It is just the reflexive pronoun, as we saw in *Chapter 14 Pronouns*. In reflexive verbs like "afeitarse" (= to shave oneself), the infinitive is "afeit**ar**". So you can see verbs ending in **ar**se, -**er**se, -**ir**se, but the infinitives are still –AR, -ER, –IR.
> He is going **to shave himself** tomorrow.
> (él) Va a **afeitarse** mañana.
> Reflexive verbs are discussed in detail in *Chapter 33 Reflexive Verbs*.

In the following chapters we'll introduce the verb tenses. In each, we'll give the endings that correspond to the **regular** verbs of each conjugation (AR, ER or IR). Right after giving the endings, you will find those endings applied to three regular verbs that serve as model: cant**ar**, beb**er** and part**ir**. (Don't get confused by the fact that "to sing," "to drink" and "to split" are irregular in English). From now on, in the end of each chapter, you'll find a corollary devoted to irregular verbs with a list of those verbs that are irregular and their irregularities.

In English and in Spanish, the infinitive doesn't change with the person and the infinitive can't go with any subject alone.

In English and in Spanish, there are three forms (infinitive, gerund and past participle) that have this invariability in common: They need an **auxiliary word** in order to function.

~~I to go to the school~~	→	I have **to go** to school.
~~(yo) ir a la escuela~~	→	Tengo que ir a la escuela.
~~I going to Peru~~	→	I am **going** to Peru.
~~(yo) yendo a Perú~~	→	Estoy yendo a Perú.
~~I gone to work~~	→	I have **gone** to work.
~~(yo) ido al trabajo~~	→	He ido al trabajo.

Corollary 1: Nouns Derived from Verbs

In theory, every verb gives rise to a noun just by using its infinitive. For example, the verb "trabajar" (= to work) functions as a noun in:

<u>Trabajar</u> es mi adicción (= working is my addiction).
  NOUN   VERB

In those cases, it is optional to put the article "el" (not "la").

Working is my addiction.
Trabajar es mi adicción.
El trabajar es mi adicción.

Singing is my passion.
Cantar es mi pasión.
El cantar es mi pasión.

Notice that English uses the gerund (or ING-words, like singing, drinking, living) instead of the infinitive for that structure.

The equivalent of: "(In order) to + INFINITIVE + Rest of the Sentence" is "Para + INFINITIVE + Rest of the Sentence"

(In order) to have better results, you need to study harder.
Para tener mejores resultados necesitas estudiar más duro.

Corollary 2: Verbal Periphrases: Two Verbs in Tandem

In many occasions, two verbs come in a pair. They are called periphrases.

Please, **help** me **find** my ring.
He **can work** hard when he wants.
I **started studying** medicine.
Avoid using this room.

There are two types of periphrases: those where the second verb is in the infinitive form (with or without "to"); and those where the second verb is in the gerund form (with or without any preposition).

It's important that as you learn verbs (such as "to help," "can," "to start," "to avoid"), you learn which form to use for the second verb (either infinitive or gerund). In most of the cases Spanish and English coincide.

19. INFINITIVE

He **can work** hard when he wants.
(él) **Puede trabajar** duro cuando quiere.

But not always:

Avoid using this room.
Evita usar esta habitación (not ~~Evita usando~~).

Don't confuse periphrases with compound tenses. In the compound tenses (I have sung, I was singing" etc.), the first verb is an auxiliary verb whose only function is to create the tense. For example in the sentences: "I have to study;" "I am studying," the verb is "to study," the others (to have and to be) don't provide any meaning, only structure.

The verb "to want" forms periphrases in English, but does not in Spanish.

I **want** you to go.
Quiero que vayas (literally: "I want that you go").

Corollary 3: I am going to + INFINITIVE = Voy a + INFINITIVE

To create a tense of an immediate future, both English and Spanish use the verb "to go" ("ir," in Spanish) followed by the infinitive.

The following are the conjugations in the present tense for the verb "ir:"

Present (I go)	ir
(I)	voy
(you singular)	vas
(he/she/it)	va
(we)	vamos
(you guys) –Spain	vais
(you guys / they)	van

Examples of use:

The party is going to be a surprise for Richard. I'm not going to prepare the enchiladas and you are not going to prepare the sangria; Clara and Fernando are going to play guitar. We all are going to make her laugh.

La fiesta va a ser una sorpesa para Richard. Yo no voy a preparar las enchiladas y tú no vas a preparar la sangría; Clara y Fernando van a tocar la guitarra. Todos nosotros vamos a hacerla reír.

Corollary 4: Irregular Verbs in the Infinitive

Let's remember the golden rule of the beginning of this chapter:

> **All** verbs have their infinitive ending in AR, ER or IR. The stem of the verb is what is left when you take out the ending AR, ER, or IR from its infinitive.

An immediate consequence is that no verb is irregular in the infinitive.

Notice that in Appendix F, A List of Irregular Verbs, the list of tenses with irregularities skips the infinitive.

Exercises

Translate:

> Acting in front of a large audience is my dream.
> He's not going to accept a no as an answer.
> We're going to abandon the car.
> We are not going to abort that military operation
> Are you guys going to accompany me home?

Answers

> Actuar en frente de una gran audiencia es mi sueño.
> No va a aceptar un no como respuesta.
> Vamos a abandonar el carro.
> No vamos a abortar esa operación militar.
> ¿Van (Vais –Spain-)a acompañarme a casa?

19. INFINITIVE

Vocabulary

The following is some advice about the vocabulary for the following chapters.

Only the auxiliary verbs are grammatical words. They don't have a meaning by themselves; they just serve to construct the sentence. Some of the auxiliary verbs have two uses: as an auxiliary verb and as a main verb.

haber	i	=	to have (auxiliary) "I have sung"
tener	i	=	to have (to posses) "I have a dog"
ser	i	=	to be (for permanent attributes)
estar	i	=	to be (for non permanent attributes)
ir	i	=	to go

i indicates irregular.

Remember that the infinitive of all verbs (with no exception) has the stress in the last vowel, e.g. cant<u>a</u>r, beb<u>e</u>r, part<u>i</u>r.

In the same way that you learn the nouns together with the information about masculine/feminine (el carro, la casa…), when you learn every verb (every infinitive) you need to learn if it's regular or irregular, e.g. cantar (regular), beber (regular), partir (regular), ser (irregular), estar (irregular). Appendices F and G show two lists of regular and irregular verbs.

20. GERUND "SINGING"
EL GERUNDIO "CANTANDO"

Gerund (singing)	AR Verbs	ER Verbs	IR Verbs
	-ando	-iendo	-iendo
	cantar	**beber**	**partir**
	cantando	bebiendo	partiendo

In English, the gerund corresponds to the form –ing (e.g. singing, studying, drinking, being etc).

As said in the previous chapter, the gerund (as the infinitive and as the Past Participle we'll see next chapter) needs an **auxiliary word** in order to function.

~~I going to Peru.~~
~~Yendo a Perú.~~

I am going to Peru.
Estoy yendo a Perú.

20. GERUND

Corollary 1: Adverbs Derived from Verbs

In theory, you can generate adverbs from verbs by just using the gerund. In the sentence "By working I will achieve my goal," **how** will you achieve your goal? Working, which is functioning as an adverb (Remember "how" is the key word to identify an adverb).

> I have avoided the traffic **studying** at home.
> He evitado el tráfico **estudiando** en casa.

Corollary 2: "I am singing = "Estoy cantando"

Both English and Spanish have a tense to express an action that is occuring at the moment. For this, both languages use the verb estar (= to be) followed by the verb in gerund.

> I am sing**ing**.
> Estoy cant**ando**.

Below are the conjugations in the present tense for the verb "estar" (introduced in *Chapter 18 Verbs*).

Present (I am, you are...)	**estar**
(I)	estoy
(you singular)	estás
(he/she/it)	está
(we)	estamos
(you guys) –Spain-	estáis
(you guys/ they)	están

Example of use:

> We four are living in Santa Cruz now. Marta is working downtown; I am painting; Ernesto and Carlos are teaching at the University. Only you are not living with us.

> Los cuatro estamos viviendo en Santa Cruz ahora. Marta está trabajando en el centro; yo estoy pintando; Ernesto y Carlos están enseñando en la universidad. Sólo tú no estás viviendo con nosotros.

Corollary 3: Irregular Verbs in the Gerund

An example of an irregular verb in the gerund is "atribuir" (= to attribute). Its gerund is not ~~atribuiendo,~~ but atribuyendo.

There are four types of irregularities:

Type 1. Affects all verbs ending with -aer, -eer, -oer, -oír, -uir. e.g. atribuir.

These verbs insert a "y" between the stem and the ending, (otherwise it would sound strange with three vowels together) e.g. atribu-ir → atribuiendo → atribuyendo (= attributing).

Infinitive		Gerund
atribuir	= to attribute	atribuyendo
caer	= to fall	cayendo
construir	= to construct	construyendo
contribuir	= to contribute	contribuyendo
creer	= to believe	creyendo
destruir	= to destruct	destruyendo
distribuir	= to distribute	distribuyendo
huir	= to flee	huyendo
incluir	= to include	incluyendo
leer	= to reed	leyendo
oír	= to hear	oyendo
poseer	= to posses	poseyendo
proveer	= to supply	proveyendo
traer	= to bring	trayendo

We'll see the same irregularity in the present tense (*Chapter 22 Present*).

Type 2. Affects two verbs. Those IR verbs whose infinitive have an –o- in the second to last syllable.

These verbs change o → u, in order to form the gerund.

dor-mir → durmiendo   (= sleeping)

20. GERUND

Infinitive		Gerund
dormir	= to sleep	durmiendo
morir	= to die	muriendo

We'll see the same irregularity in the present tense (*Chapter 22 The Present*).

Notice that this irregularity affects those verbs that are irregular in the Preterite in the form "ellos." See *Chapter 23 Preterite*.

Type 3. Affects all verbs of the third conjugation (IR verbs) whose infinitive have an -e- in the second to last syllable.

These verbs change e → i to form the gerund.

a-rre-pen-tir → arrepintiendo   (= repenting)

Examples:

Infinitive		Gerund
arrepentir	= to repent	arrepintiendo
conseguir	= to achieve	consiguiendo
convertir	= to convert	convirtiendo
corregir	= to correct	corrigiendo
decir	= to say	diciendo
despedir	= to see so. off./ to fire	despidiendo
divertir	= to have fun	divirtiendo
elegir	= to choose	eligiendo
freír	= to fry	friendo
gemir	= to wine	gimiendo
herir	= to cause a wound	hiriendo
hervir	= to boil	hirviendo
inferir	= to infer	infiriendo
invertir	= to invert	invirtiendo
medir	= to measure	midiendo
mentir	= to lie	mintiendo
pedir	= to ask for	pidiendo
preferir	= to prefer	prefiriendo
reír	= to laugh	riendo
rendir	= to surrender	rindiendo

Infinitive		Gerund
reñir	= to quarrel	riñendo
repetir	= to repeat	repitiendo
seguir	= to go on	siguiendo
sentir	= to feel	sintiendo
servir	= to serve	sirviendo
sonreír	= to smile	sonriendo
sugerir	= to suggest	sugiriendo
venir	= to come	viniendo
vestir	= to dress	vistiendo

Notice that this irregularity affects those verbs that are irregular in the Preterite in the form "ellos." See *Chapter 23 The Preterite*.

    e → ie   sentir → sintieron → sintiendo
    e → i   sugerir → sugirieron → sugiriendo

We'll also see similar irregularities in the present tense (*Chapter 22 The Present*).

Type 4. Others.

There are only two verbs that don't admit any rule for their irregularity. These are:

Infinitive		Gerund
ir	= to go	yendo
poder	= can	pudiendo

Note about irregular verbs.

Certain tenses share the same irregularities. You will see similar types of irregularities of the Gerund when you study the Preterite (*Chapter 23*) and the Past Subjunctive (*Chapter 29*).

In those chapters, you will find the golden rule that links them. Appendix F, a List of Irregular Verbs, shows a synopsis of all tenses, and their types of irregularities.

20. GERUND

Exercises

Translate:
> In this class we're learning to admire the avant-gardes.
> With Pedro, Juan is acquiring a lot of experience.
> I'm educating my voice by singing in the shower.
> Are not you guys altering the document by eliminating the appendices?
> The Police are taking note of his declaration.

Answers
> En esta clase de arte estamos aprendiendo a admirar las vanguardias.
> Con Pedro, Juan está adquiriendo mucha experiencia.
> Estoy educando mi voz cantando en la ducha.
> ¿No están (estáis –Spain-) alterando el documento al eliminar los apéndices?
> La policía está tomando nota de su declaración.

Vocabulary

The following are some verbs and verb expressions that require a comment about their meanings.

ver	i	=	to see
ver la televisión	i	=	to watch TV
mirar		=	to look
oír	i	=	to hear
oír la radio	i	=	to listen to the radio
escuchar		=	to listen
tocar		=	to touch
tocar		=	to play (an musical instrument)
oler		=	to smell (to expel smell)
oler, oler bien	i	=	to have smell, to smell good
oler mal	i	=	to stink
hablar con		=	to speak with
decir	i	=	to say, to tell
contar	i	=	to tell
contar	i	=	to count

i indicates irregular

21. PAST PARTICIPLE "SUNG"
EL PARTICIPIO "CANTADO"

Past Participle (sung)	AR Verbs	ER Verbs	IR Verbs
	-ado	-ido	-ido

	cantar	beber	partir
	cantado	bebido	partido

The Past Participle corresponds to the English form "sung" of the verb "to sing." Other examples are: gone, seen, forgotten, been, sunk, rotten, eaten, forbidden). To recognize the Past Participle in English you simply use the Present Perfect:

>I have **sung**. I have **gone**. I have **seen**. I have **eaten**.

In English regular verbs, the past participle ends with "ed," like: studied, worked, analyzed, distributed, or repaired. We omit those as examples because they get confused with the simple past tense.

As said in the previous two chapters, the Past participle (as the infinitive and the gerund) needs an **auxiliary word** to function.

>~~I gone to work.~~
>~~(yo) ido al trabajo.~~

>I have **gone** to work.
>(yo) He **ido** al trabajo.

21. PAST PARTICIPLE 193

Corollary 1: Adjectives Derived from Verbs

In Spanish, the past participle forms an adjective. Remember that any word can function as an adjective when placed after "to be." For example, the verbs "to bore" and "to tire" generate bored and tired.

>I am bored.   I'm tired.
>Estoy aburrido. Estoy cansado.

Warning

> In English, the gerund can also form adjectives. Spanish can not. Spanish will use the Past Participle and will use "ser" instead of estar.

Example: Soy aburrido = I am boring.

Corollary 2: "I have sung = He cantado;" "I had sung" ="Había cantado"

Both English and Spanish form the compound tenses of a given verb by conjugating the verb "to have" (haber) followed by the past participle of the verb.

Below are the conjugations in the present tense for the verb "haber"

Present (I have)	haber
(I)	he
(you singular)	has
(he/she/it)	ha
(we)	hemos
(you guys) –Spain-	habéis
(you guys/ they)	han

Past (I had)	haber
(I)	había
(you singular)	habías
(he/she/it)	había
(we)	habíamos
(you guys) –Spain-	habíais
(you guys/ they)	habían

The use is explained in further detail in *Chapter 30 The Tenses with To Have*.

Example of use:

> Last rains have caused the catastrophe. The river had accumulated too much water.
>
> Las últimas lluvias han causado la catástrofe. El río había acumulado demasiada agua.

Corollary 3: Irregular Verbs in the Past Participle

There are only 13 verbs with an irregular participle.

> escrito, not ~~escribido~~   (= written)

Below you'll find **the** list of verbs that are irregular in the Past Participle.

Infinitive		Past Participle
abrir	= to open	abierto
cubrir	= to cover	cubierto
escribir	= to write	escrito
decir	= to say	dicho
hacer	= to do	hecho
morir	= to die	muerto
poner	= to put	puesto
resolver	= to resolve	resuelto
romper	= to break	roto
satisfacer	= to satisfy	satisfecho
soltar	= to loosen up	suelto
volver	= to come back	vuelto
ver	= to see	visto

Another small group of verbs accept either the regular or the irregular form e.g. imprimido/impreso (= printed).

21. PAST PARTICIPLE

Exercises

Translate:

> The forgotten victims of the accident are the relatives.
> The movie is: The night of the living dead.
> I've acquired a collection of Picasso's replicas.
> He's in jail because he accepted a bribe.
> We are affected, tired and offended.

Answers

> Las víctimas olvidadas del accidente son los familiars.
> La película es: La noche de los muertos vivientes.
> He adquirido una colección de réplicas de Picasso.
> Está en la cárcel porque había aceptado una mordida.
> Estamos afectados, cansados y ofendidos.

Vocabulary

tener 40 años	i	=	to be 40 years old
tener calor / frío	i	=	to be hot/cold "I'm hot"
tener miedo de	i	=	to be afraid of
tener que ver con	i	=	to have to do with
tener sueño	i	=	to be asleep
tener hambre / sed	i	=	to be hungry / thirsty

i indicates irregular

22. PRESENT "I SING"
EL PRESENTE "CANTO"

Regular Verbs

	AR Verbs	ER Verbs	IR Verbs
(I)	-o	-o	-o
(you singular)	-as	-es	-es
(he/she/it)	-a	-e	-e
(we)	-amos	-emos	-imos
(you guys)- Spain-	-ais	-eis	-ís
(you guys/ they)	-an	-en	-en

	cantar	beber	partir
(I)	canto	bebo	parto
(you singular)	cantas	bebes	partes
(he/she/it)	canta	bebe	parte
(we)	cantamos	bebemos	partimos
(you guys)- Spain-	cantáis	bebéis	partís
(you guys/ they)	cantan	beben	parten

We marked the persons in parentheses to denote that in Spanish, it is redundant to put it because the information on who did the action is already in the ending. You don't need to say "Yo canto" (I sing), but just "Canto."

22. PRESENT

Examples of use of the present tense:

> I sing, you sing, he sings, we sing, you guys sing, they sing
> Canto, cantas, canta, cantamos, cantáis, cantan
>
> I drink, you drink, he drinks, we drink, you guys drink, they drink
> Bebo, bebes, bebe, bebemos, bebéis, beben
>
> I live, you live, he lives, we live, you guys live, they live
> Vivo, vives, vive, vivimos, vivís, viven

Unlike English, in Spanish you can use the present tense to describe historical facts.

> Columbus discovered America in 1492.
> Colón descubre America en 1492.

Corollary 1: Spelling-changing or False-irregular Verbs

It may happen that the verb needs to alter its spelling to accommodate the right pronunciation. An example is **vencer** (= to defeat). If we add the endings to form the present tense, we obtain a wrong pronunciation of its forms. Venc-er /benthér/ → it should sound /benth-o/, but ~~venco~~ gives /benko/ instead.

	vencer
(I)	venzo
(you singular)	vences
(he/she/it)	vence
(we)	vencemos
(you guys)	vencéis
(they)	vencen

If you take the stem venc- and then add the suffix -o, the result is venco, but the "c" with "o" doesn't sound as "s" of vencer. That's why the spelling needs to change.

This happens with the verbs ending in:

-cer → -zo
-cir → -zo
-ger → -jo
-gir → -jo
-guir → -go
-quir → -co

Warning

> You don't have to memorize these endings. As you learn the rules of spelling of this book, you will notice when you write them (remember: pronunciation wise, they are regular). Notice that it is the same tranformation of:
> poco (= little of) + ito → poquito (= little bit of), not pocito

Examples:

	-cer → -zo	-cir → -zo	-ger → -jo
	vencer	esparcir	proteger
	= to defeat	= to spread	= to protect
(I)	venzo	esparzo	protejo
(you singular)	vences	esparces	proteges
(he/she/it)	vence	esparce	protege
(we)	vencemos	esparcimos	protegemos
(you guys)-Sp.	vencéis	esparcís	protegéis
(you guys/ they)	vencen	esparcen	protegen

	-gir → jo	-guir → -go	quie → -co
	exigir	distinguir	delinquir
	= to demand	= to distinguish	= to commit a crime
(I)	exijo	distingo	delinco
(you singular)	exiges	distingues	delinques
(he/she/it)	exige	distingue	delinque
(we)	exigimos	distinguimos	delinquimos
(you guys)-Sp.	exigís	distinguís	delinquís
(you guys/ they)	exigent	distinguen	delinquen

All these verbs are the spelling-changing verbs. Those that happen to be regular can also be called false-irregular verbs.

Also notice that these alterations can also happen when the verb is irregular for other reasons. For example "seguir" (= to follow) is truly irregular (not what we called "false irregular"). As it is explained in the following Corollary, Type 4, with the verb "seguir" forms "sigo" (I follow). So, it changes its stem; it is irregular. It is in addition to that, that it needs to alter its "u" to accommodate to the right pronunciation, according to the above rules ("sigo," not ~~sigue~~).

These alterations only take place with the Present tense, Preterite (*Chapter 23 Preterite*) and Present Subjunctive (*Chapter 28 Present Subjunctive*).

Corollary 2: The Irregular Verbs in the Present Tense

There are six types of irregularities:

Type 1 Affects all verbs ending in –uir

These verbs add "y" after the stem to form present tense, except for the forms nosotros and vosotros.

Example: construir (= to construct) construo → construyo

(I)	construyo
(you singular)	construyes
(he/she/it)	construye
(we)	construimos
(you guys) -Spain	construís
(you guys/ they)	construyen

Shading indicates irregularity

The rule of the slipper. Some Californian teachers use the term "la regla de la zapatilla" based on the shape that results when you display the conjugation in two columns:

construyo	construimos
construyes	construís
construye	construyen

Other examples are: atribuir, contribuir, distribuir (= to attribute, to contribute, to distribute).

Type 2. Affects most verbs with an -o- in the second to last syllable.

These verbs change -o- → -ue- , except for the forms nosotros and vosotros, to form present tense.

Example: dor-mir (= to sleep)

(I)	duermo
(you singular)	duermes
(he/she/it)	duerme
(we)	dormimos
(you guys) –Spain-	dormís
(you guys/ they)	duermen

Shading indicates irregularity

Notice the "rule of the slipper" explained above.

Other examples are: poder, morir, mover, contar (= can, to die, to move, to count).

Nonetheless, there are verbs like "co-mer," or "co-ser" (= to eat, to sew) which are regular.

Type 3. Affects most verbs with an –e- in the second to last syllable.

Some of these verbs change –e- → -ie- , except for the forms nosotros and vosotros. **Other verbs** of this type change according to the **type 4**.

Example: pre-fe-rir (= to prefer)

(I)	prefiero
(you singular)	prefieres
(he/she/it)	prefiere
(we)	preferimos
(you guys) –Spain-	preferís
(you guys/ they)	prefieren

Shading indicates irregularity

Notice that we have here the "rule of the slipper" explained above.

Other examples are: entender, querer, sentir (= to understand, to want, to feel).

Nonetheless, there are verbs like "be-ber" or "pesar" (= to drink, to weigh) which are regular.

Type 4. Affects most verbs with an –e- in the second to last syllable.

Some of these verbs change –e- → -i- , except for the forms nosotros and vosotros. Other verbs of this type change according to the previous type.

Example: re-pe-tir (= to repeat)

(I)	repito
(you singular)	repites
(he/she/it)	repite
(we)	repetimos
(you guys) –Spain-	repetís
(you guys/ they)	repiten

Shading indicates irregularity

Notice that we have here the "rule of the slipper" explained above.

Other examples are: seguir, conseguir, pedir (= to follow, to achieve, to ask for).

So, a verb with an –e- in the second to last syllable can be irregular ie-irregular i-irregular or regular (pref**e**rir, rep**e**tir, p**e**nsar).

Nonetheless, notice that, as in the previous type, there are verbs like "be-ber" or "pesar" (= to drink, to weigh) which are regular.

Type 5. Affects most verbs ending with –cer or –cir , except "decir."

These verbs add "z" before the "c," for the form "I." Example: producir (= to produce)

(I)	produzco

(you singular)	produces
(he/she/it)	produce
(we)	producimos
(you guys) –Spain-	producís
(you guys/ they)	producen

Shading indicates irregularity

Other examples are: conocer, conducir, crecer, (= to know, to drive, to grow up).

Nonetheless, there are verbs as "vencer" or "convencer" (= to defeat, to convince) which are regular.

Type 6. Others.

There are **21 verbs** which don't follow any rule. However they can be grouped by their similar changes.

12 verbs end with "**–go**" for the form of "I" (instead of "-o"). These are:

tener, venir, decir, bendecir, hacer, satisfacer, valer, traer, poner, salir, caer, oír.
(to have, to come, to say, to bless, to do, to satisfy, to be worth, to bring, to put, to go out, to fall, to hear)

	tener	**venir**
(I)	tengo	vengo
(you singular)	tienes	vienes
(he/she/it)	tiene	viene
(we)	tenemos	venimos
(you guys) –Spain-	tenéis	venís
(you guys/ they)	tienen	vienen

	decir	**bendecir** *
(I)	digo	bendigo
(you singular)	dices	bendices
(he/she/it)	dice	bendice
(we)	decimos	bendecimos
(you guys) –Spain-	decís	bendecís
(you guys/ they)	dicen	bendicen

22. PRESENT

	hacer	satisfacer *
(I)	hago	satisfago
(you singular)	haces	satisfaces
(he/she/it)	hace	satisface
(we)	hacemos	satisfacemos
(you guys) –Spain-	hacéis	satisfacéis
(you guys/ they)	hacen	satisfacen

	traer	valer	poner
(I)	traigo	valgo	pongo
(you singular)	traes	vales	pones
(he/she/it)	trae	vale	pone
(we)	traemos	valemos	ponemos
(you guys) –Spain-	traéis	valéis	ponéis
(you guys/ they)	traen	valen	ponen

	salir	caer	oír
(I)	salgo	caigo	oigo
(you singular)	sales	caes	oyes
(he/she/it)	sale	cae	oye
(we)	salimos	caemos	oímos
(you guys) –Spain-	salís	caéis	oís
(you guys/ they)	salen	caen	oyen

Shading indicates irregularity

(*) The rules are also applicable to all verbs that derive from them like "poner" and "suponer" (= to put and to suppose). However, although "satisfacer" and "bendecir" look like derivative verbs of hacer and decir respectively, they are not. You will see that they are not linked in other tenses.

Four verbs end with "–y" for the form of "I" (instead of "–o"). These are: dar, estar, ser, and ir (= to give, to be, to be, to go).

	dar	estar	ser	ir
(I)	doy	estoy	soy	voy
(you singular)	das	estás	eres	vas
(he/she/it)	da	está	es	va
(we)	damos	estamos	somos	vamos
(you guys) –Spain–	dais	estáis	sois	vais
(you guys/ they)	da	están	son	van

Shading indicates irregularity

Five verbs don't have any specific ending. These are: saber, ver, caber, jugar, haber (= to know, to see, to fit, to play, to have – auxiliary).

	saber	ver	caber	jugar *	haber
(I)	sé	veo	quepo	juego	he
(you s.)	sabes	ves	cabes	juegas	has
(he/she/it)	sabe	ve	cabe	juega	ha
(we)	sabemos	vemos	cabemos	jugamos	hemos
(you guys) –Spain–	sabéis	veis	cabéis	jugáis	habéis
(you guys/ they)	saben	ven	caben	juegan	han

Shading indicates irregularity

(*) Notice that the verb "jugar" seems to fit into the type-2 irregularity (o → ue); however this verb does not have a "o," but an "u," in the second to last syllable.

Note about irregular verbs.

Certain tenses share the same irregularities. You will see similar types of irregularities of the Present when you study the Present Subjunctive (*Chapter 28*).

Appendix F, A List of Irregular Verbs, shows a synopsis of all tenses, and their types of irregularities.

22. PRESENT

Exercises

Translate:

Those companies threaten to declare bankruptcy if the government doesn't intervene.
Earth attracts Moon in its orbit.
We don't approve the law in the form it's written.
Do you not repent that decision?
I aspire to obtain an A in this class.

Answers

Esas compañías amenazan con declarar la bancarrota si el gobierno no interviene.
La Tierra atrae a la luna en su órbita.
No aprobamos la ley en la forma en que está escrita.
¿No te arrepientes de esa decision?
Aspiro a obtener una A en esa clase.

Vocabulary

aprender	=	to learn
aprender de memoria	=	to learn by heart
pedir prestado i	=	to borrow
prestar	=	to lend
dejar	=	to lend
dejar	=	to leave, to drop
dejar de	=	to quit

i indicates irregular

23. PRETERITE "I SANG"
EL PASADO INDEFINIDO "CANTÉ"

Regular Verbs

	AR Verbs	ER Verbs	IR Verbs
(I)	-é	-í	-í
(you singular)	-aste	-iste	-iste
(he/she/it)	-ó	-ió	-ió
(we)	-amos	-imos	-imos
(you guys) - Spain	-asteis	-isteis	-isteis
(you guys/ they)	-aron	-ieron	-ieron

	cantar	beber	partir
(I)	canté	bebí	partí
(you singular)	cantaste	bebiste	partiste
(he/she/it)	cantó	bebió	partió
(we)	cantamos	bebimos	partimos
(you guys) - Spain	cantasteis	bebisteis	partisteis
(you guys/ they)	cantaron	bebieron	partieron

In Spanish, there are two past tenses: the Preterite (also called Indefinite Past, or Simple Past) and the Imperfect Past.

Corollary 1: Difference between the Preterite and the Imperfect Past

The English past tense "I sang" corresponds with two tenses in Spanish.

> **I sang** that song five times and every time that **I sang** it I cried.
> **Canté** esa canción cinco veces y cada vez que la **cantaba**, lloraba.

The second use of the past tense "I sang" is equivalent to "I was singing." We can state that:

Golden Rule

> If you can't substitute the past tense with the structure "I was singing" or "I used to sing," then it is the Preterite (versus the Imperfect Past tense).

> In 1939 Great Britain **declared** war on Germany.
> En 1939 Gran Bretaña **declaró** la guera a Alemania.

> In 1939 Britain ~~was declaring/used to declare~~ war on Germany.
> En 1939 Gran Bretaña ~~declaraba~~ la guera a Alemania.

In other cases, when it's clear that you mean an action with some duration or frequency, you don't have a choice.

> When I **was** in school, I **sang** in the choir.
> Cuando **estaba** en el colegio, **cantaba** en el coro.

Notice that the sentence "when I was in school" equals "when I was being a student."

Corollary 2: Spelling-changing or False-irregular Verbs

As we saw in Chapter 3, it may happen that the verb needs to alter its spelling to accommodate the right pronunciation. An example is **buscar** (= to seek). If we add the endings to form the preterite tense, we obtain a wrong pronunciation of its forms. Busc-e /bus-cé/ → it should sound /busk-é/.

This happens with the verbs ending in: "car," "gar," and "zar."

-car → -qué   (yo busqué = I sought)
-gar → -gué   (yo llegué = I arrived)
-zar → -cé   (yo alcanzar = I reach)

The reason for the last one (-zar → -cé) is strictly orthographic. According to the Spelling Rules, the syllabe "ze," "zi" must be written "ce," "ci." thus, instead of ~~empezé~~, empecé.

Examples:

	-car → -qué	-gar → -gué	-zar → -cé
	buscar	llegar	alcanzar
	= to seek	= to arrive	= to reach
(I)	busqué	llegué	alcancé
(you singular)	buscaste	llegaste	alcanzaste
(he/she/it)	buscó	llegó	alcanzó
(we)	buscamos	llegamos	alcanzamos
(you guys)-Sp.	buscastéis	llegastéis	alcanzasteis
(you guys/ they)	buscaron	llegaron	alcanzaron

All these verbs are the spelling-changing verbs. Those that happen to be regular can also be called false-irregular verbs. These alterations only take place with the Present tense, Preterite *(Chapter 23)* and Present Subjunctive *(Chapter 28)*.

Corollary 3: Irregular Verbs in the Preterite

Golden Rule

> If a verb is irregular in the **Preterite**, then it will also be irregular in the **Past Subjunctive** and will posses the same irregularity of the form "ellos" (= they). The irregularities in the **Gerund** are also related with this tense.

Example: dormir (= to sleep)

   Preterite: (ellos) durmieron

   Past Subjunctive: durmiese, durmieses, durmiese,
                  durmiésemos, durmieseis, durmiesen
   Gerund: durmiendo

Appendix F: A List of Irregular Verbs, shows a synopsis of all tenses and their types of irregularities.

23. PRETERITE

There are five types of irregularities:

Type 1 Affects all verbs ending in –aer, –eer, –oer, –oír, -uir.

> These verbs add "y" after their stem for the person él/ella and ellos (= he/she and they). To memorize it, notice that if you didn't insert the "y" you would have three vowels in a row, which would be hard to pronounce.
>
> Example: cons**truir** (= to construct) cons-tr**uió** → cons-tru-**yó**

(I)	construí
(you singular)	construiste
(he/she/it)	**construyó**
(we)	construimos
(you guys) - Spain-	construisteis
(you guys/ they)	**construyeron**

Shading indicates irregularity

> **The rule of the sole.** As we had "la regla de la zapatilla" (rule of the slipper), here we have the "regla de la suela" (rule of the sole), based on the shape that results when you display the conjugation in two columns:
>
> | | |
> |---|---|
> | construí | construimos |
> | construiste | construisteis |
> | **construyó** | **construyeron** |
>
> Other examples are: atribuir, oír, huir, incluir, excluir, leer, creer (= to attribute, to hear, to flee, to include, to exclude, to read, to believe).

Type 2. Affects most IR-verbs with an –o– in the second to last syllable.

> These verbs change –o– → -u- , for the persons él/ella and ellos.
>
> Example: dor-mir (= to sleep)

(I)	dormí
(you singular)	dormiste
(he/she/it)	**durmió**
(we)	dormimos
(you guys) - Spain-	dormisteis
(you guys/ they)	**durmieron**

Shading indicates irregularity

Notice that we have here the "rule of the sole" explained above.

Another example is: morir (= to die).

Type 3. Affects all IR-verbs with an –e- in the second to last syllable.

These verbs change –e– → –i–, for the persons él/ella and ellos.

Example: re-pe-tir (= to repeat)

(I)	repetí
(you singular)	repetiste
(he/she/it)	**repitió**
(we)	repetimos
(you guys) - Spain-	repetisteis
(you guys/ they)	**repitieron**

Shading indicates irregularity

Notice that we have here the "rule of the sole" explained above.

Other examples are: sentir, pedir (= to feel, to ask for).

Notice that verbs like advertir (=to warn) that, in the Present tense, changed -e- → -ie-, now they change -e- → -i-

Type 4. Affects all verbs ending in -cir, except "decir" and "bendecir," which also have other irregularities.

Example: producir (= to produce)

23. PRETERITE

(I)	produje
(you singular)	produjiste
(he/she/it)	produjo
(we)	produjimos
(you guys) - Spain-	produjisteis
(you guys/ they)	produjeron

Shading indicates irregularity

Other examples are: conducir, traducir (= to drive, to translate).

Unlike the present tense, the –cer verbs are **regular** in the past tense, e.g. crecer (= to grow up): crecí, creciste, creció, crecimos, crecisteis, crecieron.

Type 5 Others.

The following 18 verbs are grouped in sets by their common characteristics:

	estar	tener	andar
	= to be	= to have	= to walk
(I)	estuve	tuve	anduve
(you singular)	estuviste	tuviste	anduviste
(he/she/it)	estuvo	tuvo	anduvo
(we)	estuvimos	tuvimos	anduvimos
(you guys) - Spain-	estuvisteis	tuvisteis	anduvisteis
(you guys/ they)	estuvieron	tuvieron	anduvieron

	poder	haber
	= can	= to have (aux.)
(I)	pude	hube
(you singular)	pudiste	hubiste
(he/she/it)	pudo	hubo
(we)	pudimos	hubimos
(you guys) - Spain-	pudisteis	hubisteis
(you guys/ they)	pudieron	hubieron

	poner	saber	caber
	= to put	= to know	= to fit
(I)	puse	supe	cupe
(you singular)	pusiste	supiste	cupiste
(he/she/it)	puso	supo	cupo
(we)	pusimos	supimos	cupimos
(you guys) - Spain-	pusisteis	supisteis	cupisteis
(you guys/ they)	pusieron	supieron	cupieron

	querer	venir	hacer	satisfacer
	= to want	= to come	= to do	= to satisfy
(I)	quise	vine	hice	satisfice
(you singular)	quisiste	viniste	hiciste	satisficiste
(he/she/it)	quiso	vino	hizo	satisfizo
(we)	quisimos	vinimos	hicimos	satisficimos
(you guys) - Spain-	quisisteis	vinisteis	hicisteis	satisficisteis
(you guys/ they)	quisieron	vinieron	hicieron	satisficieron

	decir	bendecir	traer
	= to say	= to bless	= to bring
(I)	dije	bendije	traje
(you singular)	dijiste	bendijiste	trajiste
(he/she/it)	dijo	bendijo	trajo
(we)	dijimos	bendijimos	trajimos
(you guys) - Spain-	dijisteis	bendijisteis	trajisteis
(you guys/ they)	dijeron	bendijeron	trajeron

	ser	ir	dar
	= to be	= to go	= to give
(I)	fui	fui	di
(you singular)	fuiste	fuiste	diste
(he/she/it)	fue	fue	dio
(we)	fuimos	fuimos	dimos
(you guys) - Spain-	fuisteis	fuisteis	disteis
(you guys/ they)	fueron	fueron	dieron

Shading indicates irregularity

Notice that the forms of "ser" and "ir" are identical.

23. PRETERITE

Exercises

Translate:

Finally, did you arrange a meeting with your client and the contractor?
I didn't revise it at that time, because I assumed you had revised it.
Al Gore announced his decision to the judge.
We ruined the paella with so much salt.
In the battle of Alesia, the Romans attacked first.

Answers

¿Finalmente arreglaste una reunión entre tu cliente y el contratista?
No lo revisé en ese momento porque asumí que tú lo habías revisado.
Al Gore anunció su decisión al juez.
Arruinamos la paella con tanta sal.
En la batalla de Alisia, los romanos atacaron primero.

Vocabulary

hacer	i	=	to make, to do
hacer amistad con	i	=	to make friends with
hacer los platos	i	=	to do the dishes
hacer la cama	i	=	to make the bed
hacer calor / frío	i	=	to be hot/cold "It's hot"
hace 2 años	i	=	2 years ago
hacer falta	i	=	to be necessary
hacer compañía	i	=	to make company
hay	i	=	there is/there are
faltar		=	to be missing
echar de menos	i	=	to miss someone
perder	i	=	to miss (the bus)
quedar		=	to stay
quedar 2 personas		=	to be 2 persons left

i indicates irregular

24. IMPERFECT PAST "I SANG" (I USED TO SING)
EL PASADO IMPERFECTO "CANTABA"

Regular Verbs

	AR Verbs	ER Verbs	IR Verbs
(I)	-aba	-ía	-ía
(you singular)	-abas	-ías	-ías
(he/she/it)	-aba	-ía	-ía
(we)	-ábamos	-íamos	-íamos
(you guys) - Spain-	-abais	-íais	-íais
(you guys/ they)	-aban	-ían	-ían

	cantar	beber	partir
(I)	cantaba	bebía	partía
(you singular)	cantabas	bebías	partías
(he/she/it)	cantaba	bebía	partía
(we)	cantábamos	bebíamos	partíamos
(you guys) - Spain-	cantabais	bebíais	partíais
(you guys/ they)	cantaban	bebían	partían

In Spanish there are two past tenses: the Preterite and the Imperfect Past.

24. IMPERFECT PAST

Remember the golden rule to help distinguish them:

> If you can substitute the English past tense with a structure like "I was singing" or "I used to sing," then you can translate this past tense as the Imperfect Past Tense (versus the Preterite).

So when you hear this tense you can translate it into an English past tense. But if you want to use it in Spanish you need to be referring to something that has some duration or repetition in the past.

> When Beethoven composed that piece, his son distracted him with his cooing.
> When Beethoven composed (was composing) that piece, his son distracted (used to distract) him with his cooing.
> Cuando Beethoven **componía** esa pieza, su hijo le **interrumpía** con su balbuceo.

Warning

> Distinguishing the two types of past tense can be a challenge. Above you have found the basic rule that will help you. Take time to learn more as your Spanish develops.

Corollary 1: Irregular Verbs in the Imperfect Past Tense

There are only three irregular verbs in this tense: ser, ir, ver (= to be – permanent, to go, to see).

	ser (= to be)	ir (= to go)	ver (= to see)
(I)	era	iba	veía
(you singular)	eras	ibas	veías
(he/she/it)	era	iba	veía
(we)	éramos	íbamos	veíamos
(you guys) –Spain-	erais	ibais	veíais
(you guys/ they)	eran	iban	veían

Shading indicates irregualrity

Exercises

Translate:

> When the earthquake started, Rose celebrated her birthday party.
> I didn't chat with anyone in my times of college.
> Mark Twain always concluded his chats with a joke.
> The Medici collected art.
> In that time, this hospital was the most popular one.

Answers

> Cuando el teremoto comenzó, Rose celebraba su fiesta de cumpleaños.
> (yo) No charlaba con nadie en clase en mis tiempos de la universidad.
> Mark Twain siempre concluía sus charlas con un chiste.
> Los Medici coleccionaban arte.
> En ese tiempo, este hospital era el más popular.

Vocabulary

tener lugar	i	=	to occur
ocurrir		=	to happen
pasar		=	to happen
pasar		=	to pass "pass me some sugar"
pasar		=	to come round (to pass round)
pasar		=	to pass "I pass"
pasar bien / mal		=	to have a good / bad time
pensar	i	=	to think
pensar	i	=	to think "I think you are right"

25. FUTURE "I WILL SING"
EL FUTURO "CANTARÉ"

Regular Verbs

	AR Verbs	ER Verbs	IR Verbs
(I)	-aré	-eré	-iré
(you singular)	-arás	-erás	-irás
(he/she/it)	-ará	-erá	-irá
(we)	-aremos	-eremos	-iremos
(you guys) - Spain-	-aréis	-eréis	-iréis
(you guys/ they)	-arán	-erán	-irán

	cantar	beber	partir
(I)	cantaré	beberé	partiré
(you singular)	cantarás	beberás	partirás
(he/she/it)	cantará	beberá	partirá
(we)	cantar<u>e</u>mos	beber<u>e</u>mos	partir<u>e</u>mos
(you guys) - Spain-	cantaréis	beberéis	partiréis
(you guys/ they)	cantarán	beberán	partirán

Rule of thumb. Notice that you can obtain the same forms by adding the following endings to the infinitive. This rule works for AR, ER, IR verbs:

	AR, ER, IR Verbs
(I)	-é
(you singular)	-ás
(he/she/it)	-á
(we)	-<u>e</u>mos
(you guys) - Spain-	-éis
(you guys/ they)	-án

Examples:

>CANTAR: cantar-é, cantar-ás, cantar-á, cantar-emos, etc.
>BEBER: beber-é, beber-ás, beber-á, beber-emos, etc.
>PARTIR: partir-é, partir-ás, partir-á, partir-emos, etc.

The use of the future tense is, for the most part, the same as is in English. It's normally translated by "will do."

> My brother is good at computers. He **will repair** it.
> Mi hermano es bueno en computadores. Lo **reparará**.
>
> In two weeks my book **will be** published.
> En dos semana mi libro **será** publicado.

There are only two minor uses where they don't coincide.

> One: In English you can use "will" to mean that something that insists in <u>not</u> happening. Spanish uses the verb querer (= to want). For example:
>
>> My car **won't** start.
>> Mi carro **no quiere** arrancar.
>
> Two: English does not use the future tense (will do) to express probability. Spanish does. Thus, for example when someone unexpected knocks a the door...
>
>> Who **must it be**?
>> ¿Quién **será**?

<u>Corollary 1</u>: Irregular verbs in the Future Tense

Only 13 verbs are irregular verbs in the future tense in Spanish.

> Using the rule of thumb explained above in this chapter you can conjugate all the verbs in the six persons:

These verbs are:

Infinitive		Future I'll sing
caber	= to fit	cabr-é
decir	= to say	dir-é
haber	= to have (auxiliary)	habr-é
hacer	= to do, to make	har-é
satisfacer	= to satisfy	satisfar-é
poder	= to be able to	podr-é
poner	= to put	pondr-é
querer	= to want	querr-é
saber	= to know, to taste	sabr-é
salir	= to to go out	saldr-é
tener	= to have (to posses)	tendr-é
valer	= to be worthy	vendr-é
venir	= to come	valdr-é

Use the rule of thumb explained in this chapter to conjugate all the verbs in the six persons. Use the pseudostems (cabr-, dir-, habr-, etc.) to conjugate those verbs.

	AR, ER, IR Verbs
(I)	-é
(you singular)	-ás
(he/she/it)	-á
(we)	-emos
(you guys) –Spain-	-éis
(you guys/ they)	-án

	caber	decir	haber	hacer
	cabr-	dir-	habr-	har-
(I)	cabré	diré	habré	haré
(you singular)	cabrás	dirás	habrás	harás
(he/she/it)	cabrá	dirá	habrá	hará
(we)	cabremos	diremos	habremos	haremos
(you guys) –Spain-	cabréis	diréis	habréis	haréis
(you guys/ they)	cabrán	dirán	habrán	harán

25. FUTURE

	poder	poner	querer	saber
	podr-	pondr-	querr-	sabr-
(I)	podré	pondré	querré	sabré
(you singular)	podrás	pondrás	querrás	sabrás
(he/she/it)	podrá	pondrá	querrá	sabrá
(we)	podremos	pondremos	querremos	sabremos
(you guys) –Spain-	podréis	pondréis	querréis	sabréis
(you guys/ they)	podrán	pondrán	querrán	sabrán

	salir	tener	venir	valer
	saldr-	tendr-	vendr-	valdr-
(I)	saldré	tendré	vendré	valdré
(you singular)	saldrás	tendrás	vendrás	valdrás
(he/she/it)	saldrá	tendrá	vendrá	valdrá
(we)	saldremos	tendremos	vendremos	valdremos
(you guys) –Spain-	saldréis	tendréis	vendréis	valdréis
(you guys/ they)	saldrán	tendrán	vendrán	valdrán

Shading indicates irregularity

In this list we could add those that derive from them (like, tener, entretener, mantener etc), with the exception of those deriving from decir.

Example

> **tener,** entre**tener,** man**tener,** con**tener**
> (= to have, to entertain, to maintain, to contain)
>
> tendré, entretendré, mantendré, contendré
> (= I'll have, I'll entertain, I'll maintain, I'll contain)

And the exception "decir:"

> **decir**, mal**decir**, pre**decir**, contra**decir**, ben**decir**
> (= to say, to curse, to predict, to contradict, to bless)
>
> diré, maldeciré (not ~~maldiré~~), prediciré, contradeciré, bendeciré
> (= I'll say, I'll curse, I'll predict, I'll contradict, I'll bless)

Note about irregular verbs

Certain tenses share the same irregularities. You will see similar types of irregularities of the Future tense when you study the Conditional tense in next Chapter.

Appendix F, a List of Irregular Verbs, shows a synopsis of all tenses, and their types of irregularities.

Exercises

Translate:

Next month I will calculate the profit of the company.
Those measures will cause much controversy.
Afterwards we will conduct an investigation about him.
With this inflation, homes will cost 10% more.
Won't you consider my offer?

Answers

El mes próximo calcularé el beneficio de la compañía.
Esas medidas causarán mucha controversia.
Después, conduciremos una investigación sobre él.
Con esta inflacción las casas costarán un diez por ciento más.
¿No considerarás mi oferta?

Vocabulary

poner	i	=	to put
poner a alguien nervioso	i	=	to make so. nervous
poner(se)	i	=	to put on
encontrar	i	=	to find (to look up)
encontrar	i	=	to find "I find it big"
durar		=	to last
tardar		=	to take time
tardar		=	to be late
demorar		=	to be late

i indicates irregular

26. CONDITIONAL "I WOULD SING"
EL CONDICIONAL "CANTARÍA"

Regular Verbs

	AR Verbs	ER Verbs	IR Verbs
(I)	-aría	-ería	-iría
(you singular)	-arías	-erías	-irías
(he/she/it)	-aría	-ería	-iría
(we)	-aríamos	-eríamos	-iríamos
(you guys) - Spain-	-aríais	-eríais	-iríais
(you guys/ they)	-arían	-erían	-irían

	cantar	beber	partir
(I)	cantaría	bebería	partiría
(you singular)	cantarías	beberías	partirías
(he/she/it)	cantaría	bebería	partiría
(we)	cantaríamos	beberíamos	partiríamos
(you guys) - Spain-	cantaríais	beberíais	partiríais
(you guys/ they)	cantarían	beberían	partirían

Rule of thumb. As we saw in the future tense, you can obtain the same forms by adding the following endings to the infinitive.

	AR, ER, IR Verbs
(I)	-ía
(you singular)	-ías
(he/she/it)	-ía
(we)	-íamos
(you guys) –Spain-	-íais
(you guys/ they)	-ían

26. CONDITIONAL

Examples:

    CANTAR: cantar-ía, cantar- ías, cantar-ía, cantar-íamos, etc.
    BEBER: beber-ía, beber- ías, beber-ía, beber-íamos, etc.
    PARTIR: partir-ía, partir- ías, partir-ía, partir-íamos, etc.

The use of the conditional tense is, for the most part, the same as it is in English. It is translated as "would do."

    I **would go** but I have a lot of work now.
    Iría pero tengo mucho trabajo ahora.

    My baby **woud cry** if she didn't have her pacifier.
    Mi bebé **lloraría** si no tuviera* su chupete.

    (*) This past tense will be studied in *Chapter 29 The Past Subjunctive*, and typically, accompanies the conditional sentences.

This tense is called conditional because it normally accompanies the word "if," in other words, there's normally a condition envolved in the sentence. These types of sentences (called conditional sentences) actually have two clauses: one carries what would happen, the other carries the condition.

    <u>My baby woud cry</u> if <u>she didn't have her pacifier.</u>
       MAIN CLAUSE   CONDITION

There are there were four main constructions:

    <u>IF {present},   {present}</u>
    If I study,   I need silence.
    Si estudio,   necesito silencio.

    <u>IF {past subjunctive},   {conditional}</u>
    If I studied,   I would go to the test happy.
    Si estudiase,   iría al test feliz.

    <u>IF {composite past subjunctive}, {composite conditional}</u>
    If I had studied,   I would have received an A.
    Si hubiese estudiado,   habría recibido una A.

    <u>IF {composite past subjunctive}, {composite past subjunctive}</u>
    If I had studied,   I would have received an A.
    Si hubiese estudiado,   hubiese recibido una A.

The first structure uses the Present tense; the last one uses the Past Subjunctive (*Chapter 29*); other two use the conditional.

Notice that when using "would" with "if," the other verb appears in the past tense (studied, had studied). This also happens in Spanish; however Spanish uses another past tense called Past Subjunctive (*Chapter 29*).

As we saw with the use of the future tense and "will," you can translate the conditional tense by "would." There's only one use of would that Spanish lacks. It's when you use "would" meaning "didn't want to," like "My car wouldn't start." Spanish use the verb querer (to want) for this.

>My car **would**'t start.
>Mi carro no **quería*** arrancar.

>(*) "quería" is the past tense of querer. The conditional tense would be: querría.

Notice that this structure is just the past tense of "My car won't start," as it is in Spanish with querer (Mi carro no quiere arrancar).

Corollary 1: Irregular verbs in the conditional tense

Golden Rule

> If a verb is irregular in the Future Tense, then it will also be irregular in the Conditional Tense, and it will have the same irregularity in both tenses.

Example: caber (= to fit)

>(yo) cabré [future] ---- (yo) cabría [conditional]

Appendix F, a List of Irregular Verbs, shows a synopsis of all tenses, and their types of irregularities.

Only 13 verbs are irregular in the conditional tense, the same that we saw in the future tense.

Using the rule of thumb explained above in this chapter you can conjugate all the verbs in the six persons:

26. CONDITIONAL

These verbs are:

Infinitive		Conditional (I would sing)
caber	= to fit	cabr-ía
decir	= to say	dir-ía
haber	= to have (auxiliary)	habr-ía
hacer	= to do, to make	har-ía
satisfacer	= to satisfy	satisfar-ía
poder	= to be able to	podr-ía
poner	= to put	pondr-ía
querer	= to want	querr-ía
saber	= to know, to taste	sabr-ía
salir	= to to go out	saldr-ía
tener	= to have (to posses)	tendr-ía
valer	= to be worthy	vendr-ía
venir	= to come	valdr-ía

Use the rule of thumb explained above in this chapter to conjugate all the verbs in the six persons.

AR, ER, IR Verbs

(I)	-ía
(you singular)	-ías
(he/she/it)	-ía
(we)	-íamos
(you guys) –Spain-	-íais
(you guys/ they)	-ían

	caber	decir	haber	hacer
	cabr-	dir-	habr-	har-
(I)	cabría	diría	habría	haría
(you singular)	cabrías	dirías	habrías	harías
(he/she/it)	cabrá	dirá	habrá	hará
(we)	cabríamos	diríamos	habríamos	haríamos
(you guys) –Sp.-	cabríais	diríais	habríais	haríais
(you guys/ they)	cabrían	dirían	habrían	harían

	poder	poner	querer	saber
	podr-	pondr-	querr-	sabr-
(I)	podría	pondría	querría	sabría
(you singular)	podrías	pondrías	querrías	sabrías
(he/she/it)	podría	pondría	querría	sabría
(we)	podríamos	pondríamos	querríamos	sabríamos
(you guys) –Spain-	podríais	pondríais	querríais	sabríais
(you guys/ they)	podrían	pondrían	querrían	sabrían

	salir	tener	venir	valer
	saldr-	tendr-	vendr-	valdr-
(I)	saldría	tendría	vendría	valdría
(you singular)	saldrías	tendrías	vendrías	valdrías
(he/she/it)	saldría	tendría	vendría	valdría
(we)	saldríamos	tendríamos	vendríamos	valdríamos
(you guys) –Spain-	saldríais	tendríais	vendríais	valdríais
(you guys/ they)	saldrían	tendrían	vendrían	valdrían

Shading indicates irregularity

In this list we could add derivations like tener, entretener, mantener etc, with the exception of those deriving from decir.

Example

>**tener,** entre**tener,** man**tener,** con**tener**
>(= to have, to entertain, to maintain, to contain)

>tendría, entretendría, mantendría, contendría
>(= I'd have, I'd entertain, I'd maintain, I'd contain)

And the exception: "decir":

>**decir,** mal**decir,** pre**decir,** contra**decir,** ben**decir**
>(= to say, to curse, to predict, to contradict, to bless)

>diría, maldeciría (not ~~maldiría~~), predeciría, contradeciría, bendeciría
>(= I'd say, I'd curse, I'd predict, I'd contradict, I'd bless).

26. CONDITIONAL

Exercises

Translate:

> We would construct a church, too, but the funds aren't sufficient.
> I wouldn't cooperate with the police, pero no puedo.
> At those amounts, it would be a large investment.
> You would correct your sight if you used glasses.*
> I would cover him with the blanket if he had a fever.*

Answers

> Construiríamos una iglesia pero los fondos no son suficientes.
> Cooperaría con la policía, pero no puedo.
> A esas cantidades, sería una gran inversión.
> Corregirías tu vista si usaras* gafas.
> Le cubriría con la manta si tuviera* fiebre.
>
> (*) This tense ending in "ra" normally accompanies the conditional, and it is explained in *Chapter 29 The Past Subjunctive*.

Vocabulary

Spanish lacks phrasal verbs, like: "to put down," "to put on," "to put out," "to put off," "to get in," "to get out...." In other words: in Spanish prepositions are never an intrinsec part of the verb.

We recommend that you learn the translation of some of these verbs.

ir	i	=	to go
venir	i	=	to come
entrar		=	to go in / come in
salir	i	=	to go out / come out
meter		=	to put into
sacar		=	to take out
subir		=	to go up/upstairs
bajar		=	to go down/downstairs
subir (algo)		=	to lift sth.

bajar (algo)		=	to drop, to low
andar	i	=	to walk
caminar		=	to walk
correr		=	to run
parar		=	to stop
manejar		=	to drive
estacionar		=	to park

i indicates irregular

26. CONDITIONAL

27. IMPERATIVE "SING!"
EL IMPERATIVO "¡CANTA!"

Regular Verbs

	AR Verbs	ER Verbs	IR Verbs
(I)			
(you singular)	-a	-e	-e
(he/she/it)			
(we)			
(you guys) - Spain-	-ad	-ed	-id
(you guys/ they)			

	cantar	beber	partir
(I)			
(you singular)	canta	bebe	parte
(he/she/it)			
(we)			
(you guys) - Spain-	cantad	bebed	partid
(you guys/ they)			

The person of the imperative mood are just "you" (singular and plural); in Spanish: tú and vosotros.

    Sing!   (you guys) Sing!
    ¡Canta!   ¡Cantad! (remember, in Spain only)

27. IMPERATIVE

In Spanish, the Imperative has several major diferences with respect to other tenses:

- As in English, the imperative tense in Spanish lacks the form of the person "I," since you can't give a command to yourself.

- The pronoun (tú, él, lo, la, le, etc...) goes after the verb.

    You sing! You guys sing!
    ¡Canta **tú**! ¡Cantad **vosotros**! (in Spain)

    Sing it! Sing it to him!
    ¡Cánta**la**! ¡Cánta**selo**!

- The negative of the commands ("Don´t sing!") doesn't use the Imperative form. It uses the **Present Subjunctive**. This will be explained in next *Chapter 28 The Present Subjunctive.*

- Likewise, the commands for the three persons "él," "nosotros," "ustedes/ellos" (= s/he, we, and you plural/they), so the equivalent of "Let him sing!, Let us sing!, Let them sing!, don't use the imperative form. They use the **Present Subjunctive**.

- In addition, the command for the person "nosotros" (e.g. cantemos, bebamos, partamos = Let's sing!, Let's drink!, Let's split!) loses the last "s" when the reflexive pronoun is used.

    Let's look at ourselves in the mirror.
    Mirémonos en el espejo [not: miremosnos].

- The command for the person "vosotros" (e.g. cantad, bebed, partid = Sing, you guys!; Drink, you guys!; Split, you guys!) loses the last "d" when the pronoun is used.

    You guys, look at yourselves in the mirror.
    Miraos en el espejo [not: mirados].

Corollary 1: Use of "Por Favor" (= Please)

The plain command is considered rude. It is better to use the expression "Por favor," or "Favor" (= Please) when you use imperative.

>Please, come this way.
>Por favor, ven por aquí.

Corollary 2: Irregular Verbs in the Imperative

Golden Rule

> If a verb is irregular in the Present Tense of indicative, then it will also be irregular in both the Present Subjunctive and the Imperative.

Appendix F, a List of Irregular Verbs, shows a synopsis of all tenses, and their types of irregularities.

There are two types of irregularities:

Type 1. Those verbs that can form the imperative from their form in the present tense, i.e. acertar (= to hit with a projectile or an answer).

>(él) ac**ie**rta [presente] ---- ¡ac**ie**rta! [imperativo]

The form tú of the irregular verbs is formed from the form él/ella of the present tense.

Examples. (each example below corresponds to each type of irregularities seen in *Chapter 22 The Present*)

Infinitivo		Present - *él*	Imperative
contruir	= to construct	(él) contruye	contruye (tú)
dormir	= to sleep	(él) duerme	duerme (tú)
preferir	= to prefer	(él) prefiere	prefiere (tú)
repetir	= to repeat	(él) repite	repite (tú)
producir	= to produce	(él) produce	produce (tú)
traer	= to bring	(él) trae	trae (tú)
dar	= to give	(él) da	da (tú)
saber	= to know	(él) sabe	sabe (tú)

27. IMPERATIVE

Type 2. Others.

There are **eight verbs** that make up exceptions of the rule above:

These are:

Infinitive		Imperative
decir	= to say	di (tú)
hacer	= to do	haz (tú)
ir	= to go	ve (tú)
poner	= to put	pon (tú)
salir	= to go out	sal (tú)
ser	= to be	sé (tú)
tener	= to have	ten (tú)
venir	= to come	ven (tú)

The verb estar is regular in the imperative. However, it uses the pronoun te: "esta**te**," be quiet, = estate callado.

The verb "satisfacer" admits both satisface (ú) and satisfaz (tú) imperative. This book, in its Appendix F: A list of Irreguar Verbs, treats "satisfacer" as type 1.

The other person of the imperative, "vosotros, " has **no** irregular verbs. Thus: decir → deci**d** (vosotros).

Exercises

Translate:

    Imagine it!
    [You guys] get out of there!
    Please, "you" get out of there

Answers

    ¡Imagínalo!
    ¡Salid de allí!
    ¡Por favor, sal tú de allí!

Vocabulary

There are a few verbs called "defective" that lack some forms, e.g "rain." You can't conjugate "rain:" You can't say "I rain" or "you rain." In the same way, the verb "morir" (= to die) doesn't exist for the first person of singular in the past tense...("I died")

morir	i	=	to die
llover	i	=	to rain
nevar	i	=	to snow

i indicates irregular

27. IMPERATIVE

28. PRESENT SUBJUNCTIVE "...THAT I SING"
EL PRESENTE DE SUBJUNTIVO "...QUE CANTE"

Regular Verbs

	AR Verbs	ER Verbs	IR Verbs
(I)	-e	-a	-a
(you singular)	-es	-as	-as
(he/she/it)	-e	-a	-a
(we)	-emos	-amos	-amos
(you guys) - Spain-	-éis	-áis	-áis
(you guys/ they)	-en	-an	-an

	cantar	**beber**	**partir**
(I)	cante	beba	parta
(you singular)	cantes	bebas	partas
(he/she/it)	cante	beba	parta
(we)	cantemos	bebamos	partamos
(you guys) - Spain-	cantéis	bebáis	partáis
(you guys/ they)	cante	beba	parta

This tense has two uses: one, to tell commands (in those persons, that are not covered by the imperative form); two, the present (in those cases, that are not covered by the indicative tense).

28. PRESENT SUBJUNCTIVE

Use of the Present of Subjunctive for Commands

Golden Rule

> The commands for the three persons he/she, we and they ("Let him sing!; Let us sing!; Let them sing!) use the Present Subjunctive instead of the imperative form.
> The **negative** of the command ("Don´t sing!") doesn't use the imperative form; it uses the Present Subjunctive for all persons.

Using cantar as an example:

English	Spanish
Let him sing!	¡Que cante (él)!
Let us sing!	¡Cantemos (nosotros)!
Let them sing!	¡Que canten (ellos)!

Notice that "let" is translated by "que" in two cases: he/she/it and they.

We can write the table:

	cantar	beber	partir
(I)	-	-	-
(you singular)	Canta	Bebe	Parte
(he/she/it)	Que cante	Que beba	Que parta
(we)	Cantemos	Bebamos	Partamos
(you guys) –Sp.-	Cantad	Bebed	Partid
(you guys/ they)	Canten/ Que canten	Beban/ Que beban	Partan/ Que partan

Shading indicates persons of the imperative tense.

Using "cantar" as an example, we have:

English	Spanish
Sing!	¡Canta (tú)!
Let him sing!	¡Que cante (él/ella)!
Let us sing!	¡Cantemos (nosotros)!
Sing! (you guys)	¡Cantad (vosotros)!
Sing! / Let them sing!	¡Canten (ustedes)!/¡Que canten (ellos)!

Regarding the **negative commands**,

	cantar	beber	partir
(I)	-	-	-
(you singular)	No cantes	No bebas	No partas
(he/she/it)	Que no cante	Que no beba	Que no parta
(we)	No cantemos	No bebamos	No partamos
(you guys) –Sp.-	No cantéis	No bebáis	No partáis
(you guys/ they)	No canten (ustedes)/ Que no canten (ellos)	No beban / Que no beban	No partan/ Que no partan

Using "cantar" as an example, we have:

English	Spanish
Don't sing!	¡**No** cantes (tú)!
Don't let him sing!	¡Que **no** cante (él/ella)!
Don't let us sing!	¡**No** cantemos (nosotros)!
Don't sing! (you guys)	¡**No** cantéis (vosotros)!–Spain
Don't sing! (you guys) / Don't let them sing!	¡**No** canten (ustedes)! / ¡Que **no** canten (ellos)!

Introduction to the Subjunctive Mood.

There are three moods: indicative, imperative and subjunctive.

- **Indicative** is the most common, expresses statements, a fact or what is perceived as a fact.

    I study every day.
    Estudio todos los días.

- **Imperative** expresses commands.

    Please, study for that exam.
    Por favor, estudia para ese examen.

- **Subjunctive** expresses probability, wish or doubt.

    I suggest that he study more.
    Sugiero que él estudie más.

    Notice that the sentence is compound. It has two clauses: I suggest + I study. Also notice that one clause is principal (I suggest) and the other is subordinate (I study).

28. PRESENT SUBJUNCTIVE

Golden Rule

> **The subjunctive** may only appear in compound sentences, with one clause subordinate to the other. The following two conditions must be given simultaneously: one clause is subordinate to the other, **and** the verb of the primary clause expresses a feeling, a wish, or a probability.
>
> The verb in subjunctive mood can only be the one of the subordinate sentence. The verb of the main clause is always in indicative mood.

<u>\<verb in indicative\></u> LINK <u>\<verb in subjunctive\></u>
MAIN CLAUSE   SUBORDINATE CLAUSE

Example:

<u>I'd buy this house</u>   If   <u>I were a rich man.</u>
MAIN CLAUSE   SUBORDINATE CLAUSE

So, we have 1) a compound sentence with one clause subordinate to the other and 2) The main clause expresses a feeling, a wish or a probability. Then the subordinate verb will be the one in subjunctive form.

It's probable that I **study** tonight.
Es probable que **estudie** esta noche (not "estudio"),

I'm sorry that you **are** sick.
Siento que **estés** enfermo (not "estás").

The subjunctive can't appear in one-clause sentences, this is sentences with one verb (or verbs in tandem) like:

I **practice** that pirouette every day (one clause).
Practico esa pirueta todos los días.

I **am going** to **cancel** my ticket (one clause).
Voy a cancelar mi reserva.

The subjunctive can't appear in compound sentences (multiple-clause sentences) with no clause subordinated to another, like:

<u>I copied the document correctly</u> but <u>it had an error.</u>
          CLAUSE   CLAUSE
Copié el documento correctamente pero tenía un error (no subj.)

I visited him and he explained all the details to me.
   CLAUSE   CLAUSE
Le visité y me explicó todos los detalles (no subjuctive).

The sentences above are compound (they have more than one clause), but both are at the same level: none is a subordinate clause.

Subjuctive is used in sentences that have the word "maybe." Even though they are in single-clause sentences, they imply a condition. In other words, sentences with "maybe" are clauses subordinate with a main clause that is implicit or understood.

      Maybe I go (if certain conditions occur).
      Quizás vaya.

The word "maybe" can be translated by: tal vez, quizá or quizás.

This is a list of expressions that generate subjunctive sentences:

    <INDICATIVE> that <   SUBJUNCTIVE >
    MAIN CLAUSE LINK SUBORDINATE CLAUSE

It's probable that…
Es probable que…
It's possible that…
Es posible que…
It's necessary that…
Es necesario que…
I am sorry that…
Siento que…
I want that…
Quiero que…
I may…
Puede que…
I fear that…
Temo que…
I hope that… /I expect that…
Espero que…
I thank you for..
Te agradezco que…
…so that…
…para que…

28. PRESENT SUBJUNCTIVE

Examples:

> I want you to drink this medicine.
> Quiero que **bebas** esta medicina.
>
> You may recover soon.
> Puede que te **recuperes** pronto.
>
> I work hard so that you go to college.
> (yo) Trabajo duro para que (tú) **vayas** a la universidad.
>
> I fear that the force of the impact splits the column.
> Temo que the fuerza del impacto **parta** la columna.

The word "**que**" in the expressions above is a common hint to indicate that you need to place the verb in subjunctive mood. That is why this book, in the title of this chapter, writes: "...THAT I SING"

For your information, English itself has a touch of the subjunctive mood in sentences like:

> If I were a rich man, I would buy that house.
> Si fuera rico, compraría esa casa.
>
> I suggest that your son study more.
> Sugiero que tu hijo estudie más.

Notice that "were" and "study" are used instead of "was" and "studies."

Warning

Subjunctive is truly a challenge as you begin learning Spanish. Consider the basic rule and that will help you. Take time to learn more as your Spanish develops.

Corollary 1: Spelling-changing or False-irregular Verbs

As we saw in the Present tense (*Chapter 22 Present*) and the Preterite (*Chapter 23 Preterite)*, the verb may need to alter its spelling in order to accommodate itself to the right pronunciation. This also happens in the Present Subjunctive.

An example is ven**cer** (= to defeat).

(I)	venza
(you singular)	venzas
(he/she/it)	venza
(we)	venzamos
(you guys) –Spain-	venzáis
(you guys/ they)	venzan

If you take the stem of VENCER, venc-, and then you add the suffix, -o, the result is /venko/, which doesn't sound as it should be /ventho/. That's why changes in the spelling need to be made.

This happens with the verbs ending with:

-cer → -za	e.g. vencer (= to defeat)
-car → -que	e.g. aplicar (= to apply)
-zar → -ce	e.g. alcanzar (= to reach)
-cir → -za	e.g. esparcir (to spread)
-gar → -gue	e.g. llegar (= to arrive)
-ger → -ja	e.g. proteger (= to protect)
-gir → -ja	e.g. exigir (=to demand)
-guar → -güe	e.g. apaciguar (= to calm so. down)
-guir → -ga	e.g. distinguir (=to distinguish)
-quir → -ca	e.g. delinquir (= to commit a crime)

Remember the warning (*Chapter 22 Present*, Corollary 1)

> You don't have to memorize these endings. As you learn the rules of spelling in this book, you will notice then when you write (remember, as per its pronunciation, they are regular).

28. PRESENT SUBJUNCTIVE

The rest of the models are shown below:

	car → que	zar → ce	cir → za
	aplicar = to apply	alcanzar = to reach	esparcir = to spread
(I)	aplique	alcance	esparza
(you singular)	apliques	alcances	esparzas
(he/she/it)	aplique	alcance	esparza
(we)	apliquemos	alcancemos	esparzamos
(you guys) –Spain-	apliquéis	alcancéis	esparzáis
(you guys/ they)	apliquen	alcancen	esparzan

	gar → gue	ger → ja	gir → ja
	llegar = to arrive	proteger = to protect	exigir = to demand
(I)	llegue	proteja	exija
(you singular)	llegues	protejas	exijas
(he/she/it)	llegue	proteja	exija
(we)	lleguemos	protejamos	exijamos
(you guys) –Spain-	lleguéis	protejáis	exijáis
(you guys/ they)	lleguen	protejan	exijan

	guar → güe	guir → ga	quir → ca
	apaciguar = to calm down	distinguir = to distinguish	delinquir = to commit a crime
(I)	apacigüe	distinga	delinca
(you singular)	apacigües	distingas	delincas
(he/she/it)	apacigüe	distinga	delinca
(we)	apacigüemos	distingamos	delincamos
(you guys) –Spain-	apacigüéis	distingáis	delincáis
(you guys/ they)	apacigüen	distingan	delincan

Notice that, as long as the verb can follow the spelling rules of its infinitive, it will. The infinitive vencer has a "c," so will the forms vences, vence, vencemos, vencen. It's only venzo that needs a change.

All these verbs are the spelling-changing verbs. Those that happen to be regular can also be called false irregular verbs.

Corollary 2: Irregular Verbs in the Present Subjunctive

Remember the Golden Rule

> If a verb is irregular in the Present Tense of indicative, then it will also be irregular in both the Present Subjunctive and in the Imperative.

Example: acertar (= to hit with a projectile or an answer)

    (yo) acierto [presente] ---- (yo) acierte [imperativo]

Appendix F, a List of Irregular Verbs, shows a synopsis of all tenses and their types of irregularities.

There are six types of irregularities:

Type 1 Affects all verbs ending in –uir

    These verbs add "**y**" after their stem to form present tense.

    Example: const**ruir** (= to construct)

(I)	construya
(you singular)	construyas
(he/she/it)	construya
(we)	construyamos
(you guys) –Spain-	construyáis
(you guys/ they)	construyan

    Shading indicates irregularity

Compare this table with the present tense of indicative, where the forms nosotros and vosotros were not irregular. Now they are irregular too.

28. PRESENT SUBJUNCTIVE

Remember: The irregular verbs in the present tense of indicative are also irregular in the presente Subjunctive; for example: atribuir, contribuir, distribuir (= to attribute, to contribute, to distribute).

Type 2. Affects most -verbs with an –o– in the second to last syllable. (verbs with –o- can be regular, like "co-mer").

As per their irregularities, we can define **two subtypes** shown in columns below.

AR, ER-verbs
They change:

–o– → –ue– , for: yo, tú, él/ella, ellos

e.g. po-der (= can)

(I)	pueda
(you singular)	puedas
(he/she/it)	pueda
(we)	podamos
(you guys)-Sp.	podáis
(you / they)	puedan

Other examples are: "mover" or "contar" (= can, to move, to count).

IR-verbs
They change:

–o– → –ue– for: yo, tú, él/ella, ellos
–o– → –u– for: nosotros, vosotros

e.g. dor-mir (= to sleep)

(I)	duerma
(you singular)	duermas
(he/she/it)	duerma
(we)	durmamos
(you guys)-Sp.	durmáis
(you / they)	duerman

Another example is "morir" (= to die).

Shading indicates irregularity

Type 3. Affects most verbs with an –e– in the second to last syllable. (verbs with –e- can be regular, like "pe-sar," = to weigh).

As per their irregularities, we can define two subtypes: AR and ER-verbs and IR verbs:

AR, ER-verbs

They change:

e— → –ie– , for: yo, tú, él/ella, ellos

e.g. ten-der (= to tend)

(I)	**tienda**
(you singular)	**tiendas**
(he/she/it)	**tienda**
(we)	tendamos
(you guys)-Sp.	tendáis
(you / they)	**tiendan**

Other examples are: "entender." "pensar," "querer" (= to understand, to think, can).

IR-verbs

They change:

e— → –ie– for: yo, tú, él/ella, ellos
e— → –i– for: nosotros, vosotros

e.g pre-fe-rir (= to prefer)

(I)	**prefiera**
(you singular)	**prefieras**
(he/she/it)	**prefiera**
(we)	**prefiramos**
(you guys)-Sp.	**prefiráis**
(you / they)	**prefieran**

Another example is "sentir" (= to feel).

Shading indicates irregularity

Type 4. Affects most verbs with an –e- in the second to last syllable. (verbs with –e- can be regular, like "pe-sar"). They don't differ from the type 3. However, they give rise to different irregularities:

These verbs change –e– → –i–, in all persons.

Example: pe-dir (= to ask for)

Other examples are: seguir (= to follow), conseguir (= to achieve).

(I)	**pida**
(you singular)	**pidas**
(he/she/it)	**pida**
(we)	**pidamos**
(you guys) –Spain-	**pidáis**
(you guys / they)	**pidan**

Shading indicates irregularity

28. PRESENT SUBJUNCTIVE

Type 5. Affects all verbs ending in –cer, or –cir, except decir.

These verbs add "z" after their stem, for all the form.

Example: producir (= to produce)

(I)	produzca
(you singular)	produzcas
(he/she/it)	produzca
(we)	produzcamos
(you guys) –Spain-	produzcáis
(you guys / they)	produzcan

Shading indicates irregularity

Unlike the correspondent type in the Present Pubjunctive, here the changes happen in all persons, not only in the person "yo."

Other examples are: conocer, conducir, crecer (= to know, to drive, to grow up).

Type 6. Others

There are only **20 verbs** which don't follow any rule. These are the verbs that we had in the present tense (*Chapter 22*), type Others, with the exception of "dar," which is regular in the Present Subjunctive (dé, des, de, demos, deis, den).

Twelve of those 20 verbs add a "g" for all persons (similar to what we had in the Present Tense). These are:

Tener, venir, decir, oír, hacer, valer, traer, poner, salir, caer.
(= to have, to come, to say, to hear, to do, to be worth, to bring, to put, to go out, to fall)

	tener	venir	oír	valer
(I)	tenga	venga	oiga	valga
(you singular)	tengas	vengas	oigas	valgas
(he/she/it)	tenga	venga	oiga	valga
(we)	tengamos	vengamos	oigamos	valgamos
(you guys) –Sp.-	tengáis	vengáis	oigáis	valgáis
(you guys / they)	tengan	vengan	oigan	valgan

	decir	bendecir	hacer	satisfacer
(I)	diga	bendiga	haga	satisfaga
(you singular)	digas	bendigas	hagas	satisfagas
(he/she/it)	diga	bendiga	haga	satisfaga
(we)	digamos	bendigamos	hagamos	satisfagamos
(you guys) –Sp.-	digáis	bendigáis	hagáis	satisfagáis
(you guys / they)	digan	bendigan	hagan	satisfagan

	traer	poner	salir	caer
(I)	traiga	ponga	salga	caiga
(you singular)	traigas	pongas	salgas	caigas
(he/she/it)	traiga	ponga	salga	caiga
(we)	traigamos	pongamos	salgamos	caigamos
(you guys) –Sp.-	traigáis	pongáis	salgáis	caigáis
(you guys / they)	traigan	pongan	salgan	caigan

Shading indicates irregularity

The other eight don't follow any pattern. These are: ser, ir, saber, ver, caber, jugar, haber (= to be –permanent-, to go, to know, to see, to fit, to play, to have –auxiliary-).

	ser	ir	saber	ver
(I)	sea	vaya	sepa	vea
(you singular)	seas	vayas	sepas	veas
(he/she/it)	sea	vaya	sepa	vea
(we)	seamos	vayamos	sepamos	veamos
(you guys) –Sp.-	seamos	vayáis	sepáis	veáis
(you guys / they)	seais	vayan	sepan	vean

	caber	jugar	haber	estar*
(I)	quepa	juegue	haya	esté
(you singular)	quepas	juegues	hayas	estés
(he/she/it)	quepa	juegue	haya	esté
(we)	quepamos	juguemos	hayamos	estemos
(you guys) –Sp.-	quepáis	juguéis	hayáis	estéis
(you guys / they)	quepan	jueguen	hayan	estén

Shading indicates irregularity (*) Irreg. due to the stress.

28. PRESENT SUBJUNCTIVE

Exercises

Translate:

1. Imagine!
2. Don't imagine!
3. Let's decide quickly!
4. Let it snow!
5. Don't let the enemy use the bridges!
6. I want you to cancel the investigation.
7. You may not comprehend that this situation is difficult.
8. We doubt that that method distills alcohol faster.
9. We increment the number of policemen so that it diminishes the number of thefts.
10. When you select your option, press the right button.

Answers

1. ¡Imagínalo!
2. ¡No imagines!
3. ¡Decidamos rápido!
4. ¡Que nieve!
5. ¡Que el enemigo no use los puentes!
6. Quiero que canceles la investigación.
7. Puede que no comprendas que esta situación es difícil.
8. Dudamos que ese método destile el alcohol más rápidamente.
9. Incrementamos el número de policías para que disminuya el número de robos.
10. Cuando selecciones tu opción, presiona el botón derecho.

Note that the conjuction "que" (that), like "cuando" (when), is a good hint to know that the verb that follows must go in subjunctive form.

Also notice that, unlike English, in Spanish you can't omit the word "que."

> We doubt (that) that method distills alcohol faster.
> Dudamos **que** ese método destile el alcohol más rápidamente.

Vocabulary

querer	i	=	to want	
necesitar		=	to need	
poder	i	=	can, may	
deber		=	must	
esperar		=	to expect	
esperar		=	to wait	
esperar		=	to hope	
esperar		=	to look forward to	
sentir	i	=	to feel sorry	
agradecer	i	=	to thank	

i indicates irregular

29. PAST SUBJUNCTIVE "...THAT I SANG"
EL PASADO DE SUBJUNTIVO   "...QUE CANTARA / ...QUE CANTASE"

Regular Verbs

	AR Verbs	ER Verbs	IR Verbs
(I)	-ara	-iera	-iera
(you singular)	-aras	-ieras	-ieras
(he/she/it)	-ara	-iera	-iera
(we)	-áramos	-iéramos	-iéramos
(you guys) - Spain-	-arais	-ierais	-ierais
(you guys/ they)	-aran	-ieran	-ieran

Or (identical in meaning):

	AR Verbs	ER Verbs	IR Verbs
(I)	-ase	-iese	-iese
(you singular)	-ases	-ieses	-ieses
(he/she/it)	-ase	-iese	-iese
(we)	-ásemos	-iésemos	-iésemos
(you guys) - Spain-	-aseis	-ieseis	-ieseis
(you guys/ they)	-asen	-iesen	-iesen

	cantar	beber	partir
(I)	cantara	bebiera	partiera
(you singular)	cantaras	bebieras	partieras
(he/she/it)	cantara	bebiera	partiera
(we)	cantáramos	bebiéramos	partiéramos
(you guys) - Spain-	cantarais	bebierais	partierais
(you guys/ they)	cantaran	bebieran	partieran

Or (identical in meaning):

	cantar	beber	partir
(I)	cantase	bebiese	partiese
(you singular)	cantases	bebieses	partieses
(he/she/it)	cantase	bebiese	partiese
(we)	cantásemos	bebiésemos	partiésemos
(you guys) - Spain-	cantasen	bebiesen	partiesen
(you guys/ they)	cantaseis	bebieseis	partieseis

29. PAST SUBJUNCTIVE

The two forms of the table above have identical meaning. This leads us to another golden rule:

Golden Rule

> The forms "-ra" and "-se" are identical in meaning. Both represent the Past Subjunctive. In Latin America, the form "-ra" is far more common.

> It was probable that they sung that day.
> Era probable que (ellos) cant**aran** ese día.
> Era probable que (ellos) cant**asen** ese día.

Like the Present Subjunctive, there is a Past Subjunctive (There is no future subjunctive in modern Spanish). Every sentence that may use present subjunctive, can be expressed in the past by using the past subjunctive.

> It is possible that he cancels the interview.
>   → It's possible that he cancelled the interview.
>
> Es posible que cancele la entrevista.
>   →Es posible que cancelara (or, cancelase) la entrevista.

We can apply the same golden rule that we used for the Present Subjunctive.

> **The subjunctive** may only appear in compound sentences, with one clause subordinate to the other. The following two conditions must be given simultaneously: one clause is subordinate to the other, **and** the verb of the primary clause expresses a feeling, a wish, or a probability.
> The verb in subjunctive mood can only be the one of the subordinate sentence. The verb of the main clause is always in indicative mood.

<verb in indicative>   LINK   <verb in subjective>
MAIN CLAUSE   SUBORDINATE CLAUSE

Example:

It was probable that I studied that day.
PRIMARY CLAUSE   SUBORDINATE CLAUSE

So, we have: 1) a compound sentence (two clauses) since there are two verbs. 2) The main one expresses something that may not happen. Then in Spanish the subordinate verb will be in the subjunctive form.

>It was probable that I studied that day.
>Era probable que **estudiara** ese día (or "estudiase").

It's called subjunctive because you don't express a fact or a datum, you are not just informing, you are giving either a possibility, a wish or an intention.

>I was sorry that you had problems with Math.
>Sentí que **tuvieras** problemas con las Matemáticas.

Thus there's a list of expressions that generate subjunctive sentences:

It was probable that…
Era probable que…
It was possible that…
Era posible que…
It was necessary that…
Era necesario que…
I was sorry that…
Sentí que…
I wanted that…
Quise que…
I might…
Podría ser que…
I feared that…
Temí que…
I hoped that… /I expected that…
Esperé que…
I thanked you for..
Te agradecí que…
…so that…
…para que…

Examples:

>I wanted you to drink this medicine.
>Quería que **bebieras** esta medicina (or bebieses).

>You might recover soon.
>Podría ser que te **recuperaras** pronto (or: recuperases).

>I worked hard so that you go to college.
>(yo) Trabajé duro para que (tú) **fueras** a la universidad (or fueses).

I feared that the force of the impact split the column.
Temí que the fuerza del impacto **partiera** la columna (or partiese).

Corollary 1: **The conditional sentences**

As we saw in *Chapter 26 Conditional*, in Spanish, the sentences that use "if" (conditional sentences), use the tandem: Conditional – Past Subjunctive for the most part.

Below you'll see the four conditional structures to illustrate this use:

If + PRESENT,   PRESENT
If I study,   I need silence.
Si estudio,   necesito silencio.

If + PAST SUBJ.,   CONDITIONAL
If I studied,   I would go to the test happy.
Si **estudiara**,   iría al test feliz.

If + COMPOUND PAST SUBJ., COMPOUND CONDITIONAL
If I had studied,   I would have got an A.
Si **hubiera** estudiado*,   habría sacado una A.

If + COMPOUND PAST SUBJ.,   COMPOUND PAST SUBJ.
If I had studied,   I would have got an A.
Si **hubiera** estudiado*,   **hubiera** sacado una A.

(*) *Hubiera estudiado* is just the compound form of *estudiara*. This is explained in the next chapter.

For the title of this chapter we wrote "...I sang" to indicate that, although "I sang" is the translation, it always goes in conjunction with another clause.

Corollary 2: Irregular Verbs in the Past Subjunctive

Rememeber the Golden Rule

> If a verb is irregular in the Preterite, then it will also be irregular in the **Past Subjunctive** and will posses the same irregularity of the form "ellos" (= they). The irregularities in the Gerund are also related with this tense.

    Example: dormir (= to sleep)

        Preterite: (ellos) durmieron

        Past Subjunctive: durmiese, durmieses, durmiese, durmiésemos, durmieseis, durmiesen

        Gerund: durmiendo

Appendix F, A List of Irregular Verbs, shows a synopsis of all tenses and their types of irregularities.

Golden Rule

> You can obtain the Past Subjunctive by removing **–ron** from the form "ellos" of the Preterite, and then add the forms:
>
> | | | | |
> |---|---|---|---|
> | (I) | -ra | / | -se |
> | (you singular) | -ras | / | -ses |
> | (he/she/it) | -ra | / | -se |
> | (we) | -ramos | / | -semos |
> | (you guys) –Spain- | -rais | / | -seis |
> | (you guys / they) | -ran | / | -sen |

Example: ser → (ellos) fue-ron (= they were or they went)

        fuera / fuese
        fueras / fueses
        fuera / fuese
        fuéramos / fuésemos
        fuerais / fueseis
        fueran / fuesen

29. PAST SUBJUNCTIVE

Notice that this rule is applicable to all verbs (regular and irregular verbs).

Other examples:

	poner	saber	caber
Form "they" in the definite past:	pudie-ron	supie-ron	cupie-ron
(I)	pudiera	supiera	cupiera
(you singular)	pudieras	supieras	cupieras
(he/she/it)	pudiera	supiera	cupiera
(we)	pudiéramos	supiéramos	cupiéramos
(you guys) –Spain-	pudierais	supierais	cupierais
(you guys / they)	pudieran	supieran	cupieran

Shading indicates irregularity

Exercises

Translate:

> Last week I wanted you to cancel the investigation.
> You might not comprehend that the situation is difficult.
> We doubted that that method distilled alcohol faster.
> We would construct a church.
> You would correct your sight if you used glasses.

Answers

> La semana pasada quería que cancelaras (or cancelases) la investigación.
> Podía ser que no comprendieras (or comprendieses) que la situación era difícil.
> Dudábamos que ese método destilase alcohol más rápido.
> Construiríamos la iglesia si los fondos fueran (or fuesen) suficientes.
> Corregirías tu vista si usaras (or usases) gafas.

Vocabulary

When two verbs are very similar and one ends in -ear, the verb with -ear is a reduction of the other:

jugar	i	=	to play (games)
juguetear		=	to play with no purpose or effort
tocar		=	to touch, to play an instrument
toquetear		=	to touch with no purpose or effort
llorar		=	to cry
lloriquear		=	to snivel
pintar		=	to paint
pintarrajear		=	to paint by staining or scrabbling

i indicates irregular

Rule of Thumb: The most regular and common conjugation is the first conjugation. If you invent a verb, it will be an AR verb. e.g. faxear (to send a fax) is the made-up version of "enviar un fax." Not ~~faxer~~ or ~~faxir~~.

29. PAST SUBJUNCTIVE

30. TENSES WITH TO HAVE "I HAVE SUNG"
LOS TIEMPOS CON HABER "HE CANTADO"

Like English uses the verb "to have" to create the compound tenses (I have sung); Spanish uses the verb "**haber**"

>I **have sung** a lot, and my throat is sore.
>I **had sung** there before Plácido Domingo.
>I **will have sung** an opera by the age of 23.
>I **would have sung** there, if you **had allowed** me.
>It is not decisive for the job that I **have sung** there.
>It was not decisive for the job that **I had sung** there.

The last two sentences will be translated, in Spanish, by the subjunctive. In Spanish:

>**He cantado** mucho y me duele la garganta.
>**Había cantado** allí antes que Plácido Domingo.
>**Habré cantado** ópera antes de los 23.
>**Habría cantado** allí si me **hubieses permitido.**
>No es decisivo para el trabajo que **haya cantado** allí.
>No era decisivo para el trabajo que **hubiera/ese cantado** allí.

As you probably know by now, the last two sentences in Spanish have identical meaning.

30. TENSES WITH "TO HAVE"

			CANTAR	BEBER	PARTIR
I have sung					
(I)		he	he cantado	he bebido	he partido
(you singular)		has	has cantado	has bebido	has partido
(he/she/it)		ha	ha cantado	ha bebido	ha partido
(we)		hemos	hemos cantado	hemos bebido	hemos partido
(you guys) -Spain-		habéis	habéis cantado	habéis bebido	habéis partido
(you guys/ they)		han	han cantado	han bebido	han partido
I had sung					
(I)		había	había cantado	había bebido	había partido
(you singular)		habías	habías cantado	habías bebido	habías partido
(he/she/it)		había	había cantado	había bebido	había partido
(we)		habíamos	habíamos cantado	habíamos bebido	habíamos partido
(you guys) -Spain-		habíais	habíais cantado	habíais bebido	habíais partido
(you guys/ they)		habían	habían cantado	habían bebido	habían partido
I will have sung					
(I)		habré	habré cantado	habré cantado	habré cantado
(you singular)		habrás	habrás cantado	habrás cantado	habrás cantado
(he/she/it)		habrá	habrá cantado	habrá cantado	habrá cantado
(we)		habremos	habremos cantado	habremos cantado	habremos cantado
(you guys) -Spain-		habréis	habréis cantado	habréis cantado	habréis cantado
(you guys/ they)		habrán	habrán cantado	habrán cantado	habrán cantado
I would have sung					
(I)		habría	habría cantado	habría bebido	habría partido
(you singular)		habrías	habrías cantado	habrías bebido	habrías partido
(he/she/it)		habría	habría cantado	habría bebido	habría partido
(we)		habríamos	habríamos cantado	habríamos bebido	habríamos partido
(you guys) -Spain-		habríais	habríais cantado	habríais bebido	habríais partido
(you guys/ they)		habrían	habrían cantado	habrían bebido	habrían partido
...that I have sung					
(I)		haya	haya cantado	haya bebido	haya partido
(you singular)		hayas	hayas cantado	hayas bebido	hayas partido
(he/she/it)		haya	haya cantado	haya bebido	haya partido
(we)		hayamos	hayamos cantado	hayamos bebido	hayamos partido
(you guys) -Spain-		hayáis	hayáis cantado	hayáis bebido	hayáis partido
(you guys/ they)		hayan	hayan cantado	hayan bebido	hayan partido
...that I had sung					
(I)		hubiera	hubiera cantado	hubiera bebido	hubiera partido
(you singular)		hubieras	hubieras cantado	hubieras bebido	hubieras partido
(he/she/it)		hubiera	hubiera cantado	hubiera bebido	hubiera partido
(we)		hubiéramos	hubiéramos cantado	hubiéramos bebido	hubiéramos partido
(you guys) -Spain-		hubierais	hubierais cantado	hubierais bebido	hubierais partido
(you guys/ they)		hubieran	hubieran cantado	hubieran bebido	hubieran partido
-or-					
(I)		hubiese	hubiese cantado	hubiese bebido	hubiese partido
(you singular)		hubieses	hubieses cantado	hubieses bebido	hubieses partido
(he/she/it)		hubiese	hubiese cantado	hubiese bebido	hubiese partido
(we)		hubiésemos	hubiésemos cantado	hubiésemos bebido	hubiésemos partido
(you guys) -Spain-		hubieseis	hubieseis cantado	hubieseis bebido	hubieseis partido
(you guys/ they)		hubiesen	hubiesen cantado	hubiesen bebido	hubiesen partido

Golden Rule

> To create a compound tense, you can just translate literally from English, using haber for to have.

    I **had** studi**ed** opera before.
    (yo) **había** estudi**ado** ópera antes.

Then what you need to master the use the compound tenses is to memorize the verb **haber.**

Regarding the Subjunctive, we can apply again the same golden rule: the **subjunctive** only may appear **when** these two conditions are given: the clause is subordinate **and** the primary clause expresses a feeling, doubt or a probability. When all this happens, then the secondary verb carries the subjunctive form.

    It is probable that he has studied only the day before the test.

Above we have 1) a ccomplex sentence (two sentences in one) since there're two verbs. 2) The main one expresses something that may not happen. 3) Then in Spanish the subordinate verb will be in the subjunctive form.

    It is probable that he has studied only the day before the test.
    Es probable que **haya estudiado** sólo el día antes del test.

    I am sorry that you have had problems with my class.
    Siento que **hayas tenido** problemas con mi clase.

Thus there's a list of expressions that generate subjunctive sentences:

    It was probable that...
    It was possible that
    I was sorry that...
    I wanted that...
    I might...
    ...so that...
    I feared that

Examples of the Compound Past Subjunctive:

    I wanted you guys to have studied Engineering.
    Quería que **hubierais estudiado** Ingeniería
                                   (or: hubieseis estudiado).

30. TENSES WITH "TO HAVE"

You might have recovered by having that drug.
Podría ser que te **hubieras recuperado** al tomar esa medicina
(or: hubieses recuperado).

I'd have worked harder so that you had gone to college.
(yo) Habría trabajado más duro para que (tú) **hubieras ido** a la universidad (or: hubieses ido).

I feared that the force of the impact had split the column.
Temí que la fuerza del impacto **hubiera partido** la columna
(or: hubiese partido).

Corollary 1: Irregularities in the Compound Tenses

The Irregularities in the Compound Tenses are just the irregularities of the past participle.

As we have said, the compound tenses are formed by two parts:

1) the auxiliary verb "haber" which is irregular, but it is the same verb for all compound tenses; and

2) the main verb which, regardless of if it is regular or not, you only use its the past participle to form the compound tenses.

We are repeating here the same table of irregular verbs of *Chapter 21 The Past Participle*, to see at a glance some examples:

He has broken the tray that Maria had covered.
(él) **Ha roto** la bandeja que María **había cubierto.**

Infinitive		Past Participle
abrir	= to open	abierto
cubrir	= to cover	cubierto
escribir	= to write	escrito
decir	= to say	dicho
hacer	= to do	hecho
morir	= to die	muerto
poner	= to put	puesto
resolver	= to resolve	resuelto
romper	= to break	roto

Infinitive		Past Participle
satisfacer	= to satisfy	satisfecho
soltar	= to loosen up	suelto
volver	= to come back	vuelto
ver	= to see	visto

Exercises

Translate:

    I have already declared my opinion.
    The Romans had dominated the Mediterranean totally.
    You may not have comprehend that it is a difficult situation.
    If the funds had been sufficient, we would have constructed a church too.
    You would have corrected your sight, if you had used glasses when you were a kid.

Answers

    Ya he declarado mi opinión.
    Los romanos habían dominado el mediterráneo totalmente.
    Puede que no hayas comprendido que es una situación dificil.
    Si los fondos hubieran (or hubiesen) sido suficientes, habriamos construído la iglesia también.
    Habrías corregido tu vista, si hubieras (or hubieses) usado lentes cuando eras un niño.

Vocabulary

ordenar	=	to give an order
ordenar (not standard)	=	to order (a meal, drink, etc.)
ordenar	=	to sort
beber	=	to drink
tomar	=	to drink (alcohol), to hold

30. TENSES WITH "TO HAVE"

dormir	i	=	to sleep
agarrar		=	to take, to grab
soñar	i	=	to dream of/about
sonar	i	=	to sound
enseñar		=	to show, to teach
nacer	i	=	to be born
crecer	i	=	to grow up, to grow
trabajar		=	to work (job)
trabajar		=	to work (to function)

i indicates irregular

31. TENSES WITH TO BE "I AM SINGING"
LOS TIEMPOS CON ESTAR "ESTOY CANTANDO"

As we saw with verb "to have" and the compound tenses (I have sung, I had sung…), the verb "to be" also forms tenses, called continuous tenses.

I **am singing** a lot, and my throat is sore.
I **was singing** when Plácido Domingo showed up.
I **will be singing** the end by the time you come.
I **would be singing** now, if I had gotten the right teacher.
It is important that **I be singing** at 2 o'clock.
It was important that **I was singing** at 2 o'clock.

Estoy cantando mucho y me duele la garganta.
Estaba cantando cuando Plácido Domingo llegó.
Estaré cantando el final para cuando vengas.
Estaría cantando ahora si hubiese tenido un buen profesor
Es importante que **esté cantando** a las dos en punto.*
Era importante que **estuviera cantando** a las dos en punto (or:
                                            estuviese cantando).*

(*) Notice that the last two sentences will be translated, in Spanish, by the subjunctive mood.

31. TENSES WITH "TO BE"

	CANTAR	BEBER	PARTIR
I'm singing			
(I)	estoy cantando	estoy bebiendo	estoy partiendo
(you singular)	estás cantando	estás bebiendo	estás partiendo
(he/she/it)	está cantando	está bebiendo	está partiendo
(we)	estamos cantando	estamos bebiendo	estamos partiendo
(you guys) -Spain-	estáis cantando	estáis bebiendo	estáis partiendo
(you guys/ they)	están cantando	están bebiendo	están partiendo
I was singing			
(I)	estaba cantando	estaba bebiendo	estaba partiendo
(you singular)	estabas cantando	estabas bebiendo	estabas partiendo
(he/she/it)	estaba cantando	estaba bebiendo	estaba partiendo
(we)	estábamos cantando	estábamos bebiendo	estábamos partiendo
(you guys) -Spain-	estabais cantando	estabais bebiendo	estabais partiendo
(you guys/ they)	estaban cantando	estaban bebiendo	estaban partiendo
I was singing *			
(I)	estuve cantando	estuve bebiendo	estuve partiendo
(you singular)	estuviste cantando	estuviste bebiendo	estuviste partiendo
(he/she/it)	estuvo cantando	estuvo bebiendo	estuvo partiendo
(we)	estuvimos cantando	estuvimos bebiendo	estuvimos partiendo
(you guys) -Spain-	estuvisteis cantando	estuvisteis bebiendo	estuvisteis partiendo
(you guys/ they)	estuvieron cantando	estuvieron bebiendo	estuvieron partiendo
I will be singing			
(I)	estaré cantando	estaré bebiendo	estaré partiendo
(you singular)	estarás cantando	estarás bebiendo	estarás partiendo
(he/she/it)	estará cantando	estará bebiendo	estará partiendo
(we)	estaremos cantando	estaremos bebiendo	estaremos partiendo
(you guys) -Spain-	estaréis cantando	estaréis bebiendo	estaréis partiendo
(you guys/ they)	estarán cantando	estarán bebiendo	estarán partiendo
I would be singing			
(I)	estaría cantando	estaría bebiendo	estaría partiendo
(you singular)	estarías cantando	estarías bebiendo	estarías partiendo
(he/she/it)	estaría cantando	estaría bebiendo	estaría partiendo
(we)	estaríamos cantando	estaríamos bebiendo	estaríamos partiendo
(you guys) -Spain-	estaríais cantando	estaríais bebiendo	estaríais partiendo
(you guys/ they)	estarían cantando	estarían bebiendo	estarían partiendo
...that I am singing			
(I)	esté cantando	esté bebiendo	esté partiendo
(you singular)	estés cantando	estés bebiendo	estés partiendo
(he/she/it)	esté cantando	esté bebiendo	esté partiendo
(we)	estemos cantando	estemos bebiendo	estemos partiendo
(you guys) -Spain-	estéis cantando	estéis bebiendo	estéis partiendo
(you guys/ they)	estén cantando	estén bebiendo	estén partiendo
...that I was singing			
(I)	estuviera cantando	estuviera bebiendo	estuviera partiendo
(you singular)	estuvieras cantando	estuvieras bebiendo	estuvieras partiendo
(he/she/it)	estuviera cantando	estuviera bebiendo	estuviera partiendo
(we)	estuviéramos cantando	estuviéramos bebiendo	estuviéramos partiendo
(you guys) -Spain-	estuvierais cantando	estuvierais bebiendo	estuvierais partiendo
(you guys/ they)	estuvieran cantando	estuvieran bebiendo	estuvieran partiendo
-or-			
(I)	estuviese cantando	estuviese bebiendo	estuviese partiendo
(you singular)	estuvieses cantando	estuvieses bebiendo	estuvieses partiendo
(he/she/it)	estuviese cantando	estuviese bebiendo	estuviese partiendo
(we)	estuviésemos cantando	estuviésemos bebiendo	estuviésemos partiendo
(you guys) -Spain-	estuvieseis cantando	estuvieseis bebiendo	estuvieseis partiendo
(you guys/ they)	estuviesen cantando	estuviesen bebiendo	estuviesen partiendo

The rule underneath is the same in Spanish: "to be + Gerund"

Golden Rule

> The continuous tenses are formed:
> IN ENGLISH: to be +   ... -ing
> IN SPANISH: estar +   ...   -ando/ -iendo/ -iendo (AR/ ER/ IR conj.)

Exercises

Translate:

> That couple of athletes is training their children for the Olympics.
> That policy is not generating the jobs that it promised.
> I am frying the potatoes before mixing them with the sauce.
> Tomorrow at this time I'll be having a cocktail in Rio de Janeiro.
> I have been reflecting about that for two days.

Answers

> Esa pareja de atletas está entrenandos a su hijos para las olimpiadas.
> Esa política no esta generando los puestos de trabajo que prometía.
> Estoy friendo las papas antes de mezclarlas con la salsa.
> Mañana a esta hora estaré tomando un cocktail en Río de Janeiro.
> He estado reflexionando sobre eso durante dos días.

Vocabulary

abrir		=	to open
cerrar	i	=	to close. to shut
cerrar (con llave)	i	=	to lock
encender	i	=	to turn on
apagar		=	to turn on
pagar		=	to pay
costar	i	=	to cost
comprar		=	to buy
vender		=	to sell
agarrar		=	to grab

31. TENSES WITH "TO BE"

memorizar			=	to memorize
estimar			=	to estimate
calcular			=	to calculate
ganar			=	to make money, to win
perder	i		=	to lose
perderse	i		=	to get lost
cocinar			=	to cook
comer			=	to eat
desayunar			=	to have breakfast
ayunar			=	to fast
almorzar	i		=	to have lunch
cenar			=	to have dinner
enseñar			=	to teach, to show
alquilar			=	to rent, to put up for rent
rentar (not standard)			=	to rent, to put up for rent

i indicates irregular

32. PERIPHRASES "I AM GOING TO SING"
PERÍFRASIS *"VOY A CANTAR"*

English	Spanish
to be going to + INFINITIVE	ir a + INFINITIVE
to want to + INFINITIVE	querer + INFINITIVE
to have to + INFINITIVE	tener que + INFINITIVE
to be about to + INFINITIVE	estar a punto de + INFINITIVE
to start to + INFINITIVE	comenzar a + INFINITIVE
to start + GERUND	comenzar + GERUND
to continue + GERUND	continuar + GERUND
to stop + GERUND	dejar de + INFINITIVE
to end up + GERUND	terminar + GERUND
to get to + INFINITIVE	llegar a + INFINITIVE
to come back to INFINITIVE	volver a + INFINITIVE
to have been + GERUND	llevar + GERUND
to have + just + PAST PART.	acabar de + INFINITIVE
to be used to + INFINITIVE	soler + INFINITIVE

A verbal periphrasis is a structure that joins two o more verbs.

      I <u>am</u>   <u>going</u>   to <u>sing</u>   tomorrow.
         to BE   to GO   to SING

32. PERIPHRASES 273

The conversion Spanish-English as per their periphrasis is quite straightforward and simple. The most import periphrases are in the table above.
Examples:

>Placido Domingo is going to sing in San Francisco.
>Plácido Domingo va a cantar en San Francisco.
>
>We were going to eat dinner when the earthquake started.
>Íbamos a cenar cuando el terremoto comenzó.
>
>I want you to distribute this product.
>Quiero que distribuyas este producto.
>
>You have to study harder to get an A.
>Tienes que estudiar más duro para conseguir una A.
>
>The baby was about to cry when his mother showed up.
>El bebé estaba a punto de llorar cuando su mama apareció.
>
>Mozart started to compose music when he was a kid.
>Mozart comenzó a componer musica cuando era un niño.
>
>She started her presentation talking about the city in general and ended up talking about her neighborhood.
>(ella) Comenzó su presentación hablando sobre la ciudad y terminó hablando sobre su vecindario.
>
>His detective continues investigating the case.
>Su detective continúa investigando el caso.

Corollary: Translation of the English Defective Verbs

Defective verbs are those that you can't conjugate in all their forms, like can, must, etc. You can't say: "~~I have to can~~" or "~~I will can.~~"

These uses are normally translated by different forms of the verb poder, deber, saber, and the expression "ser capaz de. "

English	Spanish
I can sing	puedo cantar / sé cantar *
I could sing	podía cantar / podría cantar **
I will be able to sing	podré cantar / seré capaz de cantar
I would be able to sing	podría / sería capaz de cantar
I must sing	tengo que cantar
I may sing	puedo cantar, es posible que cante
I might sing	podía cantar / podría cantar **
I should sing	debería cantar

(*) One or the other (puedo cantar / sé cantar) depends on whether it refers to the possibility of singing or the knowledge of how to sing.

(**) One or the other (podía cantar / podría cantar) depends on if refers to past or future possibility to sing.

Examples

If I want to be healthy, I **must** work out more often.
Si quiero estar sano, **tengo que** hacer ejecicio más frecuentemente.

May I open the window?
¿Puedo abrir la ventana?

Might you open the window?
¿Podrías abrir la ventana?

Yesterday you **could** have gone [as a reproach].
Ayer (tú) podías haber ido.

Could you go tomorrow?
¿Podrías ir mañana?

Can you swim?
¿Sabes nadar?

Can you have a bath in such cold water?
¿Puedes bañarte en agua tan fría?

32. PERIPHRASES

> **Are you able to** have a bath in such cold water?
> ¿**Eres capaz de** bañarte en agua tan fría?
>
> Other countries **should** intervene in the conflict.
> Otros países deberían intervenir en el conflicto.

As the English "must," "**tener que**" is used for obligation.

> Someone is knocking at the door. It must be him.
> Alguien llama a la puerta. **Tiene que** ser él.

As the English "should," "**deber**" is used for recommendation or moral obligation. The form "**debería**" (the conditional tense of "deber") is the most preferred way to use "deber."

> You guys should attend that lecture.
> **Deberían** (ustedes) asistir a esa conferencia.
> **Deben** (ustedes) asistir a esa conferencia.

You will find in books "deber" and "deber de." The form "**deber de**" implies possibility. However, most people use one or other with no distinction.

> Having so many tickets, you guys should win that lottery.
> Teniendo tantos tiquets, **deberían de** ganar en esa lotería.

Exercises

Translate:

> The police chief got to say that he could resign.
> Stop smoking!
> The detainee said again he was innocent.
> How long has he been in Italy? He's been there for 2 years.
> I've just sold my car.

Answers

> El jefe de policía llegó a decir que podría renunciar.
> ¡Deja de fumar!
> El detenido volvió a decir que era inocente.
> ¿Cuánto tiempo lleva en Italia? Dos años.
> Acabo de vender mi carro.

Vocabulary

Learn or review the following verbs:

comenzar	i	=	to start
empezar	i	=	to start
terminar	i	=	to finish
acabar		=	to finish
seguir	i	=	to continue
continuar		=	to continue
llegar		=	to arrive
volver	i	=	to come back

i indicates irregular

32. PERIPHRASES

33. REFLEXIVE VERBS
VERBOS REFLEXIVOS

With many verbs, one can act on oneself (I wash myself). When a verb functions this way it is called reflexive. Notice that these verbs can act on something in the same way that they can act on themselves.

Let's take the verb to bathe (= bañar) as an example. The person can either act on something (what we called a Direct Object) or on himself.

>I bathe my 3-month old baby. / I bathe myself. [or I have a bath]
>(yo) Baño a mi bebé de 3 meses. / Me baño.

When a verb acts on itself we say that the verb, in that use, is reflexive. In its reflexive form the verbs appears as the infinitive plus the particle **-se**: bañar**se**.

>Bathing oneself is a pleasure. (Having a bath is a pleasure).
>Bañarse es un placer.
>
>They bathe in the river. (They have a bath in the river).
>(ellos) Se bañan en el río.
>
>They bathe each other in the river.
>(ellos) Se bañan en el río.

33. REFLEXIVE VERBS

Infinitive (to wash oneself)
lavarse

Gerund (washing oneself)
lavándose

Past Participle (washed)
lavado

Indicative

Present (I wash myself)

(I)	me	lavo
(you singular)	te	lavas
(he/she/it)	se	lava
(we)	nos	lavamos
(you guys) -Spain-	os	laváis
(you guys/ they)	se	lavan

Preterite (I washed myself)

(I)	me	lavé
(you singular)	te	lavaste
(he/she/it)	se	lavó
(we)	nos	lavamos
(you guys) -Spain-	os	lavasteis
(you guys/ they)	se	lavaron

Imperfect Past (I was washing myself)

(I)	me	lavaba
(you singular)	te	lavabas
(he/she/it)	se	lavaba
(we)	nos	lavábamos
(you guys) -Spain-	os	lavabais
(you guys/ they)	se	lavaban

Future (I'll wash myself)

(I)	me	lavaré
(you singular)	te	lavarás
(he/she/it)	se	lavará
(we)	nos	lavaremos
(you guys) -Spain-	os	lavaréis
(you guys/ they)	se	lavarán

Conditional (I'd wash myself)

(I)	me	lavaría
(you singular)	te	lavarías
(he/she/it)	se	lavaría
(we)	nos	lavaríamos
(you guys) -Spain-	os	lavaríais
(you guys/ they)	se	lavarían

Imperative

Imperative (wash yourself)

(I)		
(you singular)		lávate
(he/she/it)		
(we)		
(you guys) -Spain-		lavaos
(you guys/ they)		

Subjunctive

Pres. (... I wash myself)

(I)	me	lave
(you singular)	te	laves
(he/she/it)	se	lave
(we)	nos	lavemos
(you guys) -Spain-	os	lavéis
(you guys/ they)	se	laven

Past (... I washed myself)

(I)	me	lavara
(you singular)	te	lavaras
(he/she/it)	se	lavara
(we)	nos	laváramos
(you guys) -Spain-	os	lavarais
(you guys/ they)	se	lavaran

-or-

(I)	me	lavase
(you singular)	te	lavases
(he/she/it)	se	lavase
(we)	nos	lavásemos
(you guys) -Spain-	os	lavaseis
(you guys/ they)	se	lavasen

For clarity, we will call "reflexive" all verbs that follow the pattern shown above (strictly speaking, some of them are called "pronominal verbs," like "arrepentirse" (= to repend).

Reflexive verbs can be classified into four types.

Type One. Verbs that function as either reflexive or not depending on the direct object being oneself or something else.
Note: In Spanish you can use the reflexive pronoun and the object in the same sentence: Me lavo el pelo (I wash "myself" my hair). e.g. **lavar** (= to wash)

>I wash my car in the garage.
>Lavo mi carro en el garaje.
>
>I wash myself with very warm water.
>Me lavo con agua muy caliente.

Type Two. Verbs that function as either reflexive or non-reflexive optionally, depending on the speaker's style.
Reflexive style is more colloquial and implies more affection, e.g. **comer** (= to eat).

>I eat my lunch in half an hour.
>Como mi almuerzo en media hora.
>
>I eat my lunch in half an hour.
>Me como mi almuerzo en media hora.

Since it is a matter of style, many verbs are subject to be used reflexively in Spanish.

Type Three. Verbs that can function as either reflexive or not depending on the meaning, e.g. **ir** (= to go/ to leave).

>On Saturdays I go to the movie theatre.
>Los sábados, voy al cine.
>
>It's late, I'm leaving.
>Es tarde, me voy.

There is a limited number of verbs of this kind. A short list is provided in the table below.

33. REFLEXIVE VERBS

Type Four. Verbs that can only function as reflexive, e.g. **quejar** (= to complain).

>This doesn't work: I am going to complain.
>Esto no funciona: me voy a quejar.

There is a very limited number of verbs of this kind.

Summary. A short list of the four types is provided below (The translation is provided at the end of this chapter, in the vocabulary among other reflexive verbs).

Type 1	Type 2	Type 3	Type 4
afeitar	morir	empeñar/empeñarse	arrepentirse
bañar	olvidar	negar/negarse	fugarse
duchar	caer	llamar/llamarse	atreverse
cepillar	escapar	levantar/levantarse	suicidarse
...etc	...etc	...etc	... etc

Corollary 1: The structure "to have something done"

In addition to the foreseen structures, the translation of the pattern: I have something to be done, is also solved in Spanish by using the reflexive.

>I have my hair cut.
>Me corté el pelo.
>
>I have my car washed.
>Me lavé el carro*.
>
>(*) Ambiguous: it also means "I washed my car myself."

Corollary 2: to get/ to become+ ADJECTIVE/ PAST PARTICIPLE

Sentences that express a transition like: I got sick, I got nervous (versus I'm sick, I'm nervous) are commonly translated in Spanish by the verbs "ponerse" (literally to put oneself).

>I became sick. I got nervous. I'll get so happy.
>Me puse enfermo. Me puse nervioso. Me pondré tan contento.

Corollary 3: The Ethic Dative

In Spanish you can use the indirect object pronouns (dative pronouns) to emphasize the idea of care about somebody or to express that somebody is part of you (figuratively). Thus, for example, a mother can say to her child:

>You don't eat much.
>No comes nada.

Or she can go further (in expressing your feelings) and say:

>You don't eat much for me.
>No **me** comes nada.

Another example: You can state that a person has died in different ways depending on how expressive you want to be:

>Murió. (= He died).
>Se murió * (= He died on me).
>Se **me** murió.** (= He died on me).

>(*) Using "morirse" as a reflexive verb, more affection.
>(**) Using "me" as the ethic dative, even more affection.

Exercises

Provide as many translations as possible:

>Complain.
>Drink it!
>My wallet fell.
>I went away.
>I went to the clinic.

Answers

>Quéja**te.**
>Bébelo. / Bébetelo.
>Mi cartera cayó. / Mi cartera **se** cayó. /Mi cartera **se** me cayó.
>**Me** fui.
>Fui a la clínica. / **Me** fui a la clínica.

33. REFLEXIVE VERBS

Vocabulary

Some verbs that can function either as reflexive or not are:

acostar	i	=	to take a baby to bed
acostarse	i	=	to go to bed
despertar	i	=	to wake so. up
despertarse	i	=	to wake up
enojar	i	=	to upset so.
enojarse	i	=	to get upset
levantar		=	to get so. up
levantarse		=	to get up
lavar		=	to wash so. or sth.
lavarse		=	to wash oneself
bañar		=	to bathe so.
bañarse		=	to bathe oneself
peinar		=	to comb so.
peinarse		=	to comb oneself
vestir	i	=	to dress so.
vestirse	i	=	to get dressed
afeitarse		=	to shave so.
afeitar		=	to shave oneself
aburrir		=	to bore so.
aburrirse		=	to get bored
cansar		=	to tire so.
cansarse		=	to get tired
duchar	.	=	to have so.to have a shower
ducharse		=	to have a shower
secar		=	to dry so.
secarse		=	to get dried
empeñar		=	to pawn
empeñarse		=	to insist
negar	i	=	to deny
negarse	i	=	to refuse
llamar		=	to call
llamarse		=	to be named
sentir	i	=	to feel a feeling, sorry etc.
sentirse	i	=	to feel good, bad, hot, cold
acordar	i	=	to get to an agreement

acordarse	i	=	to remember
despedir	i	=	to fire someone
despedirse de	i	=	to say good bye
poner	i	=	to put
ponerse	i	=	to put on
quedar con		=	to meet with someone
quedarse		=	to stay
probar	i	=	to try, to taste
probarse	i	=	To try clothes on
quitar		=	to put away
quitarse		=	to take off (clothes)
dar cuenta de	i	=	to report something
darse cuenta de	i	=	to realize
arrepentirse	i	=	to repend
fugarse		=	to escape
atreverse		=	to dare
suicidarse		=	to commit suicide

i indicates irregular

33. REFLEXIVE VERBS

34. VERBS LIKE "GUSTAR"
VERBOS COMO "GUSTAR"

The indirect transitive verbs, or the family of "gustar" (= to like), are those verbs whose indirect object functions as the subject of the clause.

English also has a few verbs with this peculiarity of being conjugated in the reverse.

> That book revolts me (not: ~~I revolt the book~~).
> Ese libro me da asco. (not: ~~Yo doy asco este libro~~).

With this in mind we can conjugate the verb sorpender (= to surprise)

English	Spanish
It surprises me	Me sorprende
It surprises you	Te sorprende
It surprises him/her	Le sorprende
It surprises us	Nos sorprende
It surprises you guys	Os sorprende –Spain–
It surprises you guys /them	Les sorprende

And, in the past tense: Notice that all forms of each tense are identical.

English	Spanish
It surprised me	Me sorprendió
It surprised you	Te sorprendió
It surprised him/her	Le sorprendió
It surprised us	Nos sorprendió
It surprised you guys	Os sorprendió – Spain–
It surprised you guys /them	Les sorprendió

34. VERBS LIKE "GUSTAR"

Infinitive (to like)

gustar

Gerund (liking)

gustando

Past Participle (liked)

gustado

Indicative

Present (I like)

(I)	me	gusta
(you singular)	te	gusta
(he/she/it)	le	gusta
(we)	nos	gusta
(you guys) - Spain-	os	gusta
(you guys/ they)	les	gusta

Preterite (I liked)

(I)	me	gustó
(you singular)	te	gustó
(he/she/it)	le	gustó
(we)	nos	gustó
(you guys) - Spain-	os	gustó
(you guys/ they)	les	gustó

Imperfect Past (I liked *)

(I)	me	gustaba
(you singular)	te	gustaba
(he/she/it)	le	gustaba
(we)	nos	gustaba
(you guys) - Spain-	os	gustaba
(you guys/ they)	les	gustaba

Future (I'll like)

(I)	me	gustará
(you singular)	te	gustará
(he/she/it)	le	gustará
(we)	nos	gustará
(you guys) - Spain-	os	gustará
(you guys/ they)	les	gustará

Conditional (I'd like)

(I)	me	gustaría
(you singular)	te	gustaría
(he/she/it)	le	gustaría
(we)	nos	gustaría
(you guys) - Spain-	os	gustaría
(you guys/ they)	les	gustaría

Imperative

Imperative (Like!)

(I)	
(you singular)	Que te guste
(he/she/it)	Que les guste
(we)	Que nos guste
(you guys) - Spain-	Que os guste
(you guys/ they)	Que les guste

Subjunctive

Pres. (...that I like)

(I)	me	guste
(you singular)	te	guste
(he/she/it)	le	guste
(we)	nos	guste
(you guys) - Spain-	os	guste
(you guys/ they)	les	guste

Past (...that I liked)

(I)	me	gustara
(you singular)	te	gustara
(he/she/it)	le	gustara
(we)	nos	gustara
(you guys) - Spain-	os	gustara
(you guys/ they)	les	gustara

-or-

(I)	me	gustase
(you singular)	te	gustase
(he/she/it)	le	gustase
(we)	nos	gustase
(you guys) - Spain-	os	gustase
(you guys/ they)	les	gustase

Below you'll find a list of this type of verbs:

aburrir		=	to bore
agradar		=	to like, as in "I like playing guitar"
apetecer	i	=	to feel like
asombrar		=	to get astonished
atraer	i	=	to appeal
caer bien/mal	i	=	to like someone./ to dislike someone
cansar		=	to tire
dar asco	i	=	to revolt
dar miedo	i	=	to be afraid of
dar pánico	i	=	to panic
dar vergüenza	i	=	to feel shame
disgustar		=	to dislike, as in "I dislike that plan"
divertir	i	=	to have fun
doler	i	=	to be sore, as in "My neck is sore"
encantar		=	to love, as in "I like playing guitar"
enojar		=	to get anoyed
entretener	i	=	to entertain
fascinar		=	to get fascinated
gustar		=	to like, as in "I like playing guitar"
importar		=	to care, as in "I don't care"
indignar		=	to get indignant
molestar		=	to get bothered
motivar		=	to give motivation
ofender		=	to get offended
parecer	i	=	to find, as in "I find this cheap"
quedar		=	to be left, as in "I have one apple left"
repugnar		=	to revolt
resultar		=	to have an opinion about something
sorprender		=	to get surprised

i indicates irregular

34. VERBS LIKE "GUSTAR"

Some of these verbs can also work as normal verbs (unlike gustar).

>I offended him. That comment offends me.
>(yo) Le ofendí. Ese comentario me ofende.

Corollary: The Optional Emphasis in the Person

In sentences where you want to put emphasis on the "person," that makes the action, you cannot use the personal pronoun (yo, tú, él...) but the expressions:

>a mí
>a ti
>a él, a ella
>a nosotros, a nosotras
>a vosotros, a vosotras (Spain)
>a usted / a ellos, a ellas

Example:

>"I" like soccer, "he" likes tennis.
>"A mí" me gusta el fútbol, "a él" le gusta el tenis.

Exercises

Translate:

>I like driving.
>I don't care if you like it or not.
>We are interested in investing in the market of plastics.
>Does the nomination surprise you?
>They love soccer.

Answers

>Me gusta manejar.
>No me importa si te gusta o no.
>Estamos interesados en (= Nos interesa) invertir en el mercado de los plásticos.
>¿Te sorprende el nombramiento?
>Les encanta el fútbol.

Vocabulary

The verbs of the **gustar** family are:

aburrir		=	to bore
agradar		=	to like, as in "I like playing guitar"
apetecer	i	=	to feel like
asombrar		=	to get as tonished
atraer	i	=	to appeal to
caer bien/mal	i	=	to like someone/ to dislike someone
cansar		=	to tire
dar asco	i	=	to revolt
dar miedo	i	=	to be afraid of
dar pánico	i	=	to panic
dar pena	i	=	to feel sorry
dar vergüenza	i	=	to feel shame
disgustar		=	to dislike, as in "I dislike that plan"
divertir	i	=	to have fun
doler	i	=	to be sore, as in "My neck is sore"
encantar		=	to love, as in "I like playing guitar"
enojar		=	to get anoyed
entretener	i	=	to entertain
fascinar		=	to get fascinated
gustar		=	to like, as in "I like playing guitar"
importar		=	to care, as in "I don't care"
indignar		=	to get indignant
molestar		=	to get bothered
motivar		=	to give motivation
ofender		=	to get offended
parecer	i	=	to find, as in "I find this cheap"
quedar		=	to be left, as in "I have one apple left"
repugnar		=	to revolt
resultar		=	to have an opinion about something
sorprender		=	to get surprised

        i indicates irregular

34. VERBS LIKE "GUSTAR"

35. THE PASSIVE VOICE "THE SONG IS SUNG"
LA VOZ PASIVA "LA CANCIÓN ES CANTADA / LA CANCIÓN SE CANTA"

A sentence is in passive voice when you have swapped the subject with the object, e.g.:

      Peter saw the robber   (ACTIVE VOICE)
      SUBJECT   OBJECT

      The robber was seen by **Peter**   (PASSIVE VOICE)
      SUBJECT   OBJECT

Spanish also has that structure:

      Peter saw the robber → The robber was seen by Peter
      Peter vio al ladrón → El ladrón fue visto por Peter

But Spanish prefers to use the pronoun "**se**" for this structure:

      Peter saw the robber → The robber was seen
      Peter vio al ladrón → **Se** vio al ladrón → **Se** le vio

Notice that the last sentence omits "Peter."

35. THE PASSIVE VOICE

Also notice that the direct object always has the preposition "a" when it refers to a person (Peter vio **a**l ladrón).

Other examples:

> Martha was told to leave the classroom (passive voice).
> Se dijo a Marta que dejase la clase.
>
> That man was found guilty.
> Se encontró culpable a ese hombre.

Corollary: The impersonal "se"

In Spanish those sentences (in passive voice or not) that have no subject also use "se."

> We Speak Spanish.
> Se habla español (or Hablamos español).
>
> Don't smoke.
> No se fuma (or Prohibido fumar).
>
> It's said that Peter escaped (or Peter is said to have escaped).
> Se dice que Peter escapó.
>
> Don Quixote was published in the XVII century.
> Don Quijote se publicó en el siglo XVII.
>
> This house was being cleaned before the hurricane.
> Esta casa se estaba limpiando antes del huracán.
>
> This tower will be constructed with no concrete.
> Esta torre se construirá sin concreto.
>
> The policeman is believed to be dead.
> Se cree que el policía está muerto.

Exercises

Translate using "se:"

> You are thought to drink too much.
> The poor vote for him because he had a humble past.
> The comma is put to separate parts of the sentence.
> A thermometer is used for measuring the temperature in the chamber.
> They treated him unfairly.

Answers

> Se piensa que bebes demasiado.
> Los pobres le votan porque tiene un pasado humilde.
> La coma se pone para separar partes de la oración.
> Se usa un termómetro para medir la temperatura en la cámara
> Se le trató injustamente.

Vocabulary

Some verb expressions only admit the reflexive use:

darse cuenta	i	=	to realize, to notice
ponerse	i	=	to put on (clothes)
quitarse		=	to take off (clothes)
probarse	i	=	to try on (clothes)
quejarse		=	to complain
arrepentirse	i	=	to repent

i indicates irregular

As a last tip for your vocabulary: the vast majority of verbs are regular. The problem is that the irregulars, although a minority in number, are commonly used (it's like with centuries of use, verbs "mutate"). On the contrary, invented verbs –the newest- always belong to the first conjugation, which happens to be the most regular one, e.g. faxe**ar**, chate**ar** (= to fax, to chat in internet).

APPENDICES

APPENDIX A

NOTES ABOUT DIALECTS
NOTAS SOBRE DIALECTOS

APPENDIX A: NOTES ABOUT DIALECTS
NOTAS SOBRE DIALECTOS

All languages have dialects. In the same way that English speakers from United Kingdom, Ireland, United States or Australia speak the same language differently; speakers from Spain, Argentina or Mexico have recognizable differences.

Nonetheless, Spanish is a very unified language. The rules of grammar and spelling are the same all over the Spanish-speaking world. The differences between dialects are limited mostly to the preference of some words over others, and some differences in the pronunciation.

English	Example 1	Example 2
US English	line	tomato /tomeito/
UK English	queue	tomato /tomatoh/
Spanish		
Mexican Spanish	fila (= line)	jitomate (= tomato)
Spanish from Spain	cola	tomate

The Spanish spoken in the southwest of United States (mostly California, Arizona, Texas and New Mexico) belongs to the realm of the Mexican dialect. In addition, Spanish in the US is, of course, influenced by the English language, and some words used in the US are not part of the standard.

APPENDIX A: NOTES ABOUT DIALECTS

	Examples		
	# 1	# 2	# 3
English	line	carpet	truck
US Spanish	línea*	carpeta*	troca*
Spanish	fila	alfombra	camión

(*) Not standard Spanish

A language can be divided into dialects and, in turn, those dialects can be subdivided into subdialects indefinitely. However, we can consider three main dialects with the following representatives:

- Spanish from Spain
- Spanish from Latin America (except Argentina)
- Spanish from Argentina

The most apparent difference among the dialects in Spanish is the use of the pronouns and the verb forms thereof, as shown in the following table:

	Spain	Latin America	Argentina
I sing	(yo) canto	← THE SAME	← THE SAME
You (singular) sing	**(tú) cantas**	← THE SAME	**(vos) cantás ***
He/She sings	(él /ella) canta	← THE SAME	← THE SAME
We sing	(nosotros) cantamos	← THE SAME	← THE SAME
You guys sing	**(vosotros) cantáis**	**(ustedes) cantan**	← THE SAME
They sing	(ellos) cantan	← THE SAME	← THE SAME

(*) Notice that the stress is on the last "a."

When addressing someone **formally**, the pronouns used are the same in all three dialects:

	Spain	Latin America	Argentina
sir/ ma'am, you sing	(usted) canta	← THE SAME	← THE SAME
sirs/ ma'ams, you sing	(ustedes) cantan	← THE SAME	← THE SAME

Thus, only in Spain there is a distinction for the form "you:" vosotros (informal), ustedes (formal).

Spanish from Spain

Except in the Southern area, Spain uses the English *th* **sound** for both the letter **z**, and the letter **c** when combined in **ce, ci** (as is taught in this book).

In Spain, they use **vosotros** (= you guys). Vosotros is one form taught in this book. In Spain, they also use "usted" (= you singular) and "ustedes" (= you plural), but only either to mark a distance from the person you are addressing, like addressing a stranger, or to show respect, like addressing a professor.

Usted uses the forms of "él/ella," e.g. "Usted estudia mucho." In the same way, "ustedes" uses the forms of "ellos," e.g. "Ustedes estudian mucho."

Only in Spain it is used the forms of the second person of plural, and its pronouns, which are:

> "**vosotros**" (or vosotras) as in "**vosotros** cantáis" (= you guys study). In Latin America: "**ustedes** cantan."

> "**vuestro**" (or "vuestra," "vuestros," "vuestras") as in "vuestro amigo" (= the friend of you guys). In Latin America: "**Su** amigo."

> "**os**" as in "Os canto" (= I sing to you guys). In Latin America: "**Les** canto."

A rule to use the forms of **vosotros** is simply to substitute the ending "mos" of **nosotros** for "is." Thus,

> Nosotros canta**mos** → Vosotros cantá**is**
> Nosotros bebe**mos** → Vosotros bebé**is**
> Nosotros viví**mos** → Vosotros viv**ís**

> (= We sing, drink, live -- You guys sing, drink, live)

This rule words for most of the irregular verbs too, e.g. dormir (= to sleep)

> Nosotros dormi**mos** → Vosotros dorm**ís**

There are three exceptions:

a) The verb "haber" (= to have)

> Nosotros he**mos** estudiado → Vosotros habé**is** estudiado
> (no: Vosotros ~~heis~~ estudiado)

(= We have studied -- You guys have studied)

b) The nosotros form when ending in "imos". In this case, the vosotros form will have only one "I," e.g. :

> Nosotros vivi**mos** → Vosotros vivís
> (not: Vosotros ~~viviis~~)
> (= We live -- You guys live)

c) The past tense. For this tense, the vosotros form can be created out of the "tú" form just by adding "is," e.g.:

> Tú cantaste → Vosotros cantaste**is**
> Tú bebiste → Vosotros bebiste**is**
> Tú viviste → Vosotros viviste**is**

Spanish from Latin America

In Latin America, **they use the /s/ sound for the letter "c" when combined in "ce," "ci," and the letter "z"** (instead of the /th/ sound used in Spain). So, they don't distinguish between caza (= hunting) and casa (= house), or between coser (= to sew) and cocer (= to boil.)

Latin America **never uses "vosotros."** Instead, "ustedes" is used. Remember: ustedes uses the forms of "ellos" e.g. Ustedes estudian mucho pero ellos estudian poco (=You guys study a lot, but he studies little).

In some areas of Latin America, they never use "tú." They use "usted" instead. Remember: "usted" uses the forms of "él/ella" e.g. Usted, Pedro, estudia mucho pero él estudia poco (=You, Pedro, study a lot, but he studies little).

Spanish from Argentina

In regards to the characteristics of Spanish spoken in Latin America, Argentina shows two specific differences: the use of **"vos,"** and the pronunciation of the **strong "ll."**

Argentina has a very strong pronunciation of both the "ll," and the "y" as a consonant. It sounds close to the English "g" in George or the "sh" in shoe, depending on the speaker.

Argentina uses vos (= you singular) instead of "tú." Generally speaking, "vos" goes with the forms of "vosotros" but eliminates the -i- of the last syllable. Example:

vosotros cantáis → vos cantás.

This rule only applies for the simple present (vos cantás).

The Imperative (the commands) also makes a transformation from the original "vosotros." It uses the form of vosotros but eliminates the final "d."

Cantad vosotros → cantá vos

The rest of the tenses follow the standard rules of conjugation.

"Vos" does not have its own set of associated pronouns, so it uses the ones of "tú." Examples:

Vos, a **tu** manera… (= you, in your way, …).
A vos **te** canta María (= Maria sings to you).
No tenés que ir**te** (= You don't have to go).

The use of vos is called "voseo." Argentina is where voseo is norm. Uruguay and Paraguay and areas of Central America use "vos," but their rules are not consistent, and don't follow the Argentinian standard.

APPENDIX A: NOTES ABOUT DIALECTS

APPENDIX B

LOCAL WORDS OF CALIFORNIA
PALABRAS LOCALES DE CALIFORNIA

APPENDIX B: LOCAL WORDS OF CALIFORNIA
PALABRAS LOCALES DE CALIFORNIA

The following is a list of local words commonly used in California and other parts of United States.

Warning

> **These words are not part of standard Spanish.** These words are not in the dictionaries, and they are not understood by other Spanish speakers from other countries. In addition, they are not used in a consistent way by the speakers, who may use the standard word instead.

	Non-standard Spanish		Standard Spanish
	actualmente (= actually)*		realmente
	aplicar (= to apply) *		solicitar
el	appointment	la	cita
el	bill * [English pronunciation]	la	factura
el	bróker	el	agente
la	carpeta (= carpet) *	el	alfombrado
	chequear (= to check)		comprobar
el	college * [English pronunciation]	la	universidad
la	condición *	la	enfermedad
	consistente *		coherente

APPENDIX B: LOCAL WORDS OF CALIFORNIA 307

Non-standard Spanish		Standard Spanish	
el	custom office [English pronunc.]	la	aduana
el	D.J. [English pronunc.]	el	pinchadiscos
el	dealer [English pronunc.]	el	agente
	doméstico (= domestic) *		nacional
el	dormitorio *	el	internado universitario
el	drive-in [English pronunc.]	el	autocine
	dureza (= hardship)		desamparo
	educado (= educated) *		culto
la	elegibilidad	los	derechos
	empacar (= to pack)		empaquetar
el	escalator [English pronunc.]	las	escaleras mecánicas
la	estufa (= stove) *	la	cocina
	eventualmente (= eventually) *		finalmente
la	forma (= form) *	el	formulario
	in cash		en efectivo
el	índice (= index) *	la	lista de términos
el	infante (= infant) *	el	bebé mayor de 3 m.
	janguear (= to hang out)		salir
el	landlord	el	casero
la	librería (= library)	la	biblioteca
	likear (= to leak)		gotear
la	línea (= line, queue)	la	fila
	llamar para atrás (= to call back)		llamar
el	lonche (= lunch)	el	almuerzo
	lonchear (= to lunch)		almorzar
el	lote (= lot, parcel)	el	terreno
el	mall [English pronunc.]	el	centro comercial
el	manager	el	gerente

Non-standard Spanish		Standard Spanish	
el	mapa (= map)	el	plano
la	marketa (= market)	la	mercado
el	marketing	el	mercadeo
el	meeting	la	junta
la	mopa (= mop)	la	fregona
el	mortgage [English pronunc.]	la	hipoteca
	mover (= to move)		mudarse de casa
la	noticia (= notice)	el	aviso
	ocurrir (= to occur)		tener lugar
	ordenar (= order an item)		pedir un artículo
el	overtime [English pronunc.]	las	horas extras
el	panel	la	mesa redonda
el	parqueadero	el	estacionamiento
	parquear		estacionar
la	parte (= auto part)	la	pieza
	part-time [English pronunc.]		a media jornada
la	pompa (= pump)	la	bomba
	puchar (= to push)		tirar
el	real estate [English pronunc.]	los	bienes raíces
el	realtor	el	agente de bienes raíces
el	recuerdo (= record) *	el	registro
	remover (= to remove) *		quitar
la	renta (= rent) *	el	alquiler
el	rin, los rines	el	tapacubos
	rostizar (= to roast)		asar
la	soda	el	refresco
	sortear (= to sort) *		ordenar
los	taxes	los	impuestos
el	ticket (= a fine)	la	multa
	trabajar (= to function)		funcionar

APPENDIX B: LOCAL WORDS OF CALIFORNIA

Non-standard Spanish		Standard Spanish	
la	transportación (= transportation)	el	transporte
el	training	el	entrenamiento
los	transcripts	el	expediente académico
la	troca (= truck)	la	camioneta
las	utilidades (= utilities)	la	luz, el agua, el gas
	wireless [English pronunc.]		inalámbrico
la	yarda (= yard)	el	patio trasero
el	yonque (= junk yard)	el	desguace

(*) Asterisk indicates that the English word is similar to another word in Spanish that has a **different meaning** (these words are called false cognates or "false friends").

APPENDIX C

REGULAR VERBS
VERBOS REGULARES

APPENDIX C: REGULAR VERBS
VERBOS REGULARES

Impersonal Forms of the Verb

Infinitive (to sing)

AR verbs	ER verbs	IR verbs
-ar	-er	-ir

Gerund (singing)

AR verbs	ER verbs	IR verbs
-ando	-iendo	-iendo

Past Participle (sung)

AR verbs	ER verbs	IR verbs
-ado	-ido	-ido

Personal Forms of the Verb: Indicative Mood

Present (I sing)

	AR verbs	ER verbs	IR verbs
(I)	-o	-o	-o
(you singular)	-as	-es	-es
(he/she/it)	-a	-e	-e
(we)	-amos	-emos	-imos
(you guys) -Spain-	-ais	-éis	-ís
(you guys/ they)	-an	-en	-en

Preterite (I sang)

	AR verbs	ER verbs	IR verbs
(I)	-é	-í	-í
(you singular)	-aste	-iste	-iste
(he/she/it)	-ó	-ió	-ió
(we)	-amos	-imos	-imos
(you guys) -Spain-	-asteis	-isteis	-isteis
(you guys/ they)	-aron	-ieron	-ieron

Imperfect Past (I sang*)

	AR verbs	ER verbs	IR verbs
(I)	-aba	-ía	-ía
(you singular)	-abas	-ías	-ías
(he/she/it)	-aba	-ía	-ía
(we)	-ábamos	-íamos	-íamos
(you guys) -Spain-	-abais	-íais	-íais
(you guys/ they)	-aban	-ían	-ían

APPENDIX C: REGULAR VERBS

Future (I will sing)	AR verbs	ER verbs	IR verbs
(I)	-aré	-eré	-iré
(you singular)	-arás	-erás	-irás
(he/she/it)	-ará	-erá	-irá
(we)	-aremos	-eremos	-iremos
(you guys) -Spain-	-aréis	-eréis	-iréis
(you guys/ they)	-arán	-erán	-irán

Conditional (I would sing)	AR verbs	ER verbs	IR verbs
(I)	-aría	-ería	-iría
(you singular)	-arías	-erías	-irías
(he/she/it)	-aría	-ería	-iría
(we)	-aríamos	-eríamos	-iríamos
(you guys) -Spain-	-aríais	-eríais	-iríais
(you guys/ they)	-arían	-erían	-irían

Personal Forms of the Verb: Imperative Mood

Imperative (Sing!)	AR verbs	ER verbs	IR verbs
(I)			
(you singular)	-a	-e	-e
(he/she/it)			
(we)			
(you guys) -Spain-	-ad	-ed	-id
(you guys/ they)			

Personal Forms of the Verb: Subjunctive Mood

Present (...that I sing)	AR verbs	ER verbs	IR verbs
(I)	-e	-a	-a
(you singular)	-es	-as	-as
(he/she/it)	-e	-a	-a
(we)	-emos	-amos	-amos
(you guys) -Spain-	-éis	-áis	-áis
(you guys/ they)	-en	-an	-an

Past (...that I sang)	AR verbs	ER verbs	IR verbs
(I)	-ara	-iera	-iera
(you singular)	-aras	-ieras	-ieras
(he/she/it)	-ara	-iera	-iera
(we)	-áramos	-iéramos	-iéramos
(you guys) -Spain-	-arais	-ierais	-ierais
(you guys/ they)	-aran	-ieran	-ieran

-or-

	AR verbs	ER verbs	IR verbs
(I)	-ase	-iese	-iese
(you singular)	-ases	-ieses	-ieses
(he/she/it)	-ase	-iese	-iese
(we)	-ásemos	-iésemos	-iésemos
(you guys) -Spain-	-aseis	-ieseis	-ieseis
(you guys/ they)	-asen	-iesen	-iesen

APPENDIX D

AUXILIARY VERBS: HABER, ESTAR, SER, IR
VERBOS AUXILIARES: HABER, ESTAR, SER, IR

APPENDIX D: AUXILARY VERBS: HABER, ESTAR, SER, IR
VERBS AUXILIARES: HABER, ESTAR, SER, IR

Impersonal Forms of the Verb

Infinitive (to sing)	HABER	ESTAR	SER	IR
	haber	estar	ser	ir

Gerund (singing)	HABER	ESTAR	SER	IR
	habiendo	estando	siendo	yendo

Past Participle (sung)	HABER	ESTAR	SER	IR
	habido	estado	sido	ido

Personal Forms of the Verb: Indicative Mood

Present (I sing)	HABER	ESTAR	SER	IR
(I)	he	estoy	soy	voy
(you singular)	has	estás	eres	vas
(he/she/it)	ha	está	es	va
(we)	hemos	estamos	somos	vamos
(you guys) -Spain-	habéis	estáis	sois	vais
(you guys/ they)	han	están	son	van

Preterite (I sang)	HABER	ESTAR	SER	IR
(I)	hube	estuve	fui	fui
(you singular)	hubiste	estuviste	fuiste	fuiste
(he/she/it)	hubo	estuvo	fue	fue
(we)	hubimos	estuvimos	fuimos	fuimos
(you guys) -Spain-	hubisteis	estuvisteis	fuisteis	fuisteis
(you guys/ they)	hubieron	estuvieron	fueron	fueron

Imperfect (I sang*)	HABER	ESTAR	SER	IR
(I)	había	estaba	era	iba
(you singular)	habías	estabas	eras	ibas
(he/she/it)	había	estaba	era	iba
(we)	habíamos	estábamos	éramos	íbamos
(you guys) -Spain-	habíais	estabais	erais	ibais
(you guys/ they)	habían	estaban	eran	iban

APPENDIX D: AUXILARY VERBS: HABER, ESTAR, SER, IR

Future (I'll sing)	HABER	ESTAR	SER	IR
(I)	habré	estaré	seré	iré
(you singular)	habrás	estarás	serás	irás
(he/she/it)	habrás	estará	será	irá
(we)	habremos	estaremos	seremos	iremos
(you guys) -Spain-	habréis	estaréis	seréis	iréis
(you guys/ they)	habrán	estarán	serán	irán

Conditional (I'd sing)	HABER	ESTAR	SER	IR
(I)	habría	estaría	sería	iría
(you singular)	habrías	estarías	serías	irías
(he/she/it)	habría	estaría	sería	iría
(we)	habríamos	estaríamos	seríamos	iríamos
(you guys)	habríais	estaríais	seríais	iríais
(they)	habrían	estarían	serían	irían

Personal Forms of the Verb:Imperative Mood

Imperative (Sing!)	HABER	ESTAR	SER	IR
(I)				
(you singular)		estate	sé	ve
(he/she/it)				
(we)				
(you guys) -Spain-		estad, estaos	sed	id
(you guys/ they)				

Personal Forms of the Verb: Subjunctive Mood

Pres. (...that I sing)	HABER	ESTAR	SER	IR
(I)	haya	esté	sea	vaya
(you singular)	hayas	estés	seas	vayas
(he/she/it)	haya	esté	sea	vaya
(we)	hayamos	estemos	seamos	vayamos
(you guys) -Spain-	hayáis	estéis	seáis	vayáis
(you guys/ they)	hayan	estén	sean	vayan

Past (...that I sang)	HABER	ESTAR	SER	IR
(I)	hubiera	estuviera	fuera	fuera
(you singular)	hubieras	estuvieras	fueras	fueras
(he/she/it)	hubiera	estuviera	fuera	fuera
(we)	hubiéramos	estuviéramos	fuéramos	fuéramos
(you guys) -Spain-	hubierais	estuvierais	fuerais	fuerais
(you guys/ they)	hubieran	estuvieran	fueran	fueran
-or-				
(I)	hubiese	estuviese	fuese	fuese
(you singular)	hubieses	estuvieses	fueses	fueses
(he/she/it)	hubiese	estuviese	fuese	fuese
(we)	hubiésemos	estuviésemos	fuésemos	fuésemos
(you guys) -Spain-	hubieseis	estuvieseis	fueseis	fueseis
(you guys/ they)	hubiesen	estuviesen	fuesen	fuesen

APPENDIX E

A LIST OF REGULAR VERBS
UNA LISTA DE VERBOS REGULARES

APPENDIX E: A LIST OF REGULAR VERBS
UNA LISTA DE VERBOS REGULARES

Warning

> For simplicity, in this book all verbs that follow the spelling pattern of the verb models "cantar, "beber" and "partir" are considered regular, regardless of the placement of their stress. Thus, verbs as "act**ua**r," or "**ai**slar," are included in this list.

These two verbs, "bailar" and "aislar" have the stress in the second-two-last syllable, as the model "cantar." Yo c**a**nto. However, even though both "b**a**ilo" (I dance) and "a**i**slo" (= I isolate) meet this requirement to be regular verbs, they have the stress in different position. One in the first vowel of the pair; the other, in the second.

        b|ai|lar   Yo b**a**ilo

        |ai|slar   Yo a**í**slo

The standard book *Nueva Gramatica de la Lengua Española* considers these verbs irregular because of the unpredictablility of their stress.

The latter book lists models (in ar, er, ir) of all verbs with diphthongs at the stem, either before or after the last consonant of the stem. In the next table, you can see these models and where the stress is placed in the form "yo" of the present tense.

Model verb	Example -Pres. tense: yo...	Pair before the consonant	Pair after the consonant
bailar	b<u>ai</u>lo	A<u>I</u>	
aislar	a<u>i</u>slo	A<u>I</u>	
aplaudir	apl<u>au</u>do	A<u>U</u>	
causar	c<u>au</u>so	A<u>U</u>	
aunar	a<u>ú</u>no	A<u>U</u>	
peinar	p<u>ei</u>no	E<u>I</u>	
descafeinar	descafe<u>í</u>no	E<u>I</u>	
adeudar	ad<u>eu</u>do	E<u>U</u>	
rehusar	reh<u>ú</u>so	E<u>U</u>	
reunir	re<u>ú</u>no	E<u>U</u>	
coitar	c<u>oi</u>to	O<u>I</u>	
prohibir	proh<u>í</u>bo	O<u>I</u>	
prohijar	proh<u>í</u>jo	O<u>I</u>	
anunciar	an<u>u</u>ncio		<u>I</u>A
enviar	env<u>í</u>o		<u>I</u>A
actuar	act<u>ú</u>o		<u>U</u>A
averiguar	aver<u>i</u>guo		<u>U</u>A

Having said that, you should study these verbs associating their trend: stress on the "first vowel" (as "b<u>ai</u>lo," "apl<u>au</u>do, c<u>au</u>so, etc.), or on the "second vowel." (as "a<u>i</u>slo," "a<u>ú</u>no," "descafe<u>í</u>no," etc.).

List of Regular Verbs

abandonar	= to abandon
abonar	= to put composite
abortar	= to abort
abrazar	= to embrace
abrochar	= to button
aburrir	= to bore

acabar	= to finish
acariciar	= to pet
aceptar	= to accept
aclarar	= to clear up
acompañar	= to accompany
actuar	= to act

adelantar	=	to pass (car)
admirar	=	to admire
adorar	=	to adore
adornar	=	to adorn
adscribir	=	to ascribe
afectar	=	to affect
aflojar	=	to loosen up
agarrar	=	to grab
agredir	=	to attack
aguantar	=	to hold
ahorrar	=	to save (money)
aislar	=	to isolate
alcanzar	=	to reach
alegrar	=	to cheer up
alquilar	=	to rent
alterar	=	to alter
amenazar	=	to menace
añadir	=	to add
anotar	=	to take note
anunciar	=	to announce
apagar	=	to turn off
aparcar	=	to park
apoyar	=	to lean against
aprender	=	to learn
aprovechar	=	to take advantage
apuntar	=	to take note
arrancar	=	to start (a car)
arreglar	=	to fix, repair
arruinar	=	to ruin
asar	=	to roast
asegurar	=	to make sure of
asesinar	=	to murder
asistir	=	to attend
aspirar	=	to aspire
asumir	=	to assume
asustar	=	to frighten
atacar	=	to attack
atar	=	to tie
atender	=	to assist
aterrizar	=	to land
atracar	=	to mug
atrever	=	to dare
atropellar	=	to run over (car)
averiguar	=	to find out
ayudar	=	to help
bailar	=	to dance
bajar	=	to lower
barrer	=	to sweep
bautizar	=	to baptize
beber	=	to drink
besar	=	to kiss
bombardear	=	to bomb
borrar	=	to delete
bostezar	=	to yawn
bromear	=	to be kidding
bullir	=	to boil
buscar	=	to look for
calcular	=	to calculate
callar	=	to be quiet
calmar	=	to calm down
cambiar	=	to change
caminar	=	to walk
cancelar	=	to cancel
cantar	=	to sing
capturar	=	to capture
casar	=	to get married
castigar	=	to punish
causar	=	to cause

APPENDIX E: A LIST OF REGULAR VERBS

cazar	=	to hunt
celebrar	=	to celebrate
cenar	=	to have dinner
chantajear	=	to blackmail
charlar	=	to chat
chillar	=	to shout
chocar	=	to crash
clasificar	=	to classify
clavar	=	to nail
cobrar	=	to charge (pay.)
cocinar	=	to to cook
coger	=	to take, grab
coincidir	=	to coincide
coleccionar	=	to collect
colocar	=	to place
combinar	=	to combine
comentar	=	to comment
comer	=	to eat
cometer	=	to commit
comparar	=	to compare
compartir	=	to share
comprar	=	to buy
comprender	=	to comprehend
condenar	=	to condemn
conformar	=	to settle for
confundir	=	to get confused
congelar	=	to freeze
conllevar	=	to imply
conquistar	=	to conquer
consentir	=	to consent
considerar	=	to consider
consistir	=	to consist on
constar	=	to consist of
contemplar	=	to contemplate

contestar	=	to answer
contratar	=	to hire
convencer	=	to convince
convidar	=	to invite
cooperar	=	to cooperate
correr	=	to run
corresponder	=	to correspond
cortar	=	to cut
coser	=	to sew
crear	=	to create
criar	=	to breed; to nurse
cuidar	=	to take care of
culpar	=	to blame
cumplir	=	to comply
cundir	=	to spread
curar	=	to cure
deber	=	to must
decidir	=	to decide
declarar	=	to declare
decorar	=	to decorate
dedicar	=	to devote
deletrear	=	to spell
demandar	=	to sue
depender	=	to depend
derrochar	=	to waste money
desayunar	=	to have breakfast
descansar	=	to rest
describir	=	to describe
descubrir	=	to discover
desear	=	to desire
desesperar	=	to lose patience
desmayar	=	to black out
desnudar	=	to get nude
desordenar	=	to disorganize

despegar	=	to take off (plane)
desperdiciar	=	to waste
destilar	=	to distill
dibujar	=	to draw
dirigir	=	to manage
disculpar	=	to apologize
discutir	=	to discuss
disgustar	=	to disgust
distinguir	=	to distinguish
dividir	=	to divide into
divorciar	=	to divorce
doblar	=	to bent
dominar	=	to dominate
duchar	=	to have a shower
dudar	=	to doubt
durar	=	to last
echar	=	to toss
editar	=	to publish
educar	=	to educate
elaborar	=	to elaborate
emborrachar	=	to get drunk
empeñar	=	to insist
empeorar	=	to worsen
empujar	=	to push
encajar	=	to fit well
encantar	=	to love something
encargar	=	to order
enchufar	=	to plug
enfadar	=	to get angry with
enfermar	=	to get sick
enfocar	=	to focus
enfriar	=	to get cold
engañar	=	to mislead
engordar	=	to get fat
empaquetar	=	to pack
enrollar	=	to wrap
enseñar	=	to show, to teach
enterar	=	to learn sth.
entrar	=	to come in
entregar	=	to turn in
entrenar	=	to train
envejecer	=	to get old
enviar	=	to send
envidiar	=	to envy
equivocar	=	to get wrong
escapar	=	to to escape
escoger	=	to to chose
esconder	=	to hide
escuchar	=	to listen
escupir	=	to spit
esperar	=	to wait
espiar	=	to spy
estornudar	=	to sneeze
estropear	=	to break down
estudiar	=	to study
exigir	=	to demand
existir	=	to exist
experimentar	=	to experience
explicar	=	to explain
explorar	=	to explore
explotar	=	to explode
exportar	=	to export
expresar	=	to express
expulsar	=	to expel
fallar	=	to fail
felicitar	=	to greet
fermentar	=	to ferment
fiar	=	to trust

fijar	= to fix, settle		irrigar	= to irrigate
financiar	= to finance		juntar	= to put together
firmar	= to sign		justificar	= to justify
fotografiar	= to photograph		juzgar	= to judge
frenar	= to put breaks		ladrar	= to bark
fumar	= to smoke		lanzar	= to launch
funcionar	= to function		marchar	= to get off, leave
ganar	= to win, gain		lavar	= to wash
generar	= to generate		levantar	= to lift
girar	= to turn, spin		levitar	= to levitate
gorronear	= to beg		limar	= to file
grabar	= to tape, record		limpiar	= to clean
gritar	= to shout		llamar	= to call, phone
gruñir	= to be grouchy		llegar	= to arrive
guardar	= to save, keep		llenar	= to fill
gustar	= to like		llevar	= to carry
hablar	= to speak		llorar	= to cry
hartar	= to get full, sick of		lograr	= to achieve
heredar	= to inherit		malcriar	= to spoil
hojear	= to browse		mandar	= to send; give order
hundir	= to sink		manejar	= to drive, manage
imaginar	= to imagine		maniobrar	= to maneuver
implicar	= to imply		maquillar	= to ut make up on
importar	= to care, to import		maquinar	= to get make up
indicar	= to indicate		marcar	= to mark
informar	= to inform		marchar	= to leave
insultar	= to insult		masticar	= to chew
intentar	= to try		matar	= to kill
interesar	= to get interested in		maullar	= to mew
interrumpir	= to interrupt		meditar	= to meditate
invadir	= to invade		mejorar	= to get better
inventar	= to invent		memorizar	= to memorize
investigar	= to investigate		mencionar	= to mention
invitar	= to to invite		meter	= to put into

mezclar	=	to mix
mimar	=	to spoil, pamper
mirar	=	to look at
mojar	=	to get wet
molestar	=	to bother
montar	=	to mount; ride
mosquear	=	to get suspicious
mudar	=	to move (home)
multar	=	to give a ticket
multiplicar	=	to multiply by
murmurar	=	to murmur
navegar	=	to navigate
necesitar	=	to need
ocasionar	=	to cause
ocultar	=	to hide
ocupar	=	to occupy
ocurrir	=	to happen
ofender	=	to offend
ofrecer	=	to to offer
olvidar	=	to forget
operar	=	to operate
opinar	=	to have an opinion
ordenar	=	to command
organizar	=	to organize
pagar	=	to pay
partir	=	to split; depart
pasar	=	to pass
pasear	=	to go for a walk
pegar	=	to glue
peinar	=	to to comb
pelar	=	to peel off
pelear	=	to have a fight
perdonar	=	to forgive
permitir	=	to permit

pesar	=	to weigh
pescar	=	to fish
picar	=	to itch, to bite
pinchar	=	to prick
pintar	=	to paint
pisar	=	to step on
planear	=	to plan
plantar	=	to plant
preguntar	=	to ask
preparar	=	to prepare
presentar	=	to present
prestar	=	to lend
presumir	=	to show off
prohibir	=	to prohibit
prometer	=	to promise
pronosticar	=	to forecast
proteger	=	to protect
protestar	=	to protest
publicar	=	to publish
pudrir	=	to get rotten
quedar	=	to stay
quejar	=	to complain
quemar	=	to burn
quitar	=	to take off
rascar	=	to scratch
razonar	=	to reason
recibir	=	to receive
reclamar	=	to claim
recoger	=	to pick up
recuperar	=	to recover
reflejar	=	to reflect
reflexionar	=	to reflect
regalar	=	to give a gift
regatear	=	to bargain

APPENDIX E: A LIST OF REGULAR VERBS

regresar	= to come back		soportar	= to bear
reinar	= to reign		sospechar	= to suspect
relajar	= to relax		subir	= to go up, upstairs
renunciar	= to renounce		suceder	= to happen
repartir	= to dish out		suicidar	= to commit suicide
repasar	= to review		sujetar	= to hold
repugnar	= to disgust		sumar	= to sum up
resbalar	= to slide		suspender	= to suspend
rescatar	= to rescue		tapar	= to cover
respetar	= to respect		tardar	= to take (time)
responder	= to answer		telefonear	= to telephone
restar	= to subtract		terminar	= to finish
resultar	= to turn out		tocar	= to touch, to play
resumir	= to summarize		tomar	= to take, have
retar	= to challenge		toser	= to cough
retrasar	= to delay		trabajar	= to work
reunir	= to get together		tragar	= to swallow
rezar	= to pray		transformar	= to transform
robar	= to rob		transportar	= to transport
roncar	= to snore		tratar	= to deal with
saborear	= to taste		unir	= to put together
sacar	= to take out		usar	= to use
saltar	= to jump		utilizar	= to utilize
saludar	= to say hello		vaciar	= to empty
salvar	= to save		variar	= to vary
sangrar	= to bleed		vencer	= to defeat
secar	= to to dry		vender	= to sell
secuestrar	= to kidnap		verificar	= to verify
seleccionar	= to select		viajar	= to travel
separar	= to separate		vigilar	= to watch
silbar	= to whistle		violar	= to violate
sobar	= to finger, fondle		vivir	= to live
sobrar	= to be left		vomitar	= to vomit
solucionar	= to solve		votar	= to vote

APPENDIX F

A LIST OF IRREGULAR VERBS
UNA LISTA DE VERBOS IRREGULARES

APPENDIX F: A LIST OF IRREGULAR VERBS
UNA LISTA DE VERBOS IRREGULARES

In this appendix you will find an extensive list of irregular verbs. As we saw in three golden rules, tenses are linked by their irregularities. These relations can be checked in the list. The following is a review of the rules with examples from the list of this appendix.

A golden rule said:

> If a verb is irregular in the Present Tense of indicative, then it will also be irregular in both the Present Subjunctive and in the Imperative.

Example: Acertar (= to hit), #2 in the list, shows "x" in Present, Imperative and Present Subjunctive.

A golden rule said:

> If a verb is irregular in the Preterite, then it will also be irregular in the Past Subjunctive and will posses the same irregularity of the form "ellos" (= they). The irregularities in the Gerund are also related with this tense.

Example: Creer (= to believe), #37 in the list, shows "x" in the Preterite and Past Subjunctive. Also notice that columns 1,2 and 3 of the Gerund are linked with columns 1,2 and 3 of the Preterite respectively.

APPENDIX F: A LIST OF IRREGULAR VERBS

A golden rule said:

> If a verb is irregular in the Future Tense, then it will also be irregular in the Conditional Tense, and it will have the same irregularity in both tenses.

Example: Caber (= to fit), #14 in the list, shows "x" in Future and Conditional (among other irregularities).

Synopsis of types of irregularities:

Chapter	Verb Tense	Type of Irregularity
19	Infinitive	None
20	Gerund	(-AER, -EER, -OER, -OIR, -UIR) → -y-
		(-IR) -o- → -u-
		(-IR) -e- → -i-
		Others (only 2 verbs)
21	Past Participle	Only 13 verbs
22	Present	(-UIR) → -y-
		-o- → -ue-
		-e- → -ie-
		-e- → -i-
		(-CER, -CIR) → -z-
		Others (only 21 verbs)
23	Preterite	(-AER, -EER, -OER, -OIR, -UIR) → -y-
		(-IR) -o- → -u-
		(-IR) -e- → -i-
		(-CIR) → -j-
		Others (only 18 verbs)
24	Imperfect	Only 3 verbs
25	Future	Only 13 verbs
26	Conditional	Only 13 verbs
27	Imperative	From Present
		Others (only 8 verbs)
28	Present Subjunctive	(-UIR) → -y-
		-o- → -ue- [two subtypes]
		-e- → -ie- [two subtypes]
		-e- → -i-
		(-CER, -CIR) → -z-
		Others (only 20 verbs)
29	Past Subjunctive	Same as Preterite

List of Irreglar Verbs (PP: Past Participle; Im.:Imperfect Past; Fu.: Futuro; Co.: Condicional; PS: Past Subjunctive)

#	Verb	Gerund 1 (-AER, -EER, -OER -OIR, -UIR) → -y-	Gerund 2 (-IR) -o- → -u-	Gerund 3 (IR) -e- → -i-	Gerund 4 Others (only 2 verbs)	PP Only 13 verbs	Present 1 (-UIR) → -y-	Present 2 -o- → -ue-	Present 3 -e- → -ie-	Present 4 -e- → -i-	Present 5 (-CER, -CIR) → -z-	Present 6 Others (only 21 verbs)	Preterite 1 (-AER, -EER, -OER, -OIR, -UIR) → -y-	Preterite 2 (-IR) -o- → -u-	Preterite 3 (-IR) -e- → -i-	Preterite 4 (-CIR) → -j-	Preterite 5 Others (only 18 verbs)	Im. Only 3 verbs
1	abrir					x												
2	acertar								x									
3	advertir		x						x						x			
4	agradecer										x							
5	andar																x	
6	aparecer										x							
7	apetecer										x							
8	apretar								x									
9	aprobar							x										
10	ascender								x									
11	atribuir	x					x						x					
12	avergonzar							x										
13	bendecir											x			x			
14	caber											x					x	
15	caer	x											x	x				
16	calentar								x									
17	cegar								x									
18	cerrar								x									
19	cocer							x										
20	colar							x										
21	colgar							x										
22	comenzar								x									
23	concernir		x						x						x			
24	conducir										x					x		
25	confesar								x									
26	conocer										x							
27	conseguir		x							x					x			
28	consolar							x										
29	construir	x					x						x					
30	contar							x										

APPENDIX F: A LIST OF IRREGULAR VERBS

Fu. Only 13 verbs	Co. Only 13 verbs	Imper. From Present	Imper. Others (only 8 verbs)	Pres.Subj. (-UIR)→-y-	Pres.Subj. -o-→-ue-	Pres.Subj. -e-→-ie-	Pres.Subj. -e-→-i-	Pres.Subj. (-CER,-CIR)→-z-	Pres.Subj. Others (only 20 verbs)	PS Same as Preterite	Verb	Meaning	#
											abrir	to open	1
		x				x					acertar	to hit	2
		x				x				x	advertir	to warn	3
		x						x			agradecer	to thank	4
										x	andar	to walk	5
		x						x			aparecer	to appear	6
		x						x			apetecer	to feel like	7
		x				x					apretar	to tie	8
		x			x						aprobar	to approve	9
		x				x					ascender	to ascend	10
		x	x							x	atribuir	to atribute	11
		x			x						avergonzar	to feel shame	12
		x							x	x	bendecir	to bless	13
x	x	x							x	x	caber	to fit	14
		x							x	x	caer	to fall	15
		x				x					calentar	to heat	16
		x				x					cegar	to blind	17
		x				x					cerrar	to close	18
		x			x						cocer	to boil	19
		x			x						colar	to funnel	20
		x			x						colgar	to hang	21
		x				x					comenzar	to begin	22
		x				x				x	concernir	to be related to	23
		x						x		x	conducir	to drive (Spain)	24
		x				x					confesar	to confess	25
		x					x				conocer	to know, to meet	26
		x					x			x	conseguir	to achieve	27
		x			x						consolar	to confort	28
		x	x							x	construir	to built	29
		x		x							contar	to cut	30

#	Verb	Gerund 1 (-AER,-EER,-OER,-OIR,-UIR)→-y-	Gerund 2 (-IR) -o-→-u-	Gerund 3 (-IR) -e-→-i-	Gerund 4 Others (only 2 verbs)	PP Only 13 verbs	Present 1 (-UIR)→-y-	Present 2 -o-→-ue-	Present 3 -e-→-ie-	Present 4 -e-→-i-	Present 5 (-CER,-CIR)→-z-	Present 6 Others (only 21 verbs)	Preterite 1 (-AER,-EER,-OER,-OIR,-UIR)→-y-	Preterite 2 (-IR) -o-→-u-	Preterite 3 (-IR) -e-→-i-	Preterite 4 (-CIR)→-j-	Preterite 5 Others (only 18 verbs)	Im. Only 3 verbs
31	contribuir	x					x						x					
32	convencer										x							
33	convertir		x						x						x			
34	corregir			x						x					x			
35	costar							x										
36	crecer										x							
37	creer	x											x					
38	cubrir					x												
39	dar											x					x	
40	decir		x			x						x					x	
41	deducir										x					x		
42	defender								x									
43	demostrar							x										
44	desaparecer										x							
45	descender								x									
46	despedir			x						x					x			
47	despertar								x									
48	destruir	x					x						x					
49	devolver							x										
50	distribuir	x					x						x					
51	divertir		x						x						x			
52	doler							x										
53	dormir		x					x						x				
54	elegir			x						x					x			
55	empezar								x									
56	encontrar							x										
57	entender								x									
58	enterrar								x									
59	entristecer										x							
60	envolver							x										

APPENDIX F: A LIST OF IRREGULAR VERBS

Fu. Only 13 verbs	Co. Only 13 verbs	Imper. From Present	Imper. Others (only 8 verbs)	Pres.Subj. (-UIR) → -y-	Pres.Subj. -o- → -ue-	Pres.Subj. -e- → -ie-	Pres.Subj. -e- → -i-	Pres.Subj. (-CER, -CIR) → -z-	Pres.Subj. Others (only 20 verbs)	PS Same as Preterite	Verb	Meaning	#
		x	x							x	contribuir	to contribute	31
		x						x			convencer	to convince	32
		x				x				x	convertir	to convert	33
		x					x			x	corregir	to correct	34
		x			x						costar	to cost	35
		x						x			crecer	to grow (up)	36
										x	creer	to believe	37
											cubrir	to cover	38
		x								x	dar	to give	39
x	x	x							x	x	decir	to say	40
		x						x		x	deducir	to deduce	41
		x				x					defender	to defend	42
		x			x						demostrar	to demostrate	43
		x						x			desaparecer	to desappear	44
		x				x					descender	to descend	45
		x					x			x	despedir	to see off	46
		x				x					despertar	to wake up	47
		x	x							x	destruir	to destroy	48
		x			x						devolver	to give back	49
		x	x							x	distribuir	to distribute	50
		x				x				x	divertir	to have fun	51
		x			x						doler	to be sore	52
		x			x						dormir	to sleep	53
		x					x			x	elegir	to choose	54
		x				x					empezar	to start	55
		x			x						encontrar	to find	56
		x				x					entender	to understand	57
		x				x					enterrar	to berry	58
		x						x			entristecer	to get sad	59
		x			x						envolver	to wrap up	60

		Gerund				PP	Present						Preterite					Im.
		(-AER, -EER, -OER, -OIR, -UIR) → -y-	(-IR) -o- → -u-	(-IR) -e- → -i-	Others (only 2 verbs)	Only 13 verbs	(-UIR) → -y-	-o- → -ue-	-e- → -ie-	-e- → -i-	(-CER, -CIR) → -z-	Others (only 21 verbs)	(-AER, -EER, -OER, -OIR, -UIR) → -y-	(-IR) -o- → -u-	(-IR) -e- → -i-	(-CIR) → -j-	Others (only 18 verbs)	Only 3 verbs
#		1	2	3	4		1	2	3	4	5	6	1	2	3	4	5	
61	errar								x									
62	escribir					x												
63	establecer										x							
64	estar											x					x	
65	favorecer										x							
66	fluir	x					x											
67	forzar							x										
68	fregar								x									
69	freir		x						x					x				
70	gobernar								x									
71	haber											x					x	
72	hacer					x						x					x	
73	herir		x						x					x				
74	hervir		x						x					x				
75	huir	x					x						x					
76	imprimir																	
77	inducir										x					x		
78	inferir		x						x					x				
79	influir	x					x											
80	instruir	x					x											
81	introducir										x					x		
82	intuir	x					x											
83	invertir		x						x					x				
84	ir	x		x								x					x	x
85	jugar											x						
86	leer	x											x					
87	llover							x										
88	medir		x							x				x				
89	mentir		x						x					x				
90	merecer										x							

APPENDIX F: A LIST OF IRREGULAR VERBS

Fu. Only 13 verbs	Co. Only 13 verbs	Imper. From Present	Imper. Others (only 8 verbs)	Pres.Subj. (-UIR)→-y-	Pres.Subj. -o-↑-ue-	Pres.Subj. -e-↑-ie-	Pres.Subj. -e-↑-i-	Pres.Subj. (-CER,-CIR)→-z-	Pres.Subj. Others (only 20 verbs)	PS Same as Preterite	Verb	Meaning	#
		x				x					errar	to mistake	61
											escribir	to write	62
		x						x			establecer	to establish	63
		x							x	x	estar	to be	64
		x					x				favorecer	to favor	65
		x	x								fluir	to flow	66
		x			x						forzar	to force	67
		x				x					fregar	to mop	68
		x								x	freir	to fry	69
		x				x					gobernar	to govern	70
x	x	x							x	x	haber	to have (aux.)	71
x	x		x						x	x	hacer	to do, to make	72
		x				x				x	herir	to hurt	73
		x				x				x	hervir	to boil	74
		x	x							x	huir	to escape	75
											imprimir	to print	76
		x						x		x	inducir	to induce	77
		x					x			x	inferir	to infer	78
		x	x								influir	to influence	79
		x	x								instruir	to instruct	80
		x						x		x	introducir	to introduce	81
		x	x								intuir	to sense	82
		x				x				x	invertir	to invest	83
			x						x	x	ir	to go	84
		x							x		jugar	to play	85
										x	leer	to reed	86
		x		x							llover	to rain	87
		x					x			x	medir	to measure	88
		x				x				x	mentir	to lie	89
		x						x			merecer	to deserve	90

#	Verb	Gerund 1 (-AER,-EER,-OER,-OIR,-UIR)→-y-	Gerund 2 (-IR)-o-→-u-	Gerund 3 (IR)-e-→-i-	Gerund 4 Others (only 2 verbs)	PP Only 13 verbs	Present 1 (-UIR)→-y-	Present 2 -o-→-ue-	Present 3 -e-→-ie-	Present 4 -e-→-i-	Present 5 (-CER,-CIR)→-z-	Present 6 Others (only 21 verbs)	Preterite 1 (-AER,-EER,-OER,-OIR,-UIR)→-y-	Preterite 2 (-IR)-o-→-u-	Preterite 3 (-IR)-e-→-i-	Preterite 4 (-CIR)→-j-	Preterite 5 Others (only 18 verbs)	Im. Only 3 verbs
91	moler							x										
92	morder							x										
93	morir		x			x		x						x				
94	mostrar							x										
95	mover							x										
96	nacer										x							
97	negar								x									
98	nevar								x									
99	obedecer										x							
100	oír	x										x	x					
101	oler							x										
102	padecer										x							
103	parecer										x							
104	pedir			x						x					x			
105	pensar								x									
106	perder								x									
107	pertenecer										x							
108	poder		x					x									x	
109	poner					x											x	
110	poseer	x											x					
111	preferir			x					x						x			
112	probar							x										
113	producir										x					x		
114	querer								x								x	
115	recomendar								x									
116	recordar							x										
117	reducir										x					x		
118	regar								x									
119	rendir			x						x					x			
120	renovar							x										

APPENDIX F: A LIST OF IRREGULAR VERBS

Fu. Only 13 verbs	Co. Only 13 verbs	Imper. From Present	Imper. Others (only 8 verbs)	Pres.Subj. 1 (-UIR)→-y-	Pres.Subj. 2 -o-→-ue-	Pres.Subj. 3 -e-→-ie-	Pres.Subj. 4 -e-→-i-	Pres.Subj. 5 (-CER,-CIR)→-z-	Pres.Subj. 6 Others (only 20 verbs)	PS Same as Preterite	Verb	Meaning	#
		x			x						moler	to grind	91
		x			x						morder	to bite	92
		x			x					x	morir	to die	93
		x			x						mostrar	to show	94
		x			x						mover	to move	95
		x						x			nacer	to be born	96
		x				x					negar	to refuse	97
		x				x					nevar	to snow	98
		x						x			obedecer	to obbey	99
		x							x	x	oír	to hear	100
		x			x						oler	to smell	101
		x						x			padecer	to undergo	102
		x						x			parecer	to look like	103
		x					x			x	pedir	to ask for	104
		x				x					pensar	to think	105
		x				x					perder	to lose	106
		x						x			pertenecer	to petain	107
x	x	x			x					x	poder	to be able to	108
x	x		x						x	x	poner	to put	109
										x	poseer	to posses	110
		x				x				x	preferir	to prefer	111
		x			x						probar	to try	112
		x						x		x	producir	to produce	113
x	x	x				x				x	querer	to want	114
		x				x					recomendar	to recommned	115
		x			x						recordar	to remember	116
		x						x		x	reducir	to reduce	117
		x				x					regar	to water	118
		x					x			x	rendir	to surrender	119
		x			x						renovar	to renew	120

#	Verb	Ger 1	Ger 2	Ger 3	Ger 4	PP	Pres 1	Pres 2	Pres 3	Pres 4	Pres 5	Pres 6	Pret 1	Pret 2	Pret 3	Pret 4	Pret 5	Im.
121	repetir		x							x					x			
122	resolver					x	x											
123	rodar						x											
124	roer	x											x					
125	rogar						x											
126	romper					x												
127	saber											x					x	
128	salir											x						
129	satisfacer					x						x					x	
130	seducir										x					x		
131	seguir			x						x					x			
132	sembrar								x									
133	sentar								x									
134	sentir			x					x						x			
135	ser											x					x	x
136	servir			x						x					x			
137	soler							x										
138	soltar					x		x										
139	sonar							x										
140	soñar							x										
141	sonreir			x						x					x			
142	sugerir			x					x						x			
143	sustituir	x					x											
144	temblar								x									
145	tender								x									
146	tener											x					x	
147	tentar								x									
148	torcer							x										
149	tostar							x										
150	traducir										x					x		

APPENDIX F: A LIST OF IRREGULAR VERBS

Fu.	Co.	Imper. From Present	Imper. Others (only 8 verbs)	Pres.Subj. 1 (-UIR)→-y-	Pres.Subj. 2 -o-→-ue-	Pres.Subj. 3 -e-→-ie-	Pres.Subj. 4 -e-→-i-	Pres.Subj. 5 (-CER, -CIR)→-z-	Pres.Subj. 6 Others (only 20 verbs)	PS Same as Preterite	Verb	Meaning	#
		x					x			x	repetir	to repeat	121
		x			x						resolver	to resolve	122
		x			x						rodar	to roll	123
										x	roer	to gnaw	124
		x			x						rogar	to beg (formal)	125
											romper	to break	126
x	x	x							x	x	saber	to know	127
x	x		x						x		salir	to go out	128
x	x	x							x		satisfacer	to satisfy	129
		x						x		x	seducir	to seduce	130
		x					x			x	seguir	to follow	131
		x				x					sembrar	to sow	132
		x				x					sentar	to sit	133
		x				x				x	sentir	to feel	134
			x						x	x	ser	to be	135
										x	servir	to serve	136
		x			x						soler	to use to	137
		x			x						soltar	to let go	138
		x			x						sonar	to sound	139
		x			x						soñar	to dream	140
		x								x	sonreir	to smile	141
		x				x				x	sugerir	tu sugest	142
		x	x								sustituir	to substitute	143
		x				x					temblar	to tremble	144
		x				x					tender	to tend	145
x	x	x							x	x	tener	to have (posses)	146
		x				x					tentar	to tempt	147
		x			x						torcer	to twist	148
		x			x						tostar	to toast	149
		x						x		x	traducir	to traduce	150

#		Gerund 1 (-AER,-EER,-OER,-OIR,-UIR) → -y-	Gerund 2 (-IR) -o- → -u-	Gerund 3 (IR) -e- → -i-	Gerund 4 Others (only 2 verbs)	PP Only 13 verbs	Present 1 (-UIR) → -y-	Present 2 -o- → -ue-	Present 3 -e- → -ie-	Present 4 -e- → -i-	Present 5 (-CER, -CIR) → -z-	Present 6 Others (only 21 verbs)	Preterite 1 (-AER,-EER,-OER,-OIR,-UIR) → -y-	Preterite 2 (-IR) -o- → -u-	Preterite 3 (-IR) -e- → -i-	Preterite 4 (-CIR) → -j-	Preterite 5 Others (only 18 verbs)	Im. Only 3 verbs
151	traer	x										x					x	
152	tropezar								x									
153	valer											x						
154	venir		x									x					x	
155	ver					x						x						x
156	verter								x									
157	vestir			x						x						x		
158	volar							x										
159	volcar							x										
160	volver					x		x										

APPENDIX F: A LIST OF IRREGULAR VERBS

Fu. (Only 13 verbs)	Co. (Only 13 verbs)	Imper. From Present (1)	Imper. Others (only 8 verbs) (2)	Pres.Subj. (-UIR)→-y- (1)	Pres.Subj. -o-→-ue- (2)	Pres.Subj. -e-→-ie- (3)	Pres.Subj. -e-→-i- (4)	Pres.Subj. (-CER,-CIR)→-z- (5)	Pres.Subj. Others (only 19 verbs) (6)	PS Same as Preterite	Verb	Meaning	#
		x						x		x	traer	to bring	151
		x				x					tropezar	to trip	152
x	x	x						x			valer	to be worth	153
x	x		x					x		x	venir	to come	154
		x						x			ver	to see	155
		x				x					verter	to pour	156
		x					x			x	vestir	to dress	157
		x			x						volar	to fly	158
		x			x						volcar	to bump	159
		x			x						volver	to come back	160

GLOSSARY
GLOSARIO

The following is a list of the linguistic terms used in this book. Every entry includes a reference to the chapter which is relevant to the term in question.

accent mark — The symbol (') that indicates where the stress is (*Chapter 4, Syllable and Stress*).

acronym — An abbreviation that actually forms a word. For example: NATO, which is **N**orth **A**tlantic **T**reaty **O**rganization (*Chapter 13 Nouns*).

active voice — Verb structure where the subject and the object of the sentence remain subject and object, in contrast with passive voice. Example: "I drove the car" is active voice; while "The car was driven by me" is passive voice (*Chapter 35 The Passive Voice* "The song is sung").

adjective — A part of the speech that describes a noun, e.g. "the **gray** car." Unlike determiners, adjectives are non-grammatical words. In Spanish, the adjective goes after the noun "*el carro **gris***" (= "the gray car"). This also defines a function within the sentence, so a group of words together can work as an adjective, e.g: "the **never-ending** story" (*Chapter 12 Adjectives*).

adverb — A part of the speech that describes a verb, an adjective or another adverb, e.g. "I drive **slowly**," This is **very** intense." "I drive **very slowly**" (*Chapter 15 Adverbs*).

GLOSSARY

article	A type of determiner. They are the words: "the," "a," and "an" (*Chapter 11 Determiners*).
auxiliary verb	A verb used to form compound tenses. An example in both Spanish and English is the verb *haber* = to have, as in: "*Había ido allí*" = "I had gone there," where "to have" does not posses an actual meaning. It is used only to create the verb structure. In English, other auxiliary verbs are: to be, to go, to do; e.g. "I **am going** to study," "**Do** you work there?" (*Chapter 7 Conjugation*).
clause	The grammatical structure with one verb (single verb, compound verb or verbal periphrasis). Subordinate clauses cannot exist independently, and they must be linked to the principal clause. For example, the sentence: "If you wanted, I would go," has two clauses: "If you wanted" and "I would go" (*Chapter 17 Conjunctions*).
cognate	A word that is similar to other word of the same meaning in another language. For example "Philosophy" in English with "*Filosofía*" in Spanish (Chapter 8, How to Learn Words Efficiently).
conditional	Verb tense that passes information on something possible due to a condition: "I **would sing** in the theater, if I were famous." = "*Cantaría en el teatro si fuera famoso*" (*Chapter 26 Conditional "I would Sing"*).
(to) conjugate	To provide the six forms of a verb representing different persons in a certain tense. To conjugate "to be" in the present is to say: "I am, you are, he/she/it is, we are, you are, and they are" (*Chapter 7 Conjugation*).
conjugation	Categorization of verbs of Latin origin corresponding to certain schedule of endings. In Spanish, there are three conjugations: verbs that end with AR, like *estudiar* (= to study), also called verbs of the first conjugation; verbs that end with AR, like *poseer* (= to posses), also called verbs of the second conjugation; and verbs that end with IR, like *distribuir* (= to distribute), also called verbs of the third conjugation (*Chapter 7 Conjugation*).
conjunction	A part of the speech that links nouns and verbs (like in "Francisco **and** John," or "They studied **and** worked together"), or that link clauses (like in "I will work unless you say something." A set of words can work as a conjunction, e.g. "I will go **even if** you say no" (*Chapter 17 Conjunctions*).

consonant	Speech sound pronounced by modifying the sound using lips, teeth, tongue, etc., in contrast with the vowels. Consonant sound represent the letters: b, c ,d, f, etc. (*Chapter 3 The Consonants*).
determiner	A part of the speech that describes a noun. Unlike adjectives, determiners are grammatical words. In both Spanish and English, determiners precede the noun, e.g. "**the** car," "**an** airplane," "**some** people." This also defines a function within the sentence; so, a group of words together can work as an determiner, e.g. "**some of those** people" (*Chapter 11 Determiners*).
dieresis	In Spanish, a pair of dots over the letter "u" (ü) indicating that the letter "u" is not silent. For example *pingüino* (= penguin) (*Chapter 3 The Consonants*).
direct object	The part of the sentence over which the verb acts, e.g. "I saw **him**," or "I saw **a cat on the roof**" (*Chapter 14 Pronouns*).
false cognate	A word that is similar to another word in another language but has a different meaning. For example, the English word "assist" looks similar to the Spanish word "*asistir*;" however "*asistir*" means "to attend" (*Chapter 8 How to Learn Words Efficiently*).
false friend	See false cognate (*Chapter 8 How to Learn Words Efficiently*).
feminine	Grammatical gender in contrast with masculine. In Spanish all nouns have grammatical gender, including objects. For example, *planta* (= plant) is feminine (*Chapter 6 Masculine / Feminine*).
future	Verb tense that passes information about the future ("Tomorrow I **will sing** in the theater" = "*Mañana cantaré en el teatro*") (*Chapter 25 Future* "I will sing").
gerund	Verb form incorporating -ING. It is a form of the verb that has no tense and no person. It can be used in English as a noun ("**Working** here is difficult.") or as a verb form ("I am **working**.") In Spanish, the equivalent -ANDO, -IENDO can only be used as a verb form (*Chapter 20 Gerund* "singing").
grammatical word	Word that does not have an absolute meaning. In general they are prepositions (of, in, etc.), conjunctions (and, or, but, etc.), pronouns (I, you, me, etc.), determiners (the, a, some, etc.), some adverbs (very), and the auxiliary verbs (*Chapter 9 Types of Words*).

imperative	Verb tense that expresses a command (**Sing!** = *¡Canta!*). The verbal moods comprise the indicative, the subjunctive and the imperative. The imperative mood only has one tense: the imperative tense itself (*Chapter 27 Imperative* "sing!").
imperfect past	One of the two past tenses of the indicative mood, together with the preterit. In English it is commonly translated by the continuous past tense ("Yesterday **I was singing**, when I saw him), in contrast with the preterite ("Yesterday I sang in that theater") (*Chapter 24 Imperfect Past* "I sang").
indicative	Set of verb tenses that pass definite information, in contrast with subjunctive tenses, which reflect emotion, doubt or possibilities ("He is going to school today"). (Indicative, subjunctive and imperative are called the verbal moods). In Spanish, the tenses of the indicative mood are: the present, the preterit, the imperfect past, the future and the conditional (*Chapter 18 Verbs*).
indirect cognate	Word that is not directly translatable (recognizable) from one language to another, but which has similar derivative words. For example "*tener*" = "to have;" which are linked by other words like "*contener*" = to contain, or "*sostener*" (= to sustain) (*Chapter 8 How to Learn Words Efficiently*).
indirect object	The part of the sentence that receives the action of the direct object, e.g. "He said that to **me**," or "He said that to **all senators**." Generally, you need a direct object in order to have an indirect object. In some constructions the direct object is understood (*Chapter 14 Pronouns*).
infinitive	A form of the verb that has no tense and no person, and that can function as a noun of the clause, e.g. "**To sing** is hard." In Spanish all infinitives end with AR, ER or IR (*Chapter 19 Infinitive* "to Sing").
interjection	A part of the speech that can form a clause by itself, e.g. "hi" (*Chapter 10 Interjections*).
irregular verb	Verb that doesn't obey a set of rules, in contrast with regular verb. For example, the verb "to brake" ("I braked") is regular, and "to break" is irregular, since, in the past tense at least, "to break" has an irregularity: "I broke" (*Chapter 18 Verbs*).
irregularity	A form of a verb in a person and a tense that does not follow the rules. If a verb has at least one irregularity, it is called "irregular." In English, the verb "to send," for example, is irregular. The form "sent" is an irregularity of the past tense (it is not "sended.") (*Chapter 18 Verbs*).

local word	Word that is used in specific areas to the exclusion of other areas. For example on the East Coast, they use the term "thru way" and "package store" instead of "freeway" and "liquor store" respectively (*Chapter 8 How to Learn Words Efficiently*).
masculine	Grammatical gender in contrast with feminine. In Spanish, all nouns have grammatical gender, including objects. For example, *carro* (= car) is masculine. (*Chapter 6 Masculine / Feminine*).
non-grammatical word	Word with actual meaning. In general, they are: nouns (table, house etc.), adjectives (red, blue, etc.), and verbs (to sing, to eat, etc.) (*Chapter 9 Types of Words*).
noun	A part of the speech that identifies an entity, and that can work as subject of the clause. A noun can be: a person, animal, plant or object, tangible or intangible, e.g. "patience" (*Chapter 13 Nouns*).
passive voice	Verb structure where the object of the sentence become the subject and vice versa, in contrast with active voice. For example: "I drove the car" is active voice; "The car was driven by me" is passive voice (*Chapter 35 The Passive Voice* "The song is sung").
past participle	A form of the verb that has no tense and no person. It can be used as an adjective ("I am **tired**") or as a verb form ("I have **tired** my students in the gym"). In Spanish, past participles end with: -ADO, -IDO (**Chapter 21 Past Participle** "sung").
past subjunctive	Tense that expresses emotion, doubt or possibility in the past. Typically it doesn't exist in English. You can only find it in rare cases like: "If I were a rich man, I'd go," where "were" is used instead of "was." An example in Spanish is: "*Esperaba que él cantara más.*" = "I expected that he **sang** more" (*Chapter 29 Past Subjunctive* "...that I sang").
periphrasis	Verb structure with more than one verb functioning as one. For example, the sentence "I **stop smoking** years ago." has two verbs in tandem; and "They **are going** to **continue trying**," has four verbs in tandem (*Chapter 32 Periphrases* "I am going to sing").
person	Each of the possible forms of the verb as defined by its subject. Persons are: I /we (first person); you (second person); he/she/it/they (third person) (*Chapter 7 Conjugation*).

GLOSSARY

plural	Grammatical number that means more than one, in contrast with singular (which means one). For example the word "lions" is plural (*Chapter 5 Singular / Plural*).
prefix	A construction at the beginning of the word that alters meaning, e.g. un-, dis-, pre- (*Chapter 8 How to Learn Words Efficiently*).
preposition	A part of the speech that introduces a noun clause, e.g. "to," "at," "in," and "on" (*Chapter 16 Prepositions*).
present indicative	Verb tense that passes information in the present. It has several uses: 1) it indicates a fact ("Two and two **equals** four"); 2) It shows a habitual action ("He **sings** everyday"). In Spanish, it has two extra uses: 3) it shows an instant action ("*¿Qué haces?* = "What are you doing?"), where English uses the continuous present tense; and 4) it shows an historic fact ("*Colon descubre America en 1492*" = "Columbus discovered America in 1492"), where English uses the past tense (*Chapter 22 Present* "I sing").
present subjunctive	Tense that expresses emotion, doubt or possibility in the present. Typically it doesn't exist in English. You can only find it in rare cases like: "I expect that he **sing** more" = "*Espero que él cante más,*" where "sing" is used instead of "sings" (*Chapter 28 Present Subjunctive* "…that I sing").
preterite	One of the two past tenses of the indicative mood, together with the imperfect past. In English, it is commonly translated by the past tense ("Yesterday I **sang** in that theater"), in contrast with the imperfect past ("Yesterday I was singing when I saw him") (*Chapter 23 Preterite* "I sang").
pronoun	A part of the speech that substitutes a noun in the third person. For example, "the man" can be substituted by "he," or "the persons" by "they." For example, "I told **him**" for "I told that man." The realm of the term pronoun is extended to other persons because of their similarities: I, me, mine, you, yours, we, us, ours (*Chapter 14 Pronouns*).
reflexive verb	A type of verb that has an object that is the same as the subject, e.g. "He is going to dress himself" (*Chapter 33 Reflexive Verbs*).
regular verb	Verb that obeys a set of rules, in contrast with irregular verb. For example, the verb "to brake" ("I braked") is regular, and "to break" is irregular. In the past tense at least, "to break" has an irregularity: "I broke" (*Chapter 18 Verbs*).

sentence	A grammatical structure that fully conveys meaning. It can have one or more clauses. A sentence must end with a period (*Chapter 17 Conjunctions*).
singular	Grammatical number that means one in quantity, in contrast with "plural," which means more than one. For example, the word "lion" is singular, "lions" is plural (*Chapter 5 Singular / Plural*).
spanglish	Code switching between Spanish and English; an English word (original or altered) used in the Spanish speech, e.g. "*Tomaré la freeway*" (= I'll take the freeway), where "freeway" is not a Spanish word. In the sentence: "*Iré a la marketa*" (= I'll go to the market"), marketa is an alteration of the English word "market" with the typical Spanish suffix of the nouns: "a" (*Chapter 8 How to Learn Words Efficiently*).
stress	The emphasis in the intonation of a word. In Spanish, stress is always on one, and only one, syllable (specifically in one vowel of it). For example, the word "computer" has the stress in the second syllable "com-pu-ter" (*Chapter 4 Syllable and Stress*).
subject	The part of the sentence (person or thing) that is or does something (*Chapter 14 Pronouns*).
subjunctive	Set of verb forms that reflect emotion, doubt or possibilities. Typically it doesn't exist in English. In English you can only find it in sentences like: "If I **were** a rich man, I'd go," in contrast with indicative tenses, which pass definite information ("He studies everyday"). Generally only the subordinate clause of a two-clause sentence can have a subjunctive tense. In the example above, "I'd go" is the principal clause, and "If I were a rich man" is the subordinate clause. Indicative, subjunctive and imperative are called the verbal moods. In Spanish, the subjunctive mood comprises two tenses: the present subjunctive and the past subjunctive (*Chapter 18 Verbs*).
suffix	A construction at the end of the word that alters meaning: -ing, -ness, -age, etc. (*Chapter 8 How to Learn Words Efficiently*).
syllable	A division of a word into separate sounds. For example, the three syllables com, pu, ter form the word "computer." Letters form syllables; and, in turn, syllables form words (*Chapter 4 Syllable and Stress*).
verb	A part of the speech that represents an action, e.g. "sing," "be," "see" (*Chapter 18 Verbs*).

GLOSSARY

verbs like "gustar"	A type of verb that has an object that functions as the subject. In the sentence "Fish revolts me." = "El pescado me revuelve." the real subject (who actually does the action) is "me;" however "me" functions as an object (since it is placed after the verb). Not the same as the passive voice, however. *"Gustar"* means "to like," and it is a common verb in Spanish that works this way (Notice that "to like" does not work the same way in English). (*Chapter 34 Verbs like "Gustar"*).
vocabulary	A set of words and their meaning (*Chapter 8 How to Learn Words Efficiently*).
vowel	Speech sound pronounced without obstacle (i.e. without using lips, tongue, teeth, etc.), in contrast with the consonants. Vowel sounds represent the letters: a, e, i, o, u, and occasionally "y" (*Chapter 2 The Vowels*).

Abbreviations & Symbols

e.g.	"Exampla gratia," Latin for "for example."
etc.	"Etcetera," Latin for "and the rest."
i.e.	"Id est," Latin for "this is."
i	In this book, "irregular verb."
ñ, Ñ	The only Spanish letter that is not part of the English alphabet. It can be seen in some English words with Spanish origin: piñata, jalapeño pepper or el niño (*Chapter 3 The Consonants*).
<u>underlined letter</u>	In this book, used to indicate pronunciation, e.g. comp<u>u</u>ter.
=	In this book, used to indicate "means" e.g. *carro* = car.
¡	Spanish symbol to begin an exclamation sentence.
¿	Spanish symbol to begin a question sentence.
→	In this book, "is converted to."

USING ENGLISH TO LEARN SPANISH

AUTHORS

Francisco de la Calle Bruquetas founded Bruquetas Publishing in 2009. A native of Madrid, Spain, Mr. De la Calle holds a M.S. from the *Universidad Politécnica de Madrid* in industrial engineering, and a M.A. from San José State University in Spanish. He has worked as an engineer, and has taught Spanish at university level. Mr. De la Calle is the co-author of the book series *Using English to Learn Spanish* as well as the author of a collection of fiction in Spanish.

Michelle de la Calle is a native born Californian. As a De Anza Nursing Program Graduate R.N. she joined the Peace Corps in Guatemala, where she taught basic hygiene and health to young rural children. She holds a B.S.N. from San José State University, and a Master's in Forensic Science from National University. Mrs. De la Calle, a Nurse Manager, has worked in the hospital setting for over ten years.

USING ENGLISH TO LEARN SPANISH
BOOKS OF THE SERIES

SPANISH FOR HEALTH CARE

Spanish for the Health Care is intended **for professionals** with no previous knowledge of Spanish. **The goal is to communicate with patients**. The book focuses on the dialogue to understand symptoms, and convey diagnostics and instructions.

The right way for professionals to learn Spanish is to learn the Spanish of the profession.

SPANISH FOR ENGINEERS

Spanish for the Engineers is intended **for professionals** with no previous knowledge of Spanish. **The goal is to communicate in your technical environment**. Each chapter focuses on one specialty, including construction, software, M&E engineering and project management.

The right way for professionals to learn Spanish is to learn the Spanish of the profession.

SPANISH FOR CALIFORNIANS

Spanish for Californians shows the Spanish of **Latin America and the U.S.** One of the twenty-two Academies that represent Spanish is in the U.S. The book teaches the common within the norm.

A textbook for beginners, and a reference data book for speakers. The easiest way to learn is by learning the simplest first.

ADVANCED SPANISH

Advanced Spanish focuses on **those topics that are an obstacle for your fluent Spanish**. The textbook explains the subjects with many examples and comparisons to English.

Now that you can communicate, it is time to get to the point and perfect your Spanish.

www.ingramcontent.com/pod-product-compliance
Lightning Source LLC
Chambersburg PA
CBHW031249230426
43670CB00005B/109